OVERCOMING MODERNITY

OVERCOMING MODERNITY

Synchronicity and Image-Thinking

YUASA YASUO

Translated by Shigenori Nagatomo & John W. M. Krummel
with an Introduction by Shigenori Nagatomo

STATE UNIVERSITY OF NEW YORK PRESS

Published by
STATE UNIVERSITY OF NEW YORK PRESS
Albany

For information, contact State University of New York Press, Albany, NY
www.sunypress.edu

Production by Kelli W. LeRoux
Marketing by Michael Campochiaro

Library of Congress Cataloging-in-Publication Data

Yuasa, Yasuo.
   Overcoming modernity : synchronicity and image-thinking / Yasuo Yuasa ; translated by
Shigenori Nagatomo and John W. M. Krummel ; with an introduction by Shigenori Nagatomo.
      p. cm.
   Includes bibliographical references and index.
   ISBN 978-0-7914-7401-3 (hardcover : alk. paper)
   1. Philosophy, Comparative.   2. Jung, C. G. (Carl Gustav), 1875–1961.   I. Nagatomo,
Shigenori.   II. Krummel, John Wesley Megumu, 1965–   III. Title.
   B799.Y79 2008
   181'.12—dc22   2007035479

10   9   8   7   6   5   4   3   2   1

Contents

PART II

PART III

Translator's Introduction

When one side is illuminated, the other side remains in darkness."
— Dōgen, "Genjōkōan"

Yuasa Yasuo's[1] *Overcoming Modernity: Synchronicity and Image-Thinking* proposes a new orientation of thinking, inviting people to reconsider the modern
Western paradigm of thinking, particularly concerning its views of nature
that were established by natural science in the seventeenth and eighteenth
centuries and of the human being that was advanced, almost in parallel with
the former's rise, by Enlightenment rationalism. In order to overcome these
views, he offers an *holistic* approach by thematizing "synchronicity" and
"image-thinking," while proposing "space-time and mind-body integration" as
their philosophical foundation. This holistic perspective, Yuasa maintains, is
necessary to overcome the modern rationalistic paradigm of thinking, for the
latter has brought about various negative consequences since its declaration
despite its "good" intention.

Because these four terms, "space-time and mind-body integration," "synchronicity," and "image-thinking," are central and hence cardinal ideas that
are developed as thematic foci in this volume, it will be helpful at the outset
to briefly indicate the relative relationship among them, so that the reader can
have a preliminary feel of, and a quick glance of, the present volume, *Overcoming Modernity: Synchronicity and Image-Thinking*. "Image-thinking" is Yuasa's neologism and may for now be understood to mean a mode of thinking
that incorporates within it image-experience that is intuitively apprehended
from the unconscious. For Yuasa's project in this volume, it serves as a philosophical foundation that underpins Jung's theory of synchronicity, that is,
an overlapping in meaning between physical and psychological phenomenon.
Because this overlapping is based on the experiential fact of "space-time and

I

mind-body integration" as its philosophical condition, Yuasa articulates their meaning, and in so doing proposes an holistic worldview.

In this introduction, I would like to provide (1) a short introduction of Yuasa Yasuo as a scholar; (2) the general background concern of this volume; (3) an organizational overview to suggest the order in which the parts may be read; (4) the thematic concern of the present volume, which will be discussed under the three headings: image-thinking, synchronicity, and space-time and mind-body integration; (5) the sources out of which the present volume has been gathered together; and (6) the translation process in bringing this project to completion.

YUASA YASUO AS A SCHOLAR

As part of introducing the present volume to an English-reading audience, I would like to first make a brief mention of Yuasa Yasuo as a scholar. Onuki Yoshihisa, a Tokyo University professor, describes Yuasa as a scholar who "has an interest in the vast region [of scholarship], and . . . [whose] inquiring mind is inexhaustible. Whenever I attend his study group, I wonder if he might not be an intellectual giant."[2] Intellectual giant he was! The vast region of his scholarly interest is reflected in his prolific writing career that spanned over fifty years, during which period he published fifty books and three hundred articles. And they are now being published as *Yuasa Yasuo's Complete Works* [*Yuasa Yasuo Zenshū*] in eighteen volumes, twelve of which have already been made available to the public. If one glances even casually through the table of contents in any of these volumes—they are composed of anywhere between five hundred and eight hundred pages—one will readily discern that Yuasa can indeed cover a "vast region of scholarship" with a wide variety of human and scholarly concerns ranging from topics of both Western and Eastern traditions in philosophy, science, ethics, history, psychology, and religion. And if he/she pages through any one of the pieces contained in his *Complete Works*, the reader will discover that Yuasa addresses each subject in depth with a comprehensive and balanced treatment. This feature is also apparent in the present volume, though naturally in a much smaller scale than his *Complete Works*. Nevertheless, I hope readers will appreciate the rich, multi-faceted and multi-disciplinary content when reading the present volume.

While the projected plans for his *Complete Works* are still under way, Yuasa published several books that are not included in the plans for the first compilation of his *Collected Works*, as if to announce to the world that these eighteen volumes were not enough to consummate his scholarly accomplishments. In May 2004, for example, he published, at the age of seventy-nine, a book, *Tetsugaku no tanjō: danseisei to joseisei no shinrigaku* [*The Birth of*

Philosophy: The Psychology of Masculinity and Femininity]. It sheds light on the role that the psychology of masculinity and femininity played in the formation of Greek philosophy, for which he spared four hundred and twenty-four pages, by examining the historical, social, and cultural milieu of ancient Greece and the Roman Empire. He wrote this book to assess how philosophical thinking came to be uniquely formed in ancient Greece, while tracing its influences up to the middle period of the Roman Empire. The translators of the present volume were fortunate to obtain a chapter in manuscript form from this recent work, and were able to include it in the present volume. It is placed as the very first chapter, "The Image-Thinking of Ancient People, East and West."

Since Yuasa Yasuo is unfortunately not that well known in the English-reading world, in comparison to his reputation as a prominent scholar in Japan, I wish to say a few words about his scholarship that is accessible to an English-reading audience. I am happy to write that Yuasa Yasuo's present volume, *Overcoming Modernity: Synchronicity and Image-Thinking*, forms a sequel to the two previous works published in English: *The Body, Self-Cultivation and Ki-Energy* (SUNY, 1993) and *The Body: Toward an Eastern Mind-Body Theory* (SUNY, 1987). Readers familiar with his previous works will find in the present volume a further development of his thought that is predicated on these two works.

A GENERAL BACKGROUND

I will now turn to the topic of this section, namely, to reflect on the general background concern that, I think, informs the making of the present work: *Overcoming Modernity: Synchronicity and Image-Thinking*. Although the term "modernity" may mean different things to different people, it is used in this volume in a way more or less commonly understood: it refers to an historical period during the seventeenth through the eighteenth centuries in Europe when natural science arose and the Enlightenment emerged to be celebrated for the bright future it promised to the European peoples. Philosophically, it designates the period in which modern European philosophy was historically ushered in almost in tandem with the rise of natural science. (Descartes initiated it and Kant completed it.) This paradigm was based on rationalistic thinking anchored in ego-consciousness, and natural science took an equally rationalistic stance of theoretically observing nature from the outside. Both agreed that in understanding the relationship between human beings and nature, the observation and knowledge of nature that is external to an observer were important. On the basis of both science and rationalism, both science and rationalism have instructed Western as well as non-Western peoples for the last few hundred years on how to view nature and the human being. Rationalistic thinking defines human nature as rooted in reason, exercised as a discursive mode of thinking, while natural science treats nature as a collection of physical substances, using mathematics as a methodological tool. In short, rationalism was declared to be the philosophical foundation for viewing nature and the human being. Yuasa's project is to question these views, particularly their narrow scope and one-sidedness in their orientation. He addresses the topic of "overcoming modernity," particularly in chapters three, four, five, and six, by critiquing, for example, the philosophical foundations of Descartes' dualism, Galilean-Newtonian science, and contemporary physics, while offering an holistic approach to them.

Why then does Yuasa take up the project of "overcoming of modernity"? As I believe that this issue is a practically necessary and urgent task for us today to tackle, I will first make an historical observation about the impact that the modern Western rationalistic paradigm of thinking has had on the whole world, while supplementing it with what I take to be Yuasa's own philosophical reflections.[3] It would seem that this paradigm has historically exposed, perhaps unintentionally or unconsciously on the part of those people who have advocated it, the darker side of humanity to the world, both European and non-European. This is in spite of its alleged "transparency" of the mind that the rationalististic thinkers of the Enlightenment claimed vis-à-vis the "apodictic certainty of ego-consciousness." Consequently, it has historically produced, to use Jung's language, "many dragons,"[4] from which people in both European and non-European worlds have unnecessarily suffered, as modern world history has amply shown. What are the dragons that Jung had in mind? Yuasa counts the following as historical events exemplifying Jung's "dragons": religious wars, class struggles, foreign wars, and colonialism.[5] We may also add to the list "imperialism" and "nationalism"[6] that understandably arose as an ethnic psychological response to modernity.

We may view most of these events as historical phenomena, and hence consider them as passé, so as to dismiss them as having no immediate bearing on our contemporary life. But the effect of this paradigm still prevails over the whole world and claims its dominion over our contemporary life though in different forms than the above-mentioned Jung's "dragons." I will just name a few areas in which this is evident. It can be witnessed in a most pronounced form in our failure to satisfactorily deal with nature. Everyone is now aware that the rapid development of scientific technology has invited the ongoing destruction of nature, posed today as an environmental issue threatening our very existence as well as that of future generations. This danger looms large before us regardless of the ethnic origin or nation to which we belong. It is a global problem. As most of us are now aware, this threat comes specifically from: global warming, the melting of ice in the Arctic regions, the thinning of the ozone layer, deforestation, the overall diminishing of the wetlands, and an increase of deserts.

These are the consequences of regarding nature as a collection of physical substances (i.e., lifeless matter) for the purpose of human control and manipulation, which are the consequences of accepting the rationalistic standpoint of natural science and its application in scientific technology. In this standpoint, the superiority of *theōria* over *prāxis* is advocated. It means that scientific rationalism must dominate and control human beings living the everyday life. It consequently has created a dilemma or a discrepancy between the scientific standpoint and the everyday standpoint. For example, when this superiority is translated into the terms of the mind-body problem, it states that the theoretical stance must accept mind-body dualism to be true, even though the practical stance confirms mind-body unity, which we experience in our daily life. Theoretically, this consequence is entailed by endowing the Cartesian *ego-cogito* with a privileged position that enables the human being to observe nature from the outside, where the human being is understood to be a "being-outside-of-nature." However, the ongoing destruction of nature has made us aware in our contemporary period that human beings are instead "beings-in-nature." This fact urges us to rethink the relationship between *theōria* and *prāxis*, or between the standpoint of scientific rationalism and the everyday standpoint, for it has exposed an inadequacy of the methodological stance on which modern rationalistic thinking rests. Yuasa casts this issue in this volume as an issue of "space-time and mind-body integration" in order to suggest an alternative to the methodological stance that regards *theōria* as superior to *prāxis*.

In the arena of interpersonal relationship, it seems that individualism now has turned into egoism, wherein it is easy to see how the Cartesian *ego-cogito* can slip into this mode, when the theoretical background to Descartes' declaration is ignored. (The idea of individualism took a definite shape at the time of the Enlightenment, though its germination may be sought in the Italian Renaissance.) Under the political and ideological slogan of "human rights" extolled in individualism, whose conceptual origin goes back to the British liberal tradition, particularly John Locke's "natural rights," Western society praises the "virtue" of insisting on one's ego-desire. For example, "being aggressive" is considered a virtue in the U.S. This aggressive ego-desire has taken the form of the will both at the personal and the collective levels *at the expense of* those peoples who do not make such a claim. Undoubtedly, it is in part fueled and propelled by a deep anxiety of various kinds that has taken hold of people, with or without conscious awareness, in the contemporary world.[7]

This is another consequence of accepting modern rationalism as a paradigm of thinking, for its philosophy does not address the problem of death within its purview. And yet it is for the human being the deepest source of anxiety. Even though it does not address the problem of death, it is self-evident that death will always exist for humanity. However, for a rationalist, death is a meaningless and valueless event because the "essence" of what it means to be human according to this conceptual paradigm lies in the exercise of reason, even if it relies not on its superior mode of what the Greek philosophers called *"nous,"* but its inferior mode of discursive reason. If death is indeed meaningless and valueless, human life itself, which is destined to die, will accordingly come to be regarded as meaningless and valueless. This will in turn lead human beings to accept the stance of nihilism as an appropriate way of life. In addition, the potential nuclear annihilation of all things, whether sentient or insentient, unconsciously defines human *psychē* as an underlying tone of existence, which is expressed today in various forms of nihilism in our contemporary period.

In the arena of economics and commerce, their activity has in recent years turned global. This can be viewed as an extension of individualism turning into egoism on the national and international scales, which is propelled by American style capitalism. The impression one gets is of the deification of the insatiable human desire for the acquisition of material goods. This involves two *magical* beliefs despite its allegedly *rationalistic* stance that the modern concept of individualism upholds: (1) that human beings can create infinity out of finitude; and (2) that the possession of material goods alone makes human beings happy, even spiritually. This is assisted and accelerated by the remarkable advance of scientific technology, as is now symbolically seen in the development of computers, DVDs, the Internet, cell phones, genetic engineering, and so on, wherein we are brought to face various new ethical issues, such as environmental ethics, medical ethics, bioethics, business ethics, and so on This is entailed by overemphasizing the *materialistic* view of nature that scientific technology promotes. It shows that, in our contemporary period, scientific technology has surpassed the theoretical pursuit of natural science. Since technology originally has to do with the human endeavor of negotiating with nature, the contemporary period is demanding us to think anew the relationship between technology and science, and between human beings and nature.

These "developments" have also increased the sense of the rapidly changing world, without, however, affording us any sense of where it is heading. Consequently, they contribute to the immense source of anxiety. This rapid change has given us the impression that the world is "shrinking." Scientific technology as is seen in jets, television, the Internet, and so on, has made travel and communication easier and quicker, diminishing as a consequence the physical distances between cultures. However it has also given rise to various conflicts with an ethical bearing in its failure to probe into the "logic of passion," which has been fostered in different cultures and countries for centuries. In the standpoint of modern rationalism, however, the problem of passion or emotion has been expelled from philosophical discourse as that which is irrational. But as Nietzsche points out in *Beyond Good and Evil* such a stance involves a self-deception because the rationalist must "rationalize" the irrational to explain the motivation for action. Terms such as "will" and "human right" also conceal this fact.

I would like to bring to the reader's attention one more point that has a bearing on Yuasa's project of thematizing synchronicity and image-thinking. This is the use of logic or mathematics that science and scientific technology have adopted to explain empirical phenomena. This is exemplified when, for example, natural science appeals to the principle of causality for its explanatory model. Granted that, among empirical phenomena, scientists may find necessary causal relationships; however, ignoring that it is a *relative* necessity, they replace it with logical necessity by applying logic and/or mathematics to it. The problem here is that empirical phenomena are time-bound, whereas logic and mathematics are not. What is the philosophical reason for superimposing that which is not time-bound onto that which is? It calls into question the distinction between form and matter, wherein is already detected a hint of the anthropomorphic manipulation of nature. This is a presupposition on the part of the rationalist, which is not brought to clear reflection. Yuasa urges us to reflect on this point because our everyday life is surrounded by, and sometimes guided by, many contingent, accidental, or coincidental thing-events. We can also frame the issue as follows: Is human life, which starts with birth and ends in death—or, more broadly, the generation of life through its evolutionary process—governed solely by mechanistic causal necessity? "Not so," Yuasa would say, because the living organism, including the human being, embraces an "interior" region that cannot be explored by observing it from outside and applying mechanistic causal necessity. These reflections invite us to reconsider the limit of the applicability of logic and mathematics in natural science and scientific technology. It in turns calls up in our mind the question whether the contingency or coincidence might not be operative in the course of life lived by a living organism. And may not nature conceal an important "meaning" in what appears to be contingent, accidental, and coincidental? These questions have led Yuasa to investigate Jung's theory of synchronicity and image-thinking.

Yuasa's proposal in this volume is in part to question the methodological foundations of natural science as well as his response to the rapid development of scientific technology, which has now taken on its own path quite independently of the many theoretically unsolved problems of science itself, infiltrating both positively and negatively into our daily lives. In the face of all the changes that have taken place and are now still taking place, academic philosophy seems to have been pushed to the land of complete oblivion in our contemporary period. Yuasa's *Overcoming Modernity: Synchronicity and Image-Experience* is a humble attempt to make philosophy and philosophical reflection pertinent and to address the preceding issues from an holistic perspective, however daring and daunting this may seem.

AN ORGANIZATIONAL OVERVIEW

Now, I would like to provide an organizational overview for the present volume. This volume is structurally organized into three parts: Part I consists of two chapters on "image-thinking," which is primarily philosophical in content and orientation. For example, chapter one deals with the "image-thinking" of ancient peoples, both East and West, whereas chapter two addresses the topic of how the understanding of Being (or being) differs between the West (after Plato) and East Asia. Part II is composed of three chapters: chapter three centers on Yuasa's clarification of Jung's theory of synchronicity and the implications he develops beyond Jung's original design, by examining the *Book of Changes* (*Yijing*), parapsychology, and contemporary theories of physics. Chapter four takes a fresh look at the *Yijing* with further details on its view of nature, focusing on how this classical text understands time and space, while chapter five is a careful examination of the issues surrounding Rhinean parapsychological research. Readers will be surprised to see Yuasa addressing these topics within the single thematic focus upon Jung's theory of synchronicity. As such, Yuasa's treatment of these topics should be intriguing and interesting at the same time, for the reader may wonder how Yuasa can pack and weave these topics into the theme of synchronicity. Part III contains the last chapter of this volume, in which Yuasa addresses the philosophical issue of space-time and mind-body integration in an attempt to connect science with philosophy.

With this organizational overview in mind, I would now like to make a suggestion to readers about the order of reading this volume. Readers who feel an attraction to Jung's theory of synchronicity may read Part II first, wherein they will find a *clear*, systematic presentation of Jung's theory as well as insightful implications Yuasa develops for an holistic worldview in its three chapters. Readers can then return to Part I to learn about the philosophical underpinning of Jung's theory. Readers will discover in Part II that Yuasa's treatment is unique and thoughtful, for all of the books that have so far appeared in English on this subject do not, to my knowledge, carry Jung's theory to its logical conclusions. On the other hand, those readers who are more interested in the philosophical underpinning of Jung's theory of synchronicity may proceed from Part I, following the organization of the book. Because it deals with a philosophical stance on "image-thinking," Part I can be read without relating it to Jung's theory per se. It contains Yuasa's creative interpretation of both Western and Eastern philosophy, presenting his novel stance on them. Next, I will try to address the thematic concern addressed in this volume.

THE THEMATIC CONCERN

The thematic concern is captured by the four ideas, "image-thinking," "synchronicity," and "space-time and mind-body integration," and so I would like to point the direction whereby readers may approach this volume. By showing what Yuasa proposes to accomplish vis-à-vis these ideas, I will at the same time indicate how his perspective differs from the modern rationalistic paradigm of thinking. For this purpose, I will first deal with "image-thinking," since it is the central topic of the first two chapters that constitute Part I. I will then move to Yuasa's articulation of Jung's theory of synchronicity, which Yuasa, as I mentioned earlier, develops far beyond its original design in chapters three, four, and five. This portion makes up Part II. Lastly, I will address "space-time integration" and "mind-body integration" together since they are one of the main thematic foci of this volume, which Yuasa develops in chapter six, the only chapter making up Part III.

Image-Thinking

Image-thinking is a central and key concept in chapters one and two, and serves as a foundational concept for chapters three, four, and five. Yuasa forms this neologism when examining the epistemological stance he excavates in the hylozoism assumed by the pre-Socratic natural philosophers of Ancient Greece. Hylozoism is the belief that nature is filled with life or spiritual energy. Yuasa points out that within hylozoism is the functioning of image-thinking that connects human beings with nature. It points to a mode of human life organized in harmony with *living* nature, while interresonating with its activity. According to Yuasa, this mode of thinking is conducive, philosophically speaking, for advancing the correlativity between the human being *qua* microcosm and nature *qua* macrocosm. What he means by "image-thinking" can for now be taken to mean a mode of thinking that connects these worlds.

Yuasa maintains that when the natural philosophers questioned the origin of the cosmos by positing *archē* such as earth, water, fire, and air, these *archai* carried a symbolic meaning involving a projection from the *psychē*. For the espistemological subject who is anchored in the standpoint of ego-consciousness, this means that the authentic understanding of Being must be *passive* in nature, because it occurs vis-à-vis intuition, which is a passive cognition involving image-experience. This is because intuition cannot occur when ego-consciousness is posited as the active agent in cognition. Generally speaking, this mode of thinking assumes a panpsychic stance in viewing nature. Yuasa observes that this mode of thinking with a panpsychic stance is also found in ancient India as well as in ancient China, although in the case of the Chinese tradition, there was no concern for substantializing these elements (through the image of the "five goings"[8]). Except for this difference, he notes that ancient peoples, whether of the West or the East, assumed a *common* epistemological stance in understanding nature. This is an innovative interpretation for it is often the case that whenever the *archē* is thematized, its material dimension has been emphasized without sufficiently incorporating the projective character of the unconscious into the inquiry.

However, Yuasa notes that a shift occurred in the Greek tradition after Plato, from this mode of thinking to a rationalistic stance, a shift that did not occur either in India or China. He thus examines various philosophical issues that arise in maintaining the stance of image-thinking—for example, he compares Aristotle's metaphysics and the Chinese concept of "that which is above form," "logic and being" in Parmenides, and "the eternal and the changing" and "physics and ethics" as understood by Aristotle and the Chinese tradition. One of the purposes for conducting these comparisons is to show that there was a stark difference between the East and the West in regard to the understanding of Being (or being), which he explores in chapter two.

When Yuasa proposes the stance of "image-thinking," the reader may wonder what he is questioning. As I mentioned previously, his concern is to overcome modernity, particularly its rationalistic views of nature and the human being. These views assume Cartesian dualism that ontologically divides the mind and the body, from which the reader can see why Yuasa proposes "mind-body integration" as an alternative thesis. Along with dualism, there are sub-issues that are called into question, for example, its either–or logical stance. This logic thinks it reasonable to divide the whole in two parts in apprehending reality. It celebrates *exclusion*, but invariably entails the fragmentation of all of that to which this logic is applied. Moreover, because it divides at the linguistic level the whole into either affirmation or negation, it favors reductionism in understanding the whole. What carries out this division is the mind, particularly in its discursive mode of reasoning, that is, the modern epistemological subject. This is the standpoint of ego-consciousness, whose activity is delimited mainly by external sensory perception and the discursive mode of reasoning. In other words, it does not thematically incorporate issues arising from the body and the unconscious.[9] Taking these points together, Yuasa questions the rationalistic paradigm of thinking for its one-sided and narrow scope. Instead, Yuasa thinks that we need to approach reality *holistically*, for holism stipulates as one of its cardinal principles for knowing that to know is to know the whole. To move toward this goal, Yuasa proposes the stance of "image-thinking," which incorporates within its mode of thinking both the body and the unconscious. In chapter two he articulates the difference between the Eastern and the Western mode of thinking regarding this point by examining how Being (or being) has traditionally been understood in the East and the West.

Synchronicity

Yuasa develops the topic of synchronicity specifically in chapters three, four and five, where he sets up two major goals. The first is to provide a theoretical explanation for the phenomenon of synchronicity, and the second is to develop through the first attempt a worldview that is *holistic*. To accomplish these goals, he offers an original and innovative interpretation of Jung's theory of synchronicity by establishing a connection with the *Yijing's* worldview, the contemporary development in physics, and Rhinean paranormal research. While bringing these multidisciplinary topics into the purview of this single thematic focus, Yuasa also critiques the methodological foundations of the modern worldview proposed by natural science and rationalism.

Jung defines synchronicity to mean the meaningful coincidence between a psychological phenomenon and a physical phenomenon, and, as Yuasa interprets it, this occurs vis-à-vis an image-experience (chapter three). Jung confined this definition to apply only to isolated individual experiences. To further clarify Jung's definition of synchronicity, Yuasa expands this definition to include the interpersonal dimension as well as the cosmological dimension, where he sees the interpersonal dimension related to ethics and the cosmological dimension related to the view of nature. This expansion is guided by Jung's reinterpretation of the collective unconscious in terms of a spatial spread. Yuasa captures this expanded sense of synchronicity as follows: "synchronistic phenomena connect these two worlds [i.e., the physical world and the psychological world], when there obtains an explicit communication between a sender and a recipient, who are psychologically connected through mutual love, or in unfortunate cases, hatred and hostility." Here, the reader will discover Yuasa's development of Jung's theory of synchronicity beyond its original designs. In fact, he offers original and unique interpretations of Jung's theory, one after another, to the end of this volume.

In dealing with the cognitive aspect of Jung's theory, which is now expanded to include the interpersonal, cosmological dimension, Yuasa thematizes the *Yijing's* divination insofar as it demonstrates an instance of synchronicity, and defines it as "a technique of externalizing to conscious awareness the unconscious intuition about a situation in which one is placed in the present." With this observation, Yuasa makes important points. First, synchronicity questions Cartesian mind-body dualism. This is because in the *Yijing's* divination, psychological conditions surrounding the person divined are incorporated into its reading, that is, thing-events are understood to occur *inseparably* from the subject. This inseparability questions the methodological foundation of natural science, for the observing subject in natural science is allegedly excluded from the investigated nature. Moreover, Yuasa points out that the *Yijing* has a strong future orientation vis-à-vis teleology, in sharp contrast to the past orientation that modern natural science accepts vis-à-vis the principle of causality for its explanatory paradigm. He cautions that this future orientation does not mean a determinism. Instead he sees in it an important ethical meaning, as he explains that the *Yijing* is fundamentally a classic dealing with ethics.

Taking these points together, Yuasa proposes "one world" as the basis for the occurrence of synchronistic phenomena. To this effect, he states: just as there is one common physical world to which everyone has access, so there is one world of *psychē* that is the collective (or interpersonal) unconscious, which is common to everyone. This is a crystallization of Jung's "one world" (*unus mundus*). Despite the apparent diversity in apprehending the outer and the inner worlds, there is one world that connects everyone. This is the philosophical basis for Yuasa to advance his main thesis of space-time and mind-body integration. (For a further elaboration on this point see chapter four and chapter six) It must be noted, however, that this "one world" is not self-evident to ego-consciousness because the dimension of the collective unconscious is "below" and/or "above" it. In other words, it cannot be experienced unless "the human being" comes to realize that he or she is "a *passive* being made to be alive," supported and affected by the movement of nature.[10] (See also the section on the eternal in chapter one and the section on the theory of time in chapter four)

In his endeavor to expand and deepen the implications of Jung's theory of synchronicity, Yuasa now brings into the purview of his inquiry contemporary developments in physics and addresses a propinquity observed, for example, between the relativization of time and space in synchronistic phenomena and in Einstein's theory, and between Jung's psychology and

Heisenberg's indeterminacy principle. In this vein, Yuasa analyzes a "psychophysical" problem Jung detected in Heisenberg's principle, that is, the separation of the psychological from the physical, although he also criticizes Jung for his impetuous attempt to connect the psychological with the physical. That is, Jung neglects the intermediary region between them, the region of life-phenomena. Yuasa remarks that it needs to be investigated before making this connection, which he discusses in terms of *ki*-energy, that is, psychophysical life-energy. What draws the reader's attention to this point is Yuasa's insight that life-phenomena are endowed with teleological intentionality (e.g., in the form of natural healing power). In the same vein, he also examines Pauli's observation about the similarity in cognition between Heisenberg's principle and Jung's psychology concerning the unknowability of the thing-in-itself and the *psychē*-in-itself.

Of all the propinquities Yuasa discusses in connection with Jung's theory, David Bohm's implicate-explicate theory is very significant. The explicate order refers to the macro-world that modern natural science investigates and that can be explained by appealing to the theory of causation. On the other hand, the implicate order cannot be accessed by this method. Taking note of this point, Yuasa brings out the similarity of Bohm's explicate-implicate order with Pauli's observation about the propinquity between contemporary quantum physics and Jung's psychology. However, he sees in Bohm's explicate-implicate order an effort to go one step beyond Pauli's observation. For this reason, his explanation of Bohm's implicate order as "the holo-movement of a whirlpool of continuous energy" is illuminating, because in a holographic dry-plate, parts contain information about the whole. He reminds the reader that this is similar to the philosophy of Huáyán Buddhism where the ideas of "all is one" and "one is all" are upheld.

In this connection, Yuasa also brings up a striking phenomenon known in contemporary physics as the EPR effect (which was initially posed as a paradox and later became recognized as the EPR principle). What is intriguing about this effect is that under it an event becomes nonlocalized or, more specifically, space becomes zero. Likewise, time also becomes zero, wherein, Yuasa notes, "events occur not diachronically but synchronically." He shows the striking similarity of the conditions under which both synchronistic phenomena and nonlocalization phenomena occur. One more point Yuasa brings up regarding Bohm's theory of the implicate order deserves a special mention. Bohm's implicate order also designates the "potential common ground where consciousness and matter" are fused together. This idea parallels Pauli's idea introduced earlier, while also echoing Jung's idea of the *psychoid*, a reality appearing where no differentiation between matter and consciousness exists. To trace Bohm's theory of the implicate order, Yuasa mentions Indian philosophy as well as the Chinese concept of *ki*-energy wherein, he notes, both are directly related to meditation experience.

When Bohm's theory is philosophically assessed, it is an attempt to give concrete meaning to Kant's idea of the "unknowable" thing-in-itself, and Yuasa points out that Bohm's theory, nonlocalization phenomenon, and Huáyán Buddhism all support an *holistic* worldview that cannot be envisioned by appealing to reductionistic thinking. Viewing Bohm's theory from the broader concern for scholarship then, Yuasa concludes: "natural science needs metaphysics that goes beyond the limitations of physics." (See also the section on physics and metaphysics in chapter six.)

In a postscript to chapter three, Yuasa relates the situation surrounding Chinese somatic science, which investigates the phenomena of *ki*-energy, a psychophysical life-energy, in the three fields of (1) traditional Chinese medicine, (2) *qìgōng* or *ki*-training, and (3) paranormal phenomena—a topic he will pick up again in chapter six to suggest that they are three fields that point to a proper methodological way of envisioning the relationship between science and philosophy.

Yuasa thematizes in chapter four "the divination of the *Yìjīng* and the mind-body relation." The reader will initially be puzzled by this thematization because we do not ordinarily think that the divination of the *Yìjīng* is related to the mind-body issue. To demonstrate it, Yuasa gives another definition of the *Yìjīng*'s divination as "a method and technique for . . . knowing the future and the past." Knowing time, Yuasa shows, is a working of the mind because perceptual consciousness and sensory organs alone do not "enable us to understand the past or the future," for they register only the *present* condition of a spatial thing-event. He supplements his analysis with Bergson's theory of "pure perception." (For a detailed explanation of Bergson's theory, see the section on Einstein and Bergson in chapter six.) The mind he speaks of also includes the unconscious, and he identifies the mode of knowing in the *Yìjīng* as "intuition arising from the unconscious." Since the intuition in this case takes the form of image-experience, Yuasa proceeds to show that the *Yìjīng* formalized this image-experience, taken symbolically, in terms of the sixty-four hexagrams. With this explication, he also compares Freud's interpretation of dreams, that is, "dream-divination," with that of Jung, while expanding his examination to a comparison between the scientific mode of knowing based on causality and the mode of knowing of the *Yìjīng*.

Given that the *Yìjīng*'s divination is an intuition arising from the unconscious with the view to apprehending the future and the past, a natural question the reader may pose is: What is the "*Yìjīng*'s theory of time"? (See chapter four.) Yuasa addresses this topic also in anticipation of his analysis of the theory of time in science in chapter six, where he compares it with those proposed by Leibniz, Bergson, Einstein, and Heidegger. For now, he explains time as understood by the *Yijīng* to mean "'timing' or the 'situation' of that temporal condition," or in light of the categories of *yīn* and *yáng*, to mean "the change of phases between *yīn* and *yáng* that demonstrates a given situation from moment to moment." As he provides concrete examples to illustrate the sense of timing, while also citing actual examples of how the *Yijīng's* divination works, the reader is enabled to readily understand the *Yijīng's* theory of time. From these examples, the reader will learn that the *Yijīng* understands time to carry a *qualitative* dimension such that one can take the appropriate action in a given situation.

How then is the *Yijīng's* theory of time related to its view of nature? (See chapter four.) This question is important for Yuasa because his project is to propose a new way of understanding nature. For this purpose, he first proceeds to examine the theory of time thematized by Paul Tillich, namely, the Greek distinction between *chronos* and *chairos*. *Chronos* designates objective, physical, quantifiable time, that is, the change of a spatial thing-event known through sensory perception, for example, change in the sun's position. Natural science utilizes this sense of time. Yuasa questions it by way of Bergson's criticism, namely, that such a grasp of time is a "spatialized time," for the experience of time involves an activity of the unconscious in terms of memory and imagination, along with the perceptual consciousness and the sensory organs that function with it. It is here that the reader will learn that the theory of time is closely related to the mind-body theory. Yuasa takes this point as raising an important question regarding "the scientific method of thinking" because it does not take into account the unconscious that is "the seat of memory and intuition." If we further pursue this line of inquiry, it will lead us, Yuasa points out, to question "the [natural science's] paradigm concerning the view of nature." On the other hand, if we adhere to the mode of thinking espoused by natural science, Yuasa warns that no new views of nature and the human being will be forthcoming; science and philosophy will remain separate with their attendant problems unsolved.

What then is *chairos*, which is differentiated from *chronos*? *Chairos*, as Yuasa defines it, refers to "the quality of timing for the subject to act under a certain situation, for it carries such meanings as 'the proper time to act' and 'the arising of an opportunity.'" It designates a *qualitative* time that is lived from within *the mind*. If this is the case, Yuasa suggests that *chairos* may be considered psychological time, but quickly points out that it cannot simply be so considered. Traditional Chinese medicine, for example, maintains that as long as one is alive, the activity of both the mind and the body cannot be separated; they are inseparably tied by way of the activity of *ki*-energy. (Here, the reader can also see how Yuasa came to the idea of mind-body integration.) This means that psychological time is connected to life-time, which Yuasa defines as "the quality of time apprehended in the surrounding situation wherein a person *is* [*passively*] *placed* in the present." Yuasa concludes that time is inseparable from space, and that is the *Yijīng's* understanding of time.

Given this theory of time, what, Yuasa asks, is the ancient Chinese view of nature? In response to this question, he explicates the idea of *Dao* as the primordial source of movement in nature vis-à-vis the activity of *ki*-energy, which undergoes its *yīn-yáng* phase change, and hence the *Yijīng's* understanding of time as tim*ing*. Accordingly, nature is viewed as being permeated with this energy. A picture the reader will obtain from this explication of the human being is that being who "as a microcosm lives in harmony with the activity of the macrocosm" while receiving nature's energy.

Yuasa now asks whether time and space are separable by examining "the traditional views of nature of the East and the West." (See chapter four.) He raises this issue to question modern natural science wherein space and time are separated. For this purpose, he compares two theories of time; one is the linear concept of time reflective of the Christian myth of creation and eschatology, while the other is the Daoist cyclic concept of time observed in nature. In this vein, Yuasa points out that Christianity's myth of *imago dei* elevates the human being to a "being-outside-of nature" because the God of Christianity is conceived to transcend nature. According to this model, the human being is thought to be "closer" to God than animals and plants. On the other hand, the Daoist view defines the human being as a "being-in-nature" with the implication that there is no essential difference between the human being and other things in nature because they all live in nature in reception of life-activity *qua ki*-energy. With this comparison, Yuasa observes that natural science's linear concept of time is an inheritance of Christian mythological time with an absolute beginning and end. Out of this secularized inheritance, he notes, Newton's concepts of absolute time *and* absolute space emerged. The principle of causality is predicated on such a view of time. On the other hand, in the traditional Chinese view, Yuasa points out, there is no theoretical speculation in order to determine the separate natures of time and space, for this tradition maintained the *inseparability* of time and space. To illustrate it, he analyzes the Chinese compound that denotes "cosmos," *yǔzhòu* [宇宙, Jap., *uchū*]. In this context, he also mentions Einstein's space-time continuum in his general theory of relativity as a scientifically correct way of understanding the relationship between time and space.

To further delve into space-time inseparability, Yuasa examines "space and the energy immanent in time" as this issue touches the heart of the *Yijīng's* divination and he accordingly articulates how energy is manifest in space. (See chapter four.) To do so, he gives still another definition of the

Yijing's divination as an attempt "to know the characteristics of the operation of time that mobilizes all things, changes them, and brings them to maturation." While time carries a sense of the activity of *"qi-energy"* [氣, Jap., *ki*] that enables living organisms to change, Yuasa interprets the *Yijing* to understand space to be a field of information. Accordingly, Yuasa reasons that all the things shaped in nature, including human beings, *receive* this energy *qua* information, though in the case of human beings, it is received in the body and the unconscious. For this reason, it will be difficult to understand this point if one *clings* to a homocentric standpoint that is defined by the Cartesian *ego-cogito*. He theorizes that this receptive activity is another reason why the *Yijing's* divination is possible, because its goal is to apprehend the tim*ing* of a thing-event in space that is a field of information.

Yuasa now brings up another important point by way of the idea of the time-zone, and it is for the purpose of showing how synchronistic phenomena occur à la *Yijing's* divination. He acknowledges that even though *"ki-*energy" changes its phases, it nevertheless preserves its quality in a given time-zone, wherein energy of the same quality "ties everything together." This implies that in a given time-zone, "thing-events, appearing far and distant, resonate and harmonize with each other." This is the view of nature on which, Yuasa explains, Jung's theory of synchronicity rests. He also introduces the custom of naming eras in China and Japan to illustrate how the same quality of *"ki-*energy" is retained, while also commenting on Alvin Toffler's idea of "durational expectancies" as well as Hegel's concept of *Zeitgeist*. The reader will see clearly that Yuasa's expansion of Jung's theory to the cosmological dimension is concretely instantiated with this idea of the time-zone.

In chapter five he clarifies the problematic issues raised against the acceptance of paranormal phenomena by examining the pros and cons regarding them, the methodological limitations of Rhinean parapsychological research, and what parapsychology means for erecting a new worldview and a new view of human beings. In this connection, it is worthwhile to keep in mind Pauli's remark that Yuasa examines: while the function of teleological intentionality and wholeness are recognized in the living organism as is suggested by Jung's theory of synchronicity, Pauli remarks that physics cannot even adequately understand "the [physical] event that stands on the material foundation." To elaborate on this point, Yuasa also mentions Neils Bohr's reservation for the applicability of the criterion of repeatability to living organisms. With the articulation of these theoretical concerns, Yuasa provides an explanation of how Jung personally came to accept the *Yijing's* divination as "beyond 'probability based on chance,'" where "beyond" means the rejection of the principle of causality. That is, it refers to a different principle, namely, an acausal principle that is operative in synchronistic phenomena. (Also see the section in chapter six where he provides methodological reflections on science.)

Now, Yuasa examines the parapsychological disputes (mainly in chapter five) to assess several objections raised against Rhinean parapsychological research, to supplement Pauli's and Bohrs' reasons for rejecting the criterion of repeatability. Here I will just mention his rationale for a counter-criticism. His rebuttal against them is based on the reason that Jung's theory of synchronicity, and hence also paranormal phenomena, goes beyond the principle of causality that the methodological assumptions of natural science uphold. Instead, he takes the stance that an inquiry into synchronistic phenomena "has a bearing on the revolution of how to view human beings and nature, including such domains as medicine, history, society, and religion." As such, he remarks, "it plays the role of the 'frontline soldier' that seeks to modify the hitherto accepted view concerning the whole relationship between human beings and nature." Accordingly, we must proceed to construct, Yuasa maintains, "a new approach" to study paranormal phenomena. This is also because synchronistic phenomena are concerned with the *qualitative* dimension of human experiences, irreducible to the quantitative research which Rhine's methodology follows. (See the section on "meaningful coincidence" in chapter five.) For this reason, he reminds the reader that Jung distinguishes between meaningful and meaningless coincidences when thematizing synchronistic phenomena.

To show the qualitative dimension intrinsic to synchronistic phenomena, Yuasa cites two reported cases that actually occurred, both involving the death of a person, to maintain that synchronicity has a bearing on the meaning of life. These cases illustrate conditions that an artificially constructed scientific experiment cannot replicate, wherein Yuasa sees the issue of understanding time as *chairos*. To properly locate where synchronicity assumes its position in academic scholarship, Yuasa states that "paranormal phenomena . . . occur on the border line between the domain of objective fact discernible by science and the historical and ethical domains that have a bearing on the value and meaning of living human life." This is the domain in which, he points out, is operative "a purposiveness different in nature from scientific causality," for science is incapable of addressing this domain, as it is simply concerned with facts. This is because causality explains the "how" of a thing-event without addressing the questions of "why" and "what," which leads to metaphysics.

Since his explanation thus far is directly related to the meaning of the collective unconscious, Yuasa reflects on the scope of the collective unconscious, which Jolande Jacobi, Jung's student, further elaborated by breaking it down to the categories of family, tribe, ethnic group, and nation. He classifies these

kinds of collective unconscious from the point of view of space-time inseparability, and discusses such ideas as the familiar, communal, historical, climatic,
and natural collective unconscious. Of these, what attracts the reader's attention is Yuasa's idea of the "natural collective unconscious," which defines the
human being as "a being which resonates with the activity of animals, plants
and physical nature," a view that goes directly counter to the orthodox Christian view.[11] This is the view of human beings Yuasa draws from Jung's theory
of synchronicity, where the reader can readily see a resonance with the Chinese concept of *ki*-energy and Greek hylozoism.

Space-Time and Mind-Body Integration

Chapter six is the final chapter of this volume, in which Yuasa proposes the
holistic standpoint of "Space-Time and Mind-Body Integration." It is easier
to understand his stance, if the reader holds an opposite image of the phrase
"space-time and mind-body integration." By "mind-body integration," he
implies the rejection of the stance that separates the mind from the body, and
time from space. Otherwise, he fears that separation would invite the prioritization of theory over practice, depriving the human being of a living sense of
reality, for the prioritization is introduced by intellectually imposing an a priori form of understanding on either time or space. To avoid this consequence,
Yuasa thematizes "space-time integration," as he states, by "compar[ing] and
contrast[ing] the idea of space-time conceived in physics and the idea of the
same seen from the points-of-view of psychology and philosophy."

When Yuasa questions science's separation of time from space, he has
primarily two points in mind for refutation: science postulates (1) time as an
a priori formal condition, prior to actual experience, as well as (2) the reversibility or symmetry of time. Instead, he advances the thesis that both the past
and the future are enfolded in the present, together with the idea of the "ripening of time." To illustrate the essential points of Yuasa's view of time, let
us first take up the dispute between Leibniz and Newton. Leibniz charged
Newton that the latter's "method postulates in advance a form of time prior
to experience [vis-à-vis the concept of absolute time], and then tries to explain
the event," but Yuasa points out that this creates a gap "between *a priori* logic
and experiential fact." As such, he remarks that it is "a theoretical fiction."
He elaborates this charge by way of Bergson's theory of time, which regards
Newton's concept of time as a spatialized time, where time is turned into a
quantity and a volume. However, as Yuasa contends, the experience of time
is *qualitative* in nature and inseparable from an integrated mind-body experience. His analysis is unsparing, as he applies it to Einstein's special theory of
relativity as a metatheory and to Heisenberg's stance on time.

Yuasa now criticizes the idea of the reversibility of time as accepted in relativity theory, quantum physics, electromagnetics, and gravity-space. To do so, he introduces Prigogine's theory of time, while examining Prigogine's interest in Daoism and Heidegger's idea of the "ripening of time." Prigogine upholds the idea of "time's arrow" in his theory of "fluctuations and dissipation," that is, the unidirectional flow of time, moving from the past to the future by way of the present. Yuasa observes that while his "time's arrow" is supported by the law of entropy (i.e., an increase of entropy drives the cosmos toward chaos with the transpiration of time), Prigogine's theory also maintains that despite this increase, a new order is created in the cosmos. The latter point, Yuasa notes, resonates with Daoism in that Daoism also recognizes in its celebration of the "ripening of time" that the cosmos is generated out of chaos. This is the idea of timing through the activity of ki-energy, by means of which the order of myriad things is generated out of chaos. Moreover, Yuasa finds Prigogine's theory of the "time's arrow" to be commensurate with Heidegger's idea of the "ripening of time," as well as Bergson's theory, for both understood the past and the future to be enfolded in the present. One might think that this enfolding of past and future in the present would, on the contrary, allow for time to unfold in either direction (past or future) and hence not be opposed to the reversibility of time. The scientific theory of time as symmetrical and/or reversible is an operational concept, introduced a priori into its methodological foundations. This operational concept of time renders time to be simply *quantitative*, as it is something thought a priori, when in fact time-experience is *qualitative*, for it cannot be understood unless it is connected to the function of the unconscious (i.e, memory). Moreover, the qualitative dimension of time cannot be apprehended if time is thought to flow uniformly with a punctuated unity of homogeneity, which the scientific theory of time presupposes. In this sense, it is dead time. On the other hand the theory of time as enfolding both the past and the future in the present designates a lived time. And, as Yuasa understands it, the enfolding of past and future in the present is *living* time.

His analysis is thorough for he also examines Einstein's puzzle of his later years, namely, whether time might be an illusion. This puzzle arose from Einstein's reflection on the special theory of relativity as a metatheory. Yuasa shows that this puzzle of Einstein occurs due to the reversibility or symmetry of time, for, according to this model, it does not make any difference what value time is given on a graph, whether it is the past, the present, or the future. (He also draws the same conclusion regarding Hawking's idea of time before the Big Bang as an imaginary number, in which case Yuasa comments that "time is nothing but a form which does not have a reality.") Einstein was led to this question because, as Yuasa explains, he ignored the factual issue that is related to mind-body integration.

By reflecting on Einstein's puzzle over the status of the present, Yuasa now offers his own thought on what the present is, by relating it to the problem of measurement. This is where he establishes an explicit connection between science and philosophy. For this purpose, he analyzes a dispute that took place between Bohm and Heisenberg. It centered on how to understand the condition of a particle movement prior to measurement—the overlapping condition of either the wave or the particle. What is referred to as "the condition" designates the mathematically formulated content; Bohm questioned it, contending that there is an order that cannot be described by the mathematical function. On the other hand, Heisenberg charged Bohm that since such an hypothesis cannot be measured, it is meaningless to postulate it; we should be content with the mathematically formulated content. Yuasa's conclusion is that Heisenberg prioritizes theory over experiment in his methodological procedure because, Yuasa reasons, the experiment has a character different in nature than the mathematical function (theory). This is the procedure of imposing a priori form on the experiment. Consequently, Yuasa advances the thesis that the act of measurement means a *determination* of the "present," because it is the way of making the present determinate on the straight line on a graph that science represents as time. When Yuasa states that the act of measurement means a determination of the present, he implies that the *interest* brought by the observer to the act of measuring must be examined, that is, the psychology of the unconscious must be clarified from a philosophical point of view. This takes Yuasa to examine later the relationship between physics and metaphysics.

With these thorough examinations of science's understanding of time, Yuasa now provides an epistemological critique by performing a "Methodological Reflection on Science." His reflection first looks into the issue of "theory-ladenness," which determines *in advance* the consequence of scientific research in a definite manner. For this purpose, Yuasa examines Kant's epistemological critique of modern science, in which Kant sets up two a priori conditions: one is that time and space are the a priori forms of cognition, and the other is the use of logic and mathematics. Because Kant's definition of time and space is a philosophical translation of Newton's "absolute time" and "absolute space," Yuasa critiques that they are empty, contentless, that is, they are *dead* time and space.

Now concerning logic and mathematics, he charges that both exemplify an instance of theory-ladenness in science. In the case of mathematics, Yuasa analyzes Gödel's incompleteness thesis, while in the case of logic he questions Aristotle's law of the excluded middle, as the latter is called into question by the former. Gödel's incompleteness thesis states that mathematics cannot consistently be maintained as a self-contained and self-sufficient system because it must refer to an element outside of it. On the other hand, Aristotle's law of the excluded middle (i.e., "A must be either true or false") relies on either–or logic as the standard for making judgments. Yuasa questions whether we can understand the whole of reality by dividing it in two in this manner. Accordingly, he mounts the critique that, when logic and mathematics are applied in formulating the principle of causality, neither of them in fact have anything to do with it, for they are both timeless (see the section on logic and being in chapter one). This is because causality is empirical in nature, which presupposes a transpiration of time. Consequently, as long as natural science accepts the principle of causality as an explanatory model, Yuasa asks whether there would not be a contradiction when science attempts to establish a logically necessary relationship between a cause and an effect by relying on logic and/ or mathematics. Instead, he contends that time must be understood from the point of view of mind-body integration, for what knows time is no other than the integrated human mind and body. This criticism also applies to Einstein's special theory of relativity as a metaprinciple, namely, that his idea of space-time continuum is divorced from the space-time integration that is intrinsically related to mind-body integration. He concludes his methodological reflection on science by proposing that in order for science and philosophy to meaningfully communicate with each other, the mind-body relation must be investigated not only from the point of view of physics, but also from the point of view of psychology and philosophy.

With these critiques he moves to reflect on the propinquity observed in contemporary physics and Eastern thought regarding their worldviews, and examines the relationship between "Physics and Metaphysics" with the question of whether or not physics can incorporate into its foundation an holistic view of nature, as suggested by its discovery of the nonlocalization principle. This question is already anticipated by his analysis of the *Yijing* and Daoism. In order to envision such an holistic view of nature, Yuasa proposes, concurring with Bohm, that the wave model rather than the particle model must be adapted in approaching nature. While also relating Bohm's association with Indian philosophy, Yuasa reinstantiates the point that this tradition understands "to measure" to mean *māyā*, illusion, reminding the reader of Plato's analogy of the cave, wherein only the shadow of reality is seen. (See the section on nature's psychoid nature in chapter three.) With this observation, Yuasa is questioning the methodological foundation of physics that relies only on sensory perception (i.e., the measuring device) and theoretical observation (i.e., the use of logic and mathematics) to build its edifice. Therefore, he concludes that physics needs metaphysics in order for it to embrace an holistic understanding of nature.

Yuasa summarizes his inquiry by suggesting how an holistic understanding of nature and the human being can be accomplished through the unification of an integrated space-time and an integrated mind-body. (See the last section of chapter six.) The issue of space-time integration involves a recasting of the ideas of time and space as suggested by the *Yijīng*'s view of space-time inseparability. In the *Yijīng*, time in the sense of timing is closely tied to the *ki*-energy that mobilizes thing-events to ripen (i.e., tim*ing*), and space is that field in which this ripening occurs. (See chapter four.) On the other hand, mind-body integration is intimately connected to the understanding of living time, involving both consciousness and the unconscious, as is shown by Yuasa's interpretation of Bergson's and Heidegger's theory of time. In Yuasa's scheme, space-time integration and mind-body integration are inseparable, for nature *qua* the activity of *ki*-energy in which time expresses itself as tim*ing* cannot be understood unless it is tied to space seen from the point of view of the integrated mind-body, which synthesizes time and space as space-time. To actually learn about the empirical investigation of this integration, Yuasa directs the reader's attention to the research the Chinese people have undertaken on *ki*-training (気功; Jap., *kikō*), because it clarifies the integrated field between mind, body, and matter existing in the external environment. He concludes Part III by remarking that this integrated field involves an activity connected to "the eternal cosmos that synthesizes the past and the future." Therein Jung's collective unconscious will be seen to form "the system of the mind's network that spreads behind the background of four-dimensional space-time which sensory perception grasps." This is the picture Yuasa proposes for a new worldview.

As we have observed, Yuasa's *Overcoming Modernity: Synchronicity and Image-Thinking* is designed to initiate a new orientation of thinking in place of the rationalistic paradigm of thinking that favors the either–or logical, dualistic, and reductionistic stance for its methodological foundation. When this aspect of either–or logical dualism is emphasized, a whole is split into two *opposing* parts. This is the formula for creating conflicts and/or contradictions, for example, not only within one's self, but also between "I" and others, between peoples, and between nature and the human being. And when this paradigm emphasizes the reductionistic stance, it results in the one-sidedness in dealing with these relationships, losing sight of the whole. That is, it celebrates exclusion in the apprehension of reality. In place of this paradigm, Yuasa offers an *holistic* paradigm. Rather than separating practice from theory, mind from body, time from space, human being from nature, it offers an integrated view of these relationships, thus allowing one to apprehend whole as whole. Yuasa captures this idea with the phrase "space-time and mind-body integration."

By thinking through and beyond Jung's theory of synchronicity Yuasa has laid down foundational ideas for us to rethink the whole relationship

between nature and the human being, while also questioning the methodological foundations of science. His proposal is a suggestion to think of the
inseparability of space that is filled with information and time that carries
energy to mobilize human beings. Yuasa thinks that the separation of science
and philosophy closes this holistic understanding of nature and the human
being. I believe that Yuasa's view will afford us to situate the human being in
its proper place in nature relative to scientific developments. In these respects,
his work is original and unique. For this very reason, however, it now stands
alone in the academic field because he has cultivated a new field in the forest
of individually disjointed fields of scholarly inquiry. However, as truth detests
being left alone, it seeks to be announced to those who can apprehend it and
appreciate it. This invitation to rethink the modern Western paradigm of
rationalistic thinking is still in the hands of the reader, and I hope that he
or she will take this opportunity to incorporate the holistic way of thinking
into his or her daily life, by utilizing the image-thinking already immanent in
every one of us.

SOURCES

As the present translation is a collection gathered together from Yuasa's different writings into a book form, I would like to indicate the sources from
which they are taken.

Chapter one, "The Image-Thinking of Ancient People, East and West"
[*Kodaijinno imējishikō*] is taken from a section from *The Birth of Philosophy:
The Psychology of Masculinity and Femininity* [*Tetsugaku no tanjō: jyoseisei to
danseisei no shinri*] (Kyoto: Jinmon shoin, 2004). Chapter two, "Image-Thinking and the Understanding of 'Being': The Psychological Basis of Linguistic
Expression" [*Imējishikōto sonnzairikai: Gengohyōgenno shinrigakutekikonkyo*]
is a translation of a chapter from Yuasa Yasuo's *The Synchronistic View of
the Cosmos: Time, Life and Nature* [*Kyōjisei no uchūkan: Jikan, Seimei, Shizen*]
(Kyoto: Jinmon shoin, 1995), pp. 81–121. Since this chapter was published
in English in the journal *Philosophy East and West* vol. 55, no. 2 (April 2005),
the translators would like to express an appreciation to Professor Roger
Ames, the editor of the journal, for granting permission to include it in the
present volume.

Chapter three, "What Is Synchronicity?," is taken from Yuasa Yasuo's
"What Is Synchronicity" [*"Kyōjisei to wa nanika"*] contained in his *Between
Religion and Science* [*Shūkyō to kagaku no aida*] (Tokyo: Meicho kankōkai,
1994), pp. 47–102. Chapter four, "Life and Space-Time: Synchronicity and
the Psychology of the *Yijīng*," [*Seimei to jikū: Eki no shinrigaku to kyōjisei*] is a
translation of a chapter in Yuasa Yasuo's *The Synchronistic View of the Cosmos*

[*Kyōjisei no uchūkan*] (Kyoto: Jinmon shoin, 1995) pp.122–162. The translators deleted the section "Living Time and Dead Time" that appears as the last section of this chapter after consulting Professor Yuasa. The reason for this deletion was primarily to avoid redundancy in light of what is contained in Chapter Six. However, whatever is not redundant was inserted in the body of the text contained in chapter six. This is noted in the notes to chapter six. Chapter five, "Synchronicity and Paranormal Phenomena" [*Kyōjisei to chōjōgenshō*], is taken from Yuasa Yasuo's *The Synchronistic View of the Cosmos* [*Kyōjisei no uchūkan*] (Kyoto: Jinmon shoin, 1995), pp. 163–192.

Chapter six, "Space-Time and Mind-Body Integration: The Resurrection of Teleology," is taken from Yuasa Yasuo's "Einstein and Bergson, Jung: The Relationship Between Space-Time Integration and Mind-Body Integration" [*"Ainshutain to beruguson, yungu: jikūtōgō to shinshintōgo no kankei"*], contained in *The Science of Space-Time To Open Up Consciousness*, ed. the Organizing Committee for the Second International Symposium on Consciousness, New Medicine, New Energy (Tokyo: Tokuma shoten, 2000), pp. 109–137.

TRANSLATION PROCESS

Nagatomo formed a reading group in the Department of Religion at Temple University in the spring semester of 2001, with a view to translating Yuasa's writings to form the present volume. Initially, the group included Jacques Fasan, Pamela Winfield, Michael Graham, and Victor Forte; Nagatomo served as the moderator. Both Michael Graham and Victor Forte could not continue to attend for they needed to prepare for their Ph.D. preliminary examinations. Pamela Winfield stayed with the group to the end of that semester, but afterward she went to Japan to do research on her dissertation. In the summer of 2001, Jacques Fasan and Nagatomo continued to work on the translation of what now constitutes chapter two, collaborating to produce the final draft. Toward the end of this summer session, John Krummel joined the Nagatomo-Fasan group to observe the translation sessions. He became interested in the translation, and thereafter he and Nagatomo started translating chapters one, three, four, and five for a few hours every Saturday afternoon until they completed the rough draft of these chapters at the end of the summer of 2002. Nagatomo translated chapter six, "Space-Time and Mind-Body Integration," in October 1998, which Professor Yuasa presented in a panel with the British physicist Brian Josephson held on November 22–23, 1998, in Tokyo, Japan. During summer 2003, Nagatomo and John Krummel worked together to complete the final draft of the present work and asked Professor Yuasa to check their work. He made many valuable corrections and suggestions to improve the draft, deleting and adding sentences and paragraphs wherever he felt necessary and appropriate. Toward the end of this project, Kristin Narcowich, Edward Godfrey, and Jacob Yeager graciously accepted our request to proofread the manuscript.

The translators would like to note that any phrase or sentence that is enclosed in brackets is an insertion that they added to the body of the text. Whenever this practice is followed, they had the goal of making the text clearer and/or the transition smoother, while also establishing cross-reference whenever appropriate. The translators took the utmost care to avoid errors and mistakes. However, if any errors and mistakes remain, it is entirely their responsibility.

Shigenori Nagatomo
Havertown, Pa.

Preface

From Synchronicity to Spirituality

COINCIDENCE BETWEEN THE INNER
AND THE OUTER

C. G. Jung (1875–1961), a psychologist, through his collaboration with Wolf-gang Pauli (1900–1958), a physicist, came up in his later years with the theory of synchronicity. It is, needless to say, based on the depth-psychological viewpoint he had pursued up to that time. But its content goes far beyond the domain of psychology: it enters into a general philosophical investigation regarding *nature and human nature*. The letters exchanged between Jung and Pauli make it evident that, on the basis of the perspectives of psychology and natural science, they sought to find a standpoint that synthesizes the two.[1]

Synchronicity refers to a unique experience that sometimes occurs in situations when one is facing nature. It is defined as a "meaningful coincidence." However, this alone does not give an [adequate] explanation as to the elements that are brought to a "meaningful coincidence." It refers to the coincidence of *a psychological event in the interior of an individual* and *an event that occurs outside* of him or her (i.e., nature as environment), a coincidence in terms of the content of their meaning and one that occurs synchronically in terms of time. Or, simply put, we can say that the inner and the outer occur simultaneously while being synchronized. Jung cites an example in an essay (1952) on the topic that he made public in a book coauthored with Pauli. Although this story may elicit in one an odd feeling, Jung relates that once when a female patient, who was receiving counseling from him, was speaking about a golden scarab, an insect quite similar to it flew indoors right before them.[2] She was quite shocked by this experience, not knowing what it meant. Although the counseling was not moving well until then, it proceeded smoothly after this emotional experience. It appears that the patient had discovered in this experience the hope that "there exists in the world, a power that brings meaning to her life." In short, synchronicity may for now be understood to mean "the coincidence in the content of meaning where an interior, psychological experience such as dreams, image-experiences, and intuitions corresponds to a (natural) experience that occurs outside." The issue now is what is to be drawn from this kind of synchronistic experience, and what sort of function is active at its foundation.

What led me to this topic is a certain concern that I felt: that it presents one of the philosophical and intellectual tasks that contemporary people face today. Having pondered upon it, I can mention first the relationship to the *Yijing*, and second the relationship with Rhine's parapsychology, both as points that support the theory of synchronicity. Neither of them, it would seem, are adequately understood, however. The New (Age) Science movement arose in the 1970s from out of a small number of scientists. [For example,] in the thought of David Bohm, a British physicist, who was considered one of the leaders of this movement, there were elements influenced by the Jung–Pauli theory of synchronicity. Since the 1980s, a practical concern and interest in Eastern thought have increased [throughout the world], having taken concrete shape after the onset of the New (Age) Science movement. [In relation to this,] a concern for various somatics and body-works related to *ki*-energy has spread globally. Furthermore, after the 1990s the concern for spirituality has become widespread, arising out of the development of medical issues. In such circumstances witnessed in the latter half of the twentieth century, I think that the theory of synchronicity has played an igniting role in triggering the emergence of new movements of thought. [Hence,] I would like to think through its significance from the point of view of the present.

THE VIEW OF THE MIND PRESUPPOSED BY THE *YIJING*

Jung first used the term "synchronicity" in a lecture, delivered in Munich in 1930 to eulogize Richard Wilhelm (1873–1930), a Sinologist. Wilhelm was a scholar who translated the *Yijing* into German, and Jung praised him for this translation work as the latter's greatest achievement. What initially led Jung to think about synchronicity was his concern for divination in the *Yijing*. It was reportedly around 1910, after he parted from Freud, when he started an "experiment" with such divination of the *Yijing*. As a result of this experiment, he came to believe that the *Yijing*'s divination works [i.e., is true], and, as he deepened his exchange with Wilhelm, he began to ponder the issue of why [and how] it works. It is clear that its hitting the bull's eye is completely different in character from [the success of] scientific prediction.

If it succeeds, we cannot but think at least for now that the primary ground for this lies in a power latent within the unconscious. Divination grasps the relationship between human being and nature by assuming a principle completely different from [that of] the scientific method that yields the same result regardless of who performs [the experiment]. Jung was led to think that the divination is performed by a power of intuition latent in the interior of the unconscious, and for him to think in this way as a psychologist was natural. Here we face the problem of how to conceive the power of intuition latent in the unconscious.

In response to this issue, Jung came to the conclusion that we ought to return to the way of thinking that had guided ancient peoples to believe in divination. For the ancients, divination meant inquiring after the divine will, and it was an activity that seeks revelation from a "sacred" dimension. When this is translated in light of the contemporary psychological point of view, the natural course would be to arrive at the idea that *the depth-psychological essence of human nature is spiritual*. Through a biography that was published posthumously, we learn of the many mystical experiences Jung had throughout his life. Although psychologists of the time could not believe in knowledge based on intuition, it would seem that Jung himself thought of the issue as one that [coming] periods will solve. (At least there is an aspect in his thought that suggests this interpretation.)

While showing the highest admiration for Wilhelm's translation of the *Yijing*, Jung claims that the value this translation possesses in the contemporary period would lie in the role it plays in responding to the spiritual demand of the Western people. However, what is meant here by "the Western people" does not refer to those who represent academia but rather to ordinary people. According to Jung's view, what the ordinary people in contemporary times are seeking is in fact something that may resonate with the occult. (Or, to sound more contemporary, we may instead use the term "spirituality.") Referring to the theosophical movement that was showing signs of popularity [in Europe,] particularly in England, he states the following: "The *Yijing* is a text which answers to the demand of an historical development in our period. Occultism today is meeting a renaissance, and we can witness the movement everywhere in our period that is seeking a similar kind of demand . . . What I have in mind here is not our academia and people representative of it. Since I am a physician, I deal with ordinary people. Consequently, I know quite well that the contemporary universities have long ceased playing the role of messenger who can bring light to the people. People are now weary of scientific specialization and rationalistic intellectualism."[3] Jung's remark here drives home closer to us living in the twenty-first century than those living in the period of the 1930s. His thought is supported by a stance that bears *a perspective toward the future of the intellectual movement in the world.* In assuming such a stance, he believed that there is in the *Yijing* something that could teach us about the issue of the mind (*psychē*) that contemporary people face.

In this eulogy lecture Jung situates the *Yijing* as a classic that sets the standard for "science" in the Chinese tradition, and states that the "science" of the *Yijing* is not based on causality but on what he tentatively calls "the principle of synchronicity." He states: "My occupation with the psychology of the unconscious processes long ago necessitated my casting around for another explanatory principle . . . Thus I found that there are psychic parallelisms which cannot be related to each other causally, but which must stand in another sort of connectedness." [4] In short, the reason he came to think of the term "synchronicity" is based on the following understanding. He took note of an activity of the inner unconscious at the foundation of the *Yijing*, and came to regard *this activity of the inner unconscious* as coinciding with *the observation of outer nature.* If such an interpretation is possible, we may discern here a form of cognition of nature different from that espoused by modern science. Put differently, when the inner and the outer coincide with each other, nature appears under a new "look" different from the way it looks under the viewpoint of modern science.

Because I am afraid that some readers may question the idea that the *Yijing* can be a classic of "science," I would like to add a few more words and would like the reader to consider the following fact. As Joseph Needam's research on the history of scientific technology in China revealed, the standard of Chinese technological science was highly advanced in the world prior to the birth of modern science, probably far exceeding that of the West. (For example, China's discovery of the artificial magnet, gunpowder, as well as the circulation of blood in medical technology goes back to its ancient periods.) In this connection, Needam takes note of the fact that the bearers of scientific technology were mainly Daoist practitioners (*Daoshi*).

THE *YIJING* IS ALSO THE CLASSIC OF ETHICS

The *Yijing* is counted as one of the five classics [of Confucianism] before Confucius. In the *Yijing* there is a text that deals with "Judgments on the Hexagrams" [*quàcí*; Jap., *kaji*] to explain the triagrams (*quà*), as well as the *Ten Wings* [*Shíyì*; Jap., *Jyūyoku*] that provide it with philosophical commentary. The latter was believed to be written by Confucius, and this shows that the *Yijing* was considered one of the classics in Confucianism. The texts valued and respected by Confucianism, needless to say, were those related to ethics and politics. That is, the *Yijing*, on the one hand, was considered a classic that studies nature, but it also possessed, on the other hand, the significance of being a classic of ethics in that it teaches us how to live our lives. Here I would like to bring to the reader's attention that this idea points to *a fundamental difference in character from the intellectual tradition of the West.*

As represented by Aristotle, *physica* (i.e., the study of nature) and *ethica* (i.e. . ethics) have been thought to be unrelated to each other in the Western tradition. The *Yijing* ignores this distinction between nature and human affairs. As long as we assume the everyday standpoint, issues regarding the cognition of nature and issues related to ethics (morality) [seem to] have nothing in common. Because we ordinarily follow such commonsensical understanding, we tend to think it natural that the cognition of nature and ethical practice, as seen in Aristotle, deal with [fundamentally] different issues. This is reasonable to a certain extent. By contrast, the essence of the *Yijing*, its raison d'être, lies in a dimension different from the everyday, commonsensical standpoint, that is, it lies in the spiritual dimension.

The divination of the *Yijing* carried the significance of inquiring after divine will for the ancients, and its responses were [taken to be] revelations from the sacred dimension. It teaches one how to cope with the situation into which one is placed. Here, we need to take note of a deeper part of the mind that is not ordinarily brought to awareness, that is, the region that since ancient times people have referred to as "the soul" (what the Greeks called *psychē*). In this case, the cognition of nature and the practice of ethics come to share a common basis. As Freud clarified, the activity of the unconscious is connected to the foundational part of moral consciousness. The so-called activity of conscience emerges from a tangential point between consciousness and the unconscious. This is where the divination of the *Yijing* stands. To divine is to inquire how one should act toward the world, by facing the spirituality that is one's original nature while standing on the field where consciousness encounters the activity of the unconscious. To characterize it à la Socrates, the answer is found in knowing oneself. Here is the reason why in the history of Chinese philosophy since ancient times the *Yijing* has been respected by both Daoism and Confucianism while possessing the unique characteristic of being a classic common to the study of [both] nature and ethics.

To add a word to the relationship between Daoism and Confucianism, one point that connects them is the idea of *ki*-energy and experiences disclosed through meditation methods. The Daoist view of nature, which is inherited from the *Yijing* and is developed in the *Dàodéjīng*, assumes the thought that all things are *generated and undergo change via the exchange of yīn* and *yáng ki-energy.* The Daoist meditation method (Jap., *naitan*) that gradually developed from the Han dynasty to the Tang dynasty conceives of its process in the following way. Through the purification of *ki*-energy in the training of the mind and body that looks into the interior of one's self, one comes to experience a spiritual realm (i.e., the kneading of *ki*-energy, transforming it into divine, subtle energy). The practitioner as an incarnate subject receives through such meditation experience an activity springing from out of the foundation of the unconscious, consequently transforming his or her libido, and he or she comes to experience oneness with the movement of outer nature. This refers to the state of the so-called micro-macro cosmic correlativity, i.e. that state wherein Heaven and man are correlated. And this also designates the ideal state of ethical personality.

In the case of Confucianism, particularly neo-Confucianism which upheld *Li-Qi* philosophy, as is represented by Zhuxi and Wang Yang-ming, nature is understood in light of *ki* (Chin., *qi*) energy. Here, the cognition of nature and personality formation are grasped as inseparable by way of the concept of *ki*-energy. The Song-Ming period (after the tenth century) is referred to as the period of exchange between the three teachings, an exchange among the three teachings of Confucianism, Daoism, and Buddhism (particularly Zen Buddhism). And it was a period when each influenced and stimulated the other. What was on the center stage in this exchange was the popularity of meditation methods. Meditation involves the training and purification of *ki*-energy, and it was thought that by means of it an ethical personality can be formed. When interpreted from a contemporary point of view, we can probably characterize the training of *ki*-energy as a process of psychologically transforming the libido. Here we need to think through [the meaning of] personality [formation], while bringing into our purview the unconscious region.[5]

NATURE'S PSYCHOID NATURE

According to Pauli, after being introduced to Rhine's parapsychological work, Jung came to engage in a methodological reflection on the concepts of psychology that he had assumed up to that time. "Jung incorporated drastic change in the concepts he had thus far used in order to deal with various fundamental issues. He made this change particularly in taking into consideration extra-sensory phenomena."[6] What Pauli is calling here "various fundamental issues" refers to such epistemological issues as the relationship between spirit (mind) and matter and the role of the observer in cognizing nature. Pauli explains that while the concept of the archetype, of which Jung speaks, was originally called "primordial image" and had the strong connotation of an image in the mind, by using the new concept "psychoid" (i.e., "like the mind"), Jung attempted to incorporate material activity into the realm of the unconscious. In other words, the sharp demarcation between the physical and the psychological is a consequence of conscious intellectual judgment, and does not [necessarily] mean that nature itself contains such a distinction.

Nature that is purely material or physical, as grasped by scientific cognition, is the consequence of observation and measurement on the basis of definite presuppositions and methods.

To view the essence of nature as psychoid in this manner, when put from a different point of view for an easier understanding, is *to grasp space as the field of unconscious activity that is universal and transcends the individual.* The experience of ESP is related to this. For example, clairvoyance is to see with the mind's eye, and telepathy is to hear with the mind's ear. At the moment when such ESP experiences occur, spatial distance that is quantitatively calculable disappears. In other words, space as a whole is imbued with a psychoid nature. By assuming such a standpoint, we can say that the synchronistic experience manifests the "face" of nature prior to its distinction between mind and matter.

THE CONTENTION OF NEW SCIENCE AND ITS RELATION TO JUNG'S PSYCHOLOGY

From among scholars in England and the United States, there arose during the 1970s, the New Age Movement of thought (to be precise, New [Age] Science). One may regard this movement as one of philosophical thought that was developed from, and based on, the foundation of the contemporary standpoints of natural science such as physics. And looking at its superficial aspect, we cannot discern any particular relationship with Jung or Pauli. However, it is possible to interpret this movement as offering the theory of synchronicity a new point of view.

Fritjof Capra's book, *The Tao of Physics,* was published in 1974 and became a best seller. This book discusses the similarities between the ways of thinking found in the Eastern mystical philosophy of India and China and contemporary theories of physics. This led to a gradual increase in the number of people who agreed with its contention that science and the Eastern traditions can coexist. As I mentioned previously, behind Jung's idea of synchronicity was his concern for the *Yijing,* and he did not think the philosophical traditions of the East were incompatible with the contemporary sciences. Thanks to the spread of the New Age Movement, it would seem that this sort of idea has come to be widely accepted.

Theoretically representative of the New Age Movement is the understanding of the world through the holographic model, shared by the neurophysiologist Carl Pribram and the physicist David Bohm. Pribram advocated at the beginning of the 1970s the idea that memory and the activity of the brain [both] function like a hologram (i.e., as a recording of a perfect copy image). In a holographic picture, each part of the picture contains information about the whole, and parts are placed in an integrated relationship with the whole. Even though functions of the brain, when seen superficially, are explained in terms of mutual relationships among its parts, because the function of the whole is operative at its foundation going beyond such mutual relations among parts, the brain can be said to be a kind of hologram. In this respect, Pribram took note of the work of the British physicist David Bohm. Bohm attempted to think of nature as consisting of a dual structure, namely, the realm that appears on the surface and the hidden realm behind it. He postulated an implicate order that is contained behind the explicate order that appears on the surface. As he proceeded to research the so-called quantum potential, he came to the conclusion that physical substances, while appearing to be discontinuous in space and in time, existing independently of each other, are in fact connected and integrated at their foundation, though this is hidden within an "interior." The former is the explicate order while the latter is the implicate order. That everything is connected at its foundation means that the world can be seen as a hologram. Thing-events exist separately from each other in the surface realm of space-time, and as such they are not continuous. However, in the hidden realm beneath the surface, all thing-events are neither spatial nor temporal but are originally one, and therefore cannot be divided.[7]

When we assume this kind of standpoint, Bohm and Pribram thought it possible to even recognize mystical religious experiences and a dimension of experience that transcends the world, which science has hitherto considered negatively. Bohm was already examining the Jung–Pauli idea of synchronicity circa 1970, and recognized that his idea of the implicate order is commensurate with the concept of synchronicity.[8] The idea of the quantum potential, which was a departing point for his thought, was not accepted in the world of physics, as it was deemed impossible to provide any experimental proof for it. Nevertheless, the contentions of Bohm and Pribram generated considerable response in the intellectual fields that are connected to philosophy, psychology, history, and literature. That science and mystical experience can coexist probably marks an important change in the ideas of the [contemporary] period.

KI-ENERGY AND SPIRITUALITY

As I touched upon earlier, according to Pauli, Jung reached the idea of the psychoid by thinking through parapsychology, particularly its research on extrasensory perception. Many New Age scientists, generally speaking, take a favorable stance on parapsychological research. There appears thus to be no necessary reason to be particular about parapsychology as in the case of Jung.

In the case of Jung, however, the experience of paranormal phenomena that followed his personal life, as well as the mystical experience and spiritualistic experience that accompanied them, exercised an influential power on the formation of his psychology, whether or not he was aware of this. (There are many instances where the opinion was divided among his students in regard to the esoteric part of his theory. For example, the pros and the cons have been sharply divided regarding the assessment of parapsychology and divination.) The ideas of both Pribram and Bohm cannot easily be approached by the general public unless one is, to a certain extent, knowledgeable about neurophysiology and quantum physics. Moreover, they have no direct bearing on parapsychology. On the other hand, paranormal and spiritualistic phenomena are themes that considerably stimulate the curiosity of the general public. Paranormal phenomena were introduced in the 1970s via the media such as television, and its subject came to be widely known. Consequently, among the researchers of New [Age] Science there arose many who pursued parapsychological research. But it is hardly the case that parapsychology was recognized [as a field] in the academic world. However, as a result of the wide dissemination of this issue, parapsychological research is no longer monopolized by psychologists. Instead there has been an increase of cases where researchers in engineering or the natural sciences, as well as those in medical science, have become interested in parapsychological research. (Given this rise, the designation of the field as parapsychology will become problematic. But at present there is no appropriate designation given to this field of research.) At any rate, as I mentioned at the beginning, there is in this issue an element that can be traced back through to the genealogy of psychic research, and because of this reason, the issue contains elements that cannot be accommodated within scholarly study. Consequently, an intermediary region has arose between academic study and personal faith. Put in reverse, the stimulus emerging from the part that goes beyond academic study, as in such elements, may become one of the forces that will propel the intellectual situation of the contemporary period forward.

In the 1980s and 1990s when the New Age Movement had subsided, research on *ki*-energy and its practical activity was transmitted from China to Japan as if to replace the New Age Movement. And subsequently this has gradually spread to the United States. The concept of *ki*-energy in China has played an important role in the history of philosophy since the ancient period of the *Yijing*, and it has been understood to be an energy that is coherently applicable in the three fields of "special extraordinary ability" (i.e., paranormal ability), *ki*-training (*qigōng*), including various bodily techniques, and traditional medicine that has been inherited by the contemporary period. Even though the English word "spirit" carries many meanings, and hence may be ambiguous, it may be appropriate to consider *ki*-energy as "spirit." Because the issues surrounding *ki*-energy cover many areas such as medical treatment, gymnastics, and the body, it has now presented a situation different from the New Age [Science] Movement where physics played a major role.

Vigorous research has recently been conducted on healing and prayer. Such research has been increasing as a new trend in England and the United States. In this case, too, what becomes important are the fields related to medical treatment and medical science. In conjunction with research on healing and prayer, the practical, experiential standpoint has come to be regarded as more important than [mere] intellectual arguments. This is one of the reasons why the concept of spirituality has become important. For spirituality is an activity that integrates the mind and the body from their ground by transcending their dichotomy. Our age accordingly appears to be approaching a "religious" context while gradually moving beyond [the traditional boundary of] religion.[9]

November 2006
Yuasa Yasuo

PART I

CHAPTER ONE

The Image-Thinking of Ancient People, East and West

THE FOUR *ARCHAI* AND THE HUMAN SOUL

The [Greek] philosophers in the ancient period used the term *archē* in order to explain the origin of nature.[1] *Archē* means the beginning or first cause of thing-events. In the Milesian school [of natural philosophy], earth, water, fire, and air came to be cited as four *archai*. In this case, it may be easier to understand if we translate *archē* as primary element, because these philosophers had in mind raw material (*stoicheia*) that makes up the natural world. The theory of the four primary elements was later to be incorporated into Aristotle's physics. However, among *archai*, there are also those of a character different from raw material. [For example,] it is difficult to maintain any concrete image of Anaximander's *to apeiron* (the infinite, or the unlimited), Democritus' *atom* (indivisibility), and so forth, because they are intellectually conceived neologisms. Furthermore, Parmenides took *on* (being) to be the *archē*, but this is something like a fundamental principle of the cosmos rather than a raw material. This was the reason why Aristotle criticized the natural philosophers for being unruly in regard to the definition of terms.

The theory of the four elements reveals a characteristic of image-thinking [*imējishikō*, イメージ思考]. A quotation survives from Thales that "[a]ll things are full of gods [*daimon*]." In fact, this has become known through the testimony of Aristotle. He states that "[c]ertain thinkers say that soul is intermingled in the whole universe, and it is perhaps for that reason that Thales came to the opinion that all things are full of gods."[2] (*De Anima/On the Soul*, 411a) The philosophy of this period is commonly referred to as *hylozoism*. This holds the view of nature according to which matter is unified with life or spiritual activity. Although it does not consider the natural environment as a collection of mere matter as in contemporary science, this view is comparable to what is referred to as animism or pantheism in the study of religion. Today it is often referred to by the word *panpsychism*, and this term is more appropriate. It designates the idea that the activity of *psychē* (i.e., spirit or soul) fills up the cosmos. Such a view indicates the stance of recognizing the activity of *divinity* within nature. In other words, even though these philosophers refused to regard gods according to anthropomorphic images, they still retained the feeling of the sacred that people of the mythological age felt toward the great nature. To put it differently, what Thales called "water" was not [just] the water we see in our everyday life, but was a symbolic expression designating the invisible power that operates within nature. Therefore, image-thinking may be understood to be a unique form of thinking that emerges at the stage when intellectual thought develops to replace the images that were chiefly based upon the intuitive feeling of the mythological age. As I will show later, in the period of transition from the mythological age to the historical period in the East as well, there emerges a stance of image-thinking very similar to that of Greece. At this juncture, what we need to take note of is that a change occurred in the methodology for cognizing the world.

I will not give an exposition in this chapter of the entirety of natural philosophy. [Instead,] I would like to narrow the topic to what I think is significant, while referring to the research of contemporary scholars and the commentaries left by ancient scholars. Among the Milesians, let us first consider Heraclitus. According to Hirokawa Yōichi, Heraclitus had used the term *psychē* the most among the philosophers of the early period.[3] While his usage of the term *psychē* newly incorporates [within it] the meaning of the seat of thinking and perception, he [also] thought deeply about the divinity immanent in nature. There is a famous episode handed down by Aristotle. When visitors to Heraclitus, noticing that he was warming himself by an oven, were hesitant [to enter], he remarked that there is no reason to hesitate, for "divinities are present even here."[4] (*On the Parts of Animals*, A5, 645a17) We may discern in this episode a panpsychic sensibility. In the case of the East, an idea emerges on the basis of this sensibility that grasps the human essence as a microcosm corresponding to the activities of the macrocosm. I will take this up later [see also chapter four]. Heraclitus regarded fire to be the most important *archē*. [According to him], all things are products transformed from the eternal "fire" through condensation and rarefaction, and change into various elements. Fire changes to water and further changes into earth through condensation, and then changes in reverse through rarefaction. The characteristic of Heraclitus' thinking is that he regarded as important the process wherein the various elements undergo generation and extinction through change. To characterize his thought, people of later generations used the well-known statement that "everything is in flux (*panta rei*)."

However, this theme of change among the elements contained, at the time, a difficult theoretical problem, which touched upon the foundation of the cosmology of the entirety of their natural philosophies. This is because the *archē* was originally assumed to exist eternally and permanently in nature. Heraclitus' thought was apparently famous from that period on for being recondite. [For this reason,] Aristotle mentions that people describe him as if he was denying the principle of contradiction (*Metaphysics*, Book IV, chapter 3, 1005b20). Parmenides of the Eleatic school held the eternal *on* (being) as the *archē*. But, according to researchers, this may have been an idea that surfaced as a critique in response to Heraclitus. In short, it is an important issue in regard to how to think of the *relationship between eternity and change*, which touches on the cosmological foundation of natural philosophy. [As an example that sided with the idea of eternity, we may mention] Plato's theory of *Ideas* [that] has received the influence of Parmenides, who pursued eternal unchangeability.

A COMPARISON WITH THE IMAGE-THINKING IN ANCIENT INDIA

The issue of the use of images employed in intellectual thought has received attention and has become a theme even within contemporary philosophy under the stimulus of linguistics. Saussure's linguistics question the relationship in linguistic expression between "that which signifies" (*signifiant*) and "that which is signified" (*signifié*). Language and words are "that which signifies;" that is, they are "*signs.*" In this case, images other than language and words can [also] take on the role of signs. The issue of *metaphor* probably comes to have a bearing on this point. In the foundation of such thought, not only intellectual logic, but intuitive psychological factors are in operation. In the research of recent years, the view is becoming prevalent that at the foundation of cognition by means of metaphor, there is the psychological relationship of self and world that is based upon mind-body integration. However, I will not enter into this theoretical issue at present. [I will take it up in chapter two in connection with Saussure's idea of "associative" meaning, and in chapter six in connection with "Space-Time and Mind-Body Integration." For now,] I would like to investigate cases of image-thinking in ancient philosophy [of the East], while undertaking a comparative examination with that of Greece.

In the process of moving from the mythological age to the historical period, the methodological attitude of understanding nature by employing sign-images [*kigōteki imēji*, 記号的イメージ][5] appeared in a variety of cultural spheres. Let us take note of the fact that cases similar to the ancient Greek theory of the four primary elements can be found in India and China in the ancient period. The idea of the "five *maṇḍala* rings" [*gorin*, 五輪] is a well-known case in India, which spread even to East Asia through Esoteric Buddhism. The five *maṇḍala* rings refer to the five elements designating earth (*prithivī*), water (*āp*), fire (*agni*), wind (*vāyu*), and sky (*ākāśa*). Of the five *maṇḍala* rings, earth, water, fire, and wind bear an image pretty similar to those conceived in Greece. While the fifth element, "sky," appears to be unique to India, there was in Greece, after Plato, a movement to think of a fifth element. I will deal with this later. The Indian idea of understanding nature in light of the five elements dates as far back as the *Upaniṣads* of the sixth century BCE. It states that everything existing in the cosmos is made out of a combination of the five elements of earth, water, fire, wind, and sky. These images eventually become associated with the yogic theories of self-cultivation and Indian medicine [*āyurveda*], and gave rise to the idea that divides the body into five parts to *correlate* the human body with nature. While the Esoteric Buddhist theory of the five *maṇḍala* rings incorporated such ancient ideas of India, it identified the fifth element with the "emptiness"[6] (*śūnyatā*) that Mahāyāna Buddhism thematizes. The term "*rin*" [ring] is derived from the *maṇḍala*. Although the *maṇḍala* is usually taken to mean the essence of the mind, it is necessary at the same time to take note of the fact that it is a symbolic sign designating the fundamental structure of the cosmos. Mahāyāna Buddhism's view of dependent origination, as represented by the [*Heart Sutra's*] statement that "form is emptiness,"[7] is originally based upon the view that takes *the psychological cosmos and the physical cosmos as one*. In this case, the theory of self-cultivation plays a methodological role for the purpose of cognizing the world. The five *maṇḍala* "rings" of earth, water, fire, wind, and sky, are made to correspond respectively with the knee, navel, chest, face, and apex of the human body. It is thought that the practitioner becomes one with the activity of the cosmos through his experience in meditation.[8] Because the stance of taking physical nature as an object of observation comes to the surface in the Greek theory of *archē*, it is easy to overlook that at its basis is the projection of the human *psychē* that is the epistemological subject. However, as we stated in connection with Heraclitus, at the foundation of image-thinking in regards to nature there is concealed a panpsychic attitude that takes the interior soul into consideration. His thought of eternal movement is similar to that of the East.

Let us note that there arose a move toward thinking of a fifth primary element in the history of Greek philosophy as well, just as in India. As concepts often used in medieval alchemy, there are terms such as *quintessence* and *prima materia* [designating] a fifth element. While these are ideas that emerge from neo-Platonism during the latter part of the Hellenistic period, they originally date as far back as Plato and Aristotle. According to Pierre Eugène Marcellin Berthelot who researched alchemical thought, the idea of the fifth element can be traced back to Plato's *Timaeus*.[9] Plato raises the question that if the various elements such as water, earth, air, and fire were things that change and come into being, none of them could be considered to be the ultimate element (*archē*). By assuming a situation where various things are made out of gold, he states: "If we were asked what each of them are, the proper reply would be to say that it is gold." Therefore, he concludes as follows:

> [T]he same account, in fact, holds also for that nature which receives all the bodies. We must always refer to it by the *same term*, for it does not depart from its own character in any way. Not only does it always receive all things, it has never in any way whatever taken on any characteristic similar to any of the things that enter it. Its nature is to be available for anything to make its impression upon and it is modified, shaped, and reshaped by the things that enter it. These are the things that make it appear different at different times.[10] (*Timaeus*, 50B–C)

Furthermore, Plato says that this is the imitation of the highest *Idea*. That is, the eternal Idea, which is the highest being, is contrasted with that which is assumed at the base of the different material alterations. This is how the idea of prime matter originated. In other words, it is the idea that there is some sort of corresponding relation between the Idea positioned highest in the investigation of the *psychē* (i.e., spirit or soul), and that which is positioned lowest and assumed as the ultimate of the material world. Plotinus (205–269 AD), adopting this idea [of schematization,] interprets "that which is positioned lowest" as signifying to mean the true state of "matter" [*hylē* or prime/pure matter] that is contrasted with "form" (*Idea*) [*eidos*]. Consequently, what Plotinus means by matter bears no stipulation at all in regard to its mode of being. It is a state like that of nothingness without even spatial characteristics. He says that when this [i.e., prime or pure matter] receives the illuminating outflow of the Idea from the highest position of being, the cosmos comes to be formed, consisting of the hierarchy of various beings [i.e., his theory of emanation (*emanatio*)]. Plotinus named the highest *Idea* "the One" (*to hen*), which, we might say, expresses "God" in an abstract and intellectual concept. If we see Plotinus's theory from the perspective of a worldview, various stages of being that range from "the One" to prime matter are distinguished. We ought to take note of his meditative experience as the precondition for such a theory of hierarchy regarding being. This is, it presupposes a process of experience that involves so-called *ek-stasis*, going out of one's self (ex-istence). [According to the account given by his student, Porphyry (232–304),] it is said that

Plotinus has had the experience of seeing God four times in his life. In other words, meditation signifies the method of knowing the world with the mind-body theory as its foundation. Accordingly, in the stance that understands the ontological state of thing-events in the world in light of the subject's inner experience, there is something comparable to the thought of ancient India that thinks of the correlative relationship between human beings and the cosmos on the basis of the *maṇḍala*.

In Aristotle as well, there is an idea comparable to Plato. In Chapter Five of Book Four of *On the Heavens* (*De Caelo*), he explains the concept of the four elements and matter as follows. "Fire" that constantly moves upwards (the lightest element) and "earth" that constantly moves downwards (the heaviest element) are two elements that bear an absolute mode of being. In contrast, because both "water" and "air" move up as well as down, they have a relative kind of being. Consequently, this means that matter has four ways of being. If we hold the view that the four elements change and develop in correlation, despite the fact that their ways of being variously differ, it is necessary to assume one common matter [among them]. [He states:] "The kinds of matter, then, must be as numerous as these bodies, i.e., four, but though they are four there must be a common matter of all—particularly if they pass into one another—which in each is in being different"[11] (*De Caelo*, 312a–b).

Aristotle called what ought to be considered the prime matter (or the fifth element), *aether* (*ether*), and postulated it as the basis of the four elements, wherein the essence of the heavenly bodies can be found. The simple material that constitutes the heavenly bodies must be distinguished even from the lightest among the four primary elements, "fire." The movements of the heavenly bodies are without beginning or end, without increase or decrease, changeless and ceaseless, and eternally the same. In the heavenly bodies that make perfect circular movements, there is neither lightness nor heaviness. The material that constitutes the heavenly bodies bearing such a characteristic must be something different from the four primary elements. [Arguing in this way, Aristotle states:] "[t]hese premises clearly give the conclusion that there is in nature some bodily substance other than the (four) formations we know, prior to them all and more divine than they"[12] (*De Caelo*, 269a30).

Although reference to the term *aether* itself is scattered among the legends relating to the early philosophers, this idea of Aristotle exercised an influence upon the alchemy that emerged in Egypt toward the end of the Hellenistic period (third to fourth century CE). During this period Alexandria was a place that was spearheading learning and culture. I would like to note that the practice of meditation was developed there, and that it can be commonly found in neo-Platonism, Gnosticism, Eastern Christianity, and so on. Although one usually tends to think of alchemy as fashionable from the Middle Ages to the

Renaissance, here we ought to take note of the idea of ancient alchemy that emerged in the Roman Empire. It is what was born upon the legacy of Egyptian civilization from a time prior to Greek philosophy, and resulted from the syncretism between the traditions of Egyptian religious science and the thought of neo-Platonism. The following is a point different from the tradition of Greek thought. While the Greeks made nature into an object of observation (theōria), they did not take the attitude of technically or experimentally relating to nature. In contrast, Egyptian civilization, as symbolized by the pyramid, erected its foundation upon engineering rather than theory, and various technical skills relating to matter had been developed since ancient times. While the Greeks placed Egypt under its dominion after the time of Alexander the Great, they reinterpreted the legacy of Egyptian science in accordance with the Greek philosophical view of matter centered in the theory of the four primary elements. The idea of a mysterious and ultimate matter, that is, the fifth primary element (or the prime matter), thus emerged there. Accordingly, it became the goal [to be achieved] in a technical investigation of nature, instead of being merely a theoretical idea. The experimental work of the alchemist has, as its purpose, the extraction of this mysterious fifth primary element. In this way, the ideas of Plato and Aristotle that attempted to overcome the theoretical difficulty in the theory of the four primary elements came to receive attention. When it was connected with the practice of meditation, it came to assume the character of a new method of cognizing the world. Here we can discover something common with the ancient East.

The reason for our allusion to alchemy is that Jung had thematized alchemy from its connection with Eastern thought. When Plato and Aristotle conceived of prime matter, they arrived at the idea of a spiritual matter by thinking through the theoretical difficulties in the theory of the four primary elements. Alchemy began its technical work with the purpose of extracting this mysterious matter. Although this project undoubtedly ended in failure, there is something that became clear to Jung when he investigated its history. This was the stance of viewing nature and matter from the psychological viewpoint. What Jung took note of was that the alchemists were hermit-like practitioners. They engaged in the practice of prayer and meditation as a precondition for their work, and interpreted the meaning of their work through the inner images they experienced [in their practice]. At this juncture, I would like the reader to take note of the fact that the reason why Jung became aware of the psychological aspect of alchemy is through his contact with the meditation methods of Daoism. In the practice of Daoism, there is the "inner elixer" that includes primarily meditation methods, and the "outer elixer" that has, as its purpose, the manufacture of medicine and chemical products (e.g., gunpowder), wherein the two are held in an inseparable relationship.[13] In other words, practical techniques were being developed in the tradition of Daoist philosophy on the basis of a standpoint that views the regions of mind and matter by integrating them. While Western alchemy eventually entered a cul-de-sac, Eastern meditation methods and medicine have been transmitted to the contemporary period, and research with new perspectives is beginning to be developed today. In short, by taking the viewpoint of psychology, we may be able to think about the common terms found in the historical traditions of the East and the West. For we can experience therein the common experience of prayer and meditation.

THE CHINESE VIEW OF NATURE BASED ON *QÌ*-ENERGY [JAP., *KI*: 氣]

Let us now take up the ancient Chinese view of nature. Because it shows a stark contrast in character when comparing it with the Greek view of nature, we may discover an issue of research significant for us, in thinking through the traditional modes of thinking of the East and the West.

We may mention the theory of five "goings"[14] [Jap., *gogyō*; Chin., *wǔháng*: 五行] as a case of ancient Chinese image-thinking. "Going" [行] signifies something that *moves and flows*. This is a theory that considers the events of the human and natural worlds in light of the relationships among the five sign-images: wood, fire, earth, metal, and water. This theory has left its impact not only on the view of nature, but on medicine and self-cultivation methods. The theory of five goings originally had no relation to early Confucianism and Daoism, as exemplified respectively by Confucius (552–479) and Lǎozǐ (fifth century BCE). This is something that the people called the *Yīn-yáng* [Jap., *Inyō*: 陰陽] School—one of the One Hundred Schools that arose toward the end of the Warring States period (third century BCE)—began to advocate, and it enters into the mainstream of the history of philosophy due to its adoption by Emperor Shǐ, when the Qín established a unified dynasty. The *Yìjīng* ["The Book of Changes"; Jap., *Ekikyō*: 易経] came to be emphasized in the world of Chinese philosophy ever since this period, and came to be considered as a foundational classic in ethics and in the investigation of nature. While the present *Yìjīng* was compiled by a Confucian scholar in the Hàn dynasty (202 BCE–8 CE), its origin dates as far back to the *Lexicon of Divination* [Chin., *bǔcí*; Jap., *bokuji*: 占辞] of the Yīn dynasty (ending in the twelfth century BCE). *The Lexicon of Divination* refers to the language for divination employed by the people of the mythological age. We may say that this language held the same psychological meaning as the oracle received by the ancient Greeks.[15]

When comparing ancient Greece and China, we come to understand that they took extremely different attitudes toward the way human beings relate to nature. China developed the stance of viewing nature while stressing practical techniques. This sharply contrasts with that of Greece, which put emphasis on observation (*theōria*). Needless to say, observation was also being conducted in China, but it was always connected to practical purposes. The period from the end of the Warring States to the Hàn (early third to the later second century) was a time when China made remarkable progress in scientific technology. To take an example from astronomy, the observation of the sun's black spots began there for the first time in the world, and furthermore a new calendar based upon Jupiter's period of revolution (about twelve years) was constructed during the time of Emperor Wǔ (reigning 140–87 BCE). The system of naming eras was instituted during this time. The utilization of magnets as well began at the end of the Warring States along with the creation of artificial magnets for their practical application. *The Yellow Emperor's Inner Medical Treatise*, a classic of acupuncture medicine, was compiled during the later Hàn (second century), and the chapter on "The Spirit-Sheath" [Chin., *língshūbiān*; Jap., *reikuhen*: 靈枢編] explains that there is a relationship between the moon's waxing and waning and the ocean tide. In fact, the intellectual reason why the ancient Chinese succeeded in such discoveries and technologies is that they took the stance of emphasizing practical application. That is, their ideas bore the characteristic of technical thinking.

One other concrete difference that draws our attention when we compare Greece and China is that the Chinese understanding of nature was founded on *the wave model*. For this reason they came to notice, early on, an agency of action in the distance between spatially separate things (e.g., magnetic force, the relationship between the moon's waxing and waning, and the high and low tides of seawater, etc.). The relation between the moon and seawater is something that was discovered when measuring the speed at which "*qi*" [Jap., *ki*: 氣] energy travels throughout the interior of the human body. That is because *qi* was thought to flow in the interior of the human body in accordance with rhythmic changes in space-time. [I will return to the topic of space-time in chapters four and six] This is one example of a stance that looks at all that is in the world, including the human being, in accordance with the model of flowing motion. In Greece, Democritus explained movement and change by conceiving of a new concept, the atom (indivisibility). This is a view of nature based on the particle model. However, since Aristotle did not adopt this notion, the idea of the atom did not develop. It was only after the rise of modernity that the wave model and the particle model came to compete with one another.[16]

As is seen, the fundamental relationship between nature and human beings was grasped from the viewpoint of the flowing *qi* motion in ancient China. If we schematize it from a theoretical viewpoint, the Dao is placed here as the origin that gives life to all things while nurturing them. Its activity is manifest in the ceaseless change of the function of *yīn* [陰気] and *yáng qì* [陽気]. Because the "*yì*" [易] of *Yìjīng* means "to change," the title is translated into English as *The Book of Changes*. *Yīn* and *yáng* are not a theoretical distinction that can be clearly demarcated from each other, but rather they are signs playing the role of metaphor. The phases of *yīn* and *yáng* are changing at every moment. This is because the essence of *qì* lies in flowing motion. Moreover, the *yīn* and *yáng qì* are divided into the "five goings" and control the natural and human worlds. A clear and simple schematization of this sort of relationship is seen in the diagram of the Great Ultimate [Chin., *Tàijítú*; Jap., *taikyokuzu*: 太極図], which the *lǐ-qì* philosophy of Neo-Confucianism employed during the Sung Dynasty (tenth to thirteenth century) (see figure 1). The circle at the top of the figure signifies the Dao that is the primordial

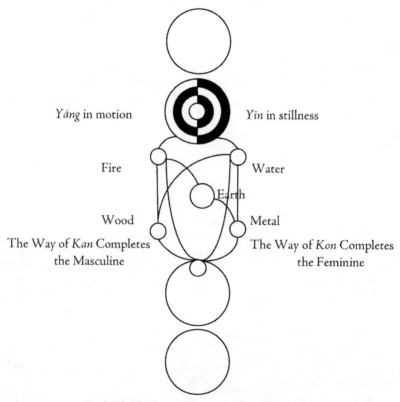

Birth of All Things Through Transformation

Figure 1. The Diagram of the Great Ultimate

origin. The circle below that is distinguished in black and white signifies that the *qì* issuing from the Dao operates by segmenting into *yīn* and *yáng*. The network drawn below designates the state of the circulation of *yīn* and *yáng* that are divided into the five goings of wood, fire, earth, metal, and water. On both sides of the circle below the network, it is inscribed: "The way of *kan* completes the masculine" [Chin., *qiándàochéngnán*; Jap., *kandōseidan*: 乾道成男] and "The way of *kon* completes the feminine" [Chin., *kūndàochéngnǚ*; Jap., *kondōseijyo*: 坤道成女] where "*kan*" designates Heaven and "*kon*" designates Earth. In other words, they are based on the idea that what nurtures all things under Heaven and on Earth is the activity of masculinity and femininity in which *qì* is divided into the *yīn-yáng* five goings. The circle at the very bottom of the figure is what is called in Lǎozǐ's *Dàodéjīng* the "gate of the female ox," that is, the "grounding place" wherein is hidden the activity of the "mysterious maternal nature" that is the origin of all life.

Although this diagram of the Great Ultimate is what the philosophers of neo-Confucianism had employed to designate the fundamental structure of the cosmos, it was originally an illustration for images used [as part of visualization training] by the practitioners of Daoism.[17] In the case of meditation method, this diagram signifies the activity of *qì* in the interior of the human body. Neo-Confucianism reinterpreted it as expressing the activity of nature vis-à-vis images. While the method of the Daoist's self-cultivation reads the diagram from the bottom up, that is, from the interior of the human body, neo-Confucianism's cosmology reads the diagram from top to bottom. In this diagram, the viewpoint of cosmology (i.e., the theory of the flowing out of *qì*) that conceives of the origin of the world, and the experience of ascension based on the incarnate subject's psychological transformation (i.e., *qì* meditation methods), are held in an inseparable relationship, wherein is conceived the so-called correlativity of Heaven and human beings [Chin., *tiānrén xiāngguān*; Jap., *tenjin sōkan*: 天人相関], that is, the inter-resonating relationship between the activity of the macrocosm and the activity of the human body as a microcosm. Here we can surmise a point commensurate with the Plotinian worldview discussed above.[18]

THE STUDY OF "THAT WHICH IS ABOVE FORM" AND METAPHYSICS

If I may be permitted to comment a little on intellectual history, the period when the traditional pattern of the history of Chinese philosophy becomes settled is during the Hàn dynasty (second century BCE to third century CE). As the most ancient literature in the history of philosophy, there are the classics called the *Six Books* [Chin., *liùshū*; Jap., *rokukyō*: 六経] that deal with religious rituals, politics, ethics, poetry, and so on that have been transmitted since the Zhōu Dynasty. These precede the time of Confucius. The Spring-Autumn, and Warring States periods after the end of Zhōu (eighth century BCE to third century CE) was a long period of disorder without any intellectual unity, and the so-called One Hundred Schools of Learning emerged. It was after the period of Emperor Wǔ of the second century BCE that the policy of adapting Confucianism as a foundational thought for the sake of national polity became accepted. The one who proposed this policy to the emperor was a person named Dǒng Zhòngshū [Jap., Tōchūjo: 董仲舒]. He was a mysterious character who, it is said, frequently performed magic for starting or stopping rain, as he was famous as a sorcerer. After this period, many new literatures called the *wìishū* [Jap., *isho*: 緯書] were produced in contrast with the *jīngshū* [Jap., *keisho*: 経書] that were written prior to them. This [group of] books investigates nature, and it bears as its background the development during this period of astronomy, and so on, as stated above. (However, because scientific theory continuously develops with its content ever-changing, the *wìishū* was hardly read in the succeeding generations.) Dǒng Zhòngshū expressed the relationship between human beings and nature with the phrase "the correlativity of Heaven and human beings" [Chin., "*tiānrén xiāngguān*"; Jap., "*tenjin sōkan*": 天人相関]. It is the idea that the heart/mind of Heaven and Earth interresonates with the human heart/mind in prayer. Between the great cosmos (i.e., macrocosm) and the small cosmos (i.e., microcosm), there is a connection by way of the flowing motion of "*qì*" acting within nature. To know this connection is the activity of the human mind. The idea of Daoism (the Daoist) that regards the relationship between nature and human beings as important gradually developed under such epochal circumstances.

It was also from the Hàn period on that the *Yìjīng* came to be emphasized. The book called *Zhōujīcāntóngqī* [Jap., *shūekisandōkei*: 周易参同契], written by Wèi Bàiyáng [Jap., Gi hakuyō: 魏伯陽] of the later Hàn period (first to third centuries), laid the foundation for the kneading technique (i.e., method of meditation), in which the *Yìjīng* was placed at the center, and below which Confucianism and Daoism were positioned. And the method of meditation (i.e., technique of kneading) is regarded as an experiential foundation that intellectually supports the integrative relationship of the three. This book, the *Yìjīng*, while highly regarded from ancient times, is the foremost of the classics in respect to the difficulty of understanding. Jung sought the key to comprehend the essence of the Chinese cultural tradition in this book. As the course of the history of philosophy shows, the thought of "changes" [*yì*] has become the principle that unifies the study of nature as represented by Daoism and the tradition of ethics as represented by Confucianism. The practitioners of Daoism [道士] in Chinese history were actually the ones who had become the important bearers of scientific technology. This is a fact that has been made clear since Needham's research. By contrast, the study of nature and ethics were separated in the tradition of the Western history of philosophy into theoretical philosophy and practical philosophy. This distinction became clear after Aristotle. It is difficult to think, even in modern philosophy, of the issues of theory and practice, cognition of nature and ethics, by treating them as one. This seems to indicate that there is a significant difference in the traditional modes of thinking between the East and the West. [I will address this topic in chapters two and four.]

If we investigate the origin of the term *keijijōgaku* [形而上学], we will find a clue for considering this point. While this term has come to be used as a translation for Aristotle's "*Metaphysika*" in contemporary Japan and China, the text where this term appears is in one of the commentaries of the *Yijīng*, collectively known as the "Ten Wings," "Commentary on the Appended Judgments" of the *Yijīng* [*xìcízhuàn*: 繋辞伝]. In this commentary, there is a famous saying: "[w]hat is above form is called *dào* [way: 道]; what is under form is called tool [Chin., *qì*; Jap., *ki*: 器]."[19] (Although this commentary was believed to have been written by Confucius, and therefore has been esteemed since ancient times, today it is regarded as having been written by a Confucian of the Hàn dynasty. We know for a fact that Confucius regarded the *Yijīng* as important, but it was not until the Hàn dynasty that the *Yijīng* was established as a text.) According to the *lǐ-qì* philosophy of neo-Confucianism that I mentioned earlier, "that which is above form" is interpreted to be "*lǐ*" [patternment], whereas "that which is under form" is interpreted to be "*qì*." (The reason why this phrase became known is due to the fact that neo-Confucianism regarded it as important.) If that is so, it would come to mean that while "*lǐ*" designates the domain of a transcendent principle that goes beyond experience, "*qì*" designates the domain of experience. In the case of Aristotle, *Metaphysika* is an ontology, while the realm of experience is relegated to his physics (*Physika*). What is called ontology has the purpose of clarifying the mode of being of everything that exists in terms of its form (rather than its content). Ontology takes as its theme so-called being *qua* being (*on hē on*). Although this is a difficult way of putting it, among existing things there are a variety of things such as physical things, living things, spiritual things, and so on, and ontology deals with the form of their being without distinguishing their content or characteristics insofar as they are all considered "to be." This is the purpose of *Metaphysika* as ontology. In contrast to this, *Physika* (physics) clarifies the being of the various beings in their modalities that are discovered within physical nature. To put this concretely, Aristotle's physics holds the purpose of systematically cognizing the various natural phenomena occurring on the earth as its center, by using the Milesian theory of the four primary elements. By contrast, *Metaphysika* introduces a system of four causes in addition to the four elements that are physical substances. This is the theory of four causes. To begin with, he recognizes the two principles of form (*idea*) and matter (*hylē*) that Plato postulated. These are the formal cause and the material cause. In addition, Aristotle postulates two other principles: efficient cause (moving cause) that moves things, and final cause toward which movement tends. These four causes become the formal principles that control nature. Accordingly, because *Metaphysika* and *Physika* designate the form and content of that which *is*, they are held in a theoretically inseparable relationship. In this sense, *Metaphysika* comes to play the limited role of clarifying the theoretical foundation of *Physika* (nature), and has nothing whatsoever to do with the ethical matter pertaining to the human world.

By contrast, "that which is above form," according to the *Yìjīng*, is the activity of the Dao, and all things (i.e., "that which is under form") are the receptacles that receive its activity (i.e., *qì*). "That which is under form" is not limited to natural objects. In this scheme, the cognition of nature and the cognition of human nature fundamentally coincide. As is seen from the analysis of the Diagram of the Great Ultimate discussed earlier, the cognition of physical nature and ethical practice investigating human nature, that is, the original human nature, are held in a relationship of oneness, two sides of the same coin. The reason for this can be found in the fact that the psychology of the subject is placed at the root connecting the two. For Aristotle, there is no such psychology of subjectivity, but instead the form of an objective logic controls nature. In other words, he observes the state of nature from the outside in light of theoretical form. Therein we can discern a standpoint that emphasizes the knowledge of *theōria* (i.e., theory or observation). Aristotle makes this explicit.

There is a famous passage in Lǎozǐ's *Dàodéjīng* that explains the *dào*:

> There is a thing confusedly formed, which arose before [the opening of] heaven and earth. Silent and formless, It depends on nothing and unchanging, It operates everywhere and yet does not weary.... For now, I call it '*dào*'. If forced to give it a name, I call it 'great.' Being great, it is receding, Receding, it is far-reaching, Far-reaching, it returns to its former origin.[20]

It would appear that the phrase cited earlier from the "Commentary on the Appended Judgments" [*xìcízhuàn*; 繋辞伝] of the *Yìjīng*, "what is above form is called *dào*," had in mind this quote from the *Dàodéjīng*. "That which is above form" is usually interpreted as transcending form, and is used to translate the *meta* of *Metaphysika*. But in the case of the *Yìjīng*, it seems more accurate to interpret this to mean temporally *prior to* form.[21] The above passage taken from Lǎozǐ addresses the image of "chaos" in flowing motion prior to its separation into Heaven and Earth. Its primordial activity is called Dao. Because the activity of the *dào* nurtures and rears all things, it is not the case that it completely transcends the domain of experience. The "Dao," which is "that which is above form," is contrasted with the "receptacle," which is "that which is under form." "Receptacle" [Chin., *qì*; Jap., *ki*: 器] signifies a tool or the container that receives activity. While "that which is under form" refers to all things containing form, it is generated by the flowing motion that emerges from chaos prior to form. In another place of the "Commentary on the Appended Judgments," it is stated that "one *yīn*, one *yáng*, this is the Dao," and it explains that the activity of the "Dao" concretizes through the interchange of the *yīn-yáng* activity. This explains the flowing motion of *qì*. The fundamental idea is that the state of all things is understood to go through generation and change by means of *qì*, that is, from chaos to order. This sort of an idea is at times called body-function theory [Chi., *tǐyònglǐlún*; Jap., *taiyōriron*: 体用理論]. *Tǐ* [body: 体] has the meaning of "original body" [Chin., *běntǐ*; Jap., *hontai*: 本体] or "real body" [Chin., *shítǐ*; Jap., *jittai*: 実体],[22] and *yòng* [use: 用] has the meaning of function or faculty, but the two are related like water and wave, and in actuality cannot be distinguished. In other words, this view [can be explained as follows: it] is not that the thing has the activity, but rather that the activity makes the thing what it is. That is, the change in the *qì*'s flowing motion is the foundation whereby all things are made to be the things that they are. This sort of image-thinking of ancient China shows a character that is in contrast with the case of ancient Greece, wherein is postulated an eternally unchanging *archē*.

LOGIC AND BEING: "WHAT IS" AND "THAT IT IS"

The activities of the Elesians arose much later than those of the Milesian school. Pythagoras was the progenitor of this school and established a religious community in Kroton in southern Italy in the sixth century BCE. As it was destroyed under the attack of the natives, people belonging to this community moved to Elea and their activity marks the origin of this school. Parmenides is the one who laid its foundation. He is known to have claimed *on* (being) as the *archē*. This word became the etymological origin of *ontology*, and it is commonly recognized that Parmenides had a great influence on Plato. Given this idea, it appears that Parmenides' thought played a significant role in the development of Greek philosophy. Nevertheless, Parmenides is an extremely difficult philosopher for the beginner to understand. I myself have the memory of having no clue as to Plato's *Parmenides* when I read it. His thought may initially give the impression that it is [too] difficult to handle and grasp, as Plato's *Parmenides* is filled with arguments [too] convoluted for the reader not familiar with philosophy. However, one would find it interesting once one starts making sense of his thought.

It is easier for the beginner to understand the *archē* when it is explained in terms of concrete images such as water or fire as the Milesian school did. But what does it mean to say that *on* (being) is the *archē*? It seems that what Parmenides problematized was probably something like an inquiry after the fundamental principle of the being of the world. To start, the term *"on"* is usually translated as "what is" [*aru mono*]. This word is the noun form of the [Greek] be-verb *"einai."* There are often cases in which the present participle *eon* is used synonymously with *on*. Then, how should *"einai"* be translated? We may, for now, translate it as "that it is." However, this in fact leads to several problems. Suzuki Teruo's great work, *The Study of Parmenides' Philosophy*, has a long, explanatory subtitle, "On being and its subject, what is (or that it is)."[23] When we think of Parmenides' *"on,"* it becomes an important issue of how to think of the relationship between "what is" and "that it is." The Chinese compound *"sonzai"* [being: 存在], carries meanings of both "what is" [*aru mono*] and "that it is" [*aru koto*].[24] If we attempt to correctly express the content of the meaning, the Japanese word *"aru"* ["to be" in the sense of both "there is . . ." and "it is . . ."] used in our daily lives is more accurate than the Chinese expression. [I will delve into an analysis of this word *"aru"* and its implications for understanding "being" in chapter two.] Now, what would then happen if we are to replace this distinction with the modern languages of the West? Heidegger called "what is," *Seiendes* (entity), in contrast to this "that it is," *Sein* (being), when he attempted to revive ontology and replace the modern epistemological paradigm with it. However, *Seiendes* is a term that is not ordinarily used in German, and perhaps we may say that this is his neologism. That is, we need to first distinguish "what *is*" [*aru mono*] and "*that* it is" [*aru koto*] in order to think about the issue of "being" [*aru*]. Heidegger was thinking that, unless he constructs a new terminology for this sake, it would be difficult to adequately explain the meaning that this situation signifies. Now, how about the case in English? While "what *is*" can be translated as *being*, how ought one to translate "*that* it is" in distinction from the former? If we follow Heidegger's distinction, it might be translated as "beingness," but it would no longer be an ordinary English expression. This is where we encounter a difficulty of comprehension and interpretation. This is because in the Western languages, the be-verb carries the meaning of both the [existential] judgment of being (i.e., "there is . . .") and the *copula* ("it is . . ."). The problematic point that led Heidegger to create a new terminology, that is, the point of dispute concerning the distinction between "what *is*" and "*that* it is," can directly be applied to the interpretation of Parmenides. I wonder if what is being questioned here is the form related to linguistic expression, that is, the relationship between the problem of logic and the existence of thing-events.

Fragment Two of Parmenides insists that the way of truth and of error [i.e., appearance] must be clearly demarcated. I will quote Mr. Hirokawa's translation.

> The one, that [*it*] *is*, and that [*it*] *cannot not be*, is the path of [the goddess of] Persuasion (for she attends upon truth); The other, that [*it*] *is not* and that [*it*] *needs must not be*, That I point out to you to be a path wholly indiscernible. For you could not know what-is-not (for that is not feasible), Nor could you point it out.[25]

Parmenides says that the way of "*is*" [*aru*] is a way that is in accord with truth, and "*is not*" [*aranu*] is a way that cannot know truth. What is translated as "is not" is *me on* [nonbeing] in Greek in its nominal form. If all that had to be done was to reject the way to error, it should be sufficient to juxtapose "not" (i.e., a pure logical negation) in contrast to "is," instead of speaking in such terms. If we look it up in the dictionary, the adverb, *me* (μη), has the meaning of *not*, but it also states that it is used only when a thing-event does not exist under a certain condition. In contrast to this, it states that the adverb *ou* (ου) is used in cases when a straightforward negation is intended. That is, the phrase *me on* carries the sense of a logical negation (i.e., *not*), while at the same time implies the negation of being. Accordingly, to put this in reverse, Parmenides is asserting that one should not think of negating what is (*on*), because it *leads* to erroneous knowledge when it is seen logically. Being and logic are not separate from each other. Here is the reason why his philosophy is difficult to understand for the beginner.

We will not enter into the details of the analyses of scholars specializing in Greek, for we amateurs would not be able to follow them in terms of linguistic ability, and because there are many different opinions regarding the interpretation of individual fragments. What interests me are the following three issues. The first point is that Parmenides' thought developed a thorough logical reflection, and this is the singular reason why Parmenides' thought had a strong influential impact. I am led to think that among the natural philosophers he was probably the one who most thoroughly thought through the role that *logos* plays. The second point I want to bring to attention is the relationship it has with Plato's theory of Ideas. This is a view that is nearly unanimously agreed upon among research specialists. They state that Parmenides proceeds from a critique of Anaximander and Heraclitus of the

Milesian school. Anaximander's idea, *to apeiron* (i.e., the indefinite), is apparently an assertion that is conceived of in consideration of the emergence and generation of the cosmos. (When Nietzsche was a young scholar of Greek, he insisted that *to apeiron* be interpreted to mean indefiniteness.[26] Put in an Eastern way, this would be taken to be *chaos*. I wonder if Anaximander's idea is similar to Zhuāngzǐ's idea that the cosmos emerged out of chaos.) If that is the case, it will lead us to think that the cosmos was generated *in time*, but Parmenides dismissed such ideas. As I stated in the previous section, Heraclitus placed a strong emphasis on change among the primary elements. Change also presupposes time [as its precondition]. By contrast, Parmenides' basic claim is that there exists something eternally unchanging (i.e., *on*) in the fundamental structure of the cosmos. Although he was critical of thinking about generation and change, this was probably connected with his stance that emphasizes logical form. This is because it is thought that logical form is unrelated to time. At the foundation of Plato's theory of Ideas is inherited this stance of conceiving of the eternal and unchanging.

A third issue that interests me as well is the question of whether Heidegger's investigation of *Sein* (being [*aru*]) might not be useful for clarifying the meaning of Parmenides' argument concerning "*on*." This is because this [route] enables us to discover a point of concern connected to the issue confronting contemporary thought and philosophy. I will therefore state next my view in regard to this point.

Aristotle's ontology is a theory that classifies all that exists in the world, while conceiving of their ways of being. *What is questioned here is the state in which a thing-event exists, that is, the mode of what exists.* Although we have no recourse in this case but to express it by using the term "to be" [*aru*] (being [*sonzai*]), what sort of meaning does the word "to be" [*aru*] have? Heidegger quotes a passage from Plato's *Sophist* at the opening of his *Being and Time*. It is the following line: "[m]anifestly you have long been aware of what you mean when you use the expression *being* [*aru*]. We used to think we understood it before. But now we are perplexed about it"[27] (244a). This is a line appearing in a scene when a visitor to Athens from Elea is having a dialogue with Socrates and his companions. This quotation symbolically shows the intention that Heidegger entrusted in this work. He thinks that when resurrecting the paradigm of ontology, one must consider *the meaning of being* of "what is" (*Seinsinn* [the meaning of being]), instead of considering, as Aristotle did, the way (mode of being) of "what is." That is, Heidegger's fundamental claim is that when philosophy considers "being" [*aru*] as an issue, what is important is not *what is* [*mono*, thing] but *that it is* [*koto*, event]. Therefore, *Being and Time*'s examination of the human being (being-(t)here [*Dasein*]) becomes an analytic concerning the *meaning of the fact* that a human being is *living* (being [*aru*]) in this world. When this [stance] is laid down as the foundation, the meaning of the being of everything else besides human beings (i.e., the fact that they are) will come to be clarified. His basic structure emerges from here, namely, that *Being and Time* is the fundamental ontology that leads to the foundation of a general ontology.

While the discussion becomes somewhat complicated, if we first investigate the periods of Plato's work, *The Sophist* is a work that belongs to the beginning of the period of his later dialogues. By contrast, *Parmenides* belongs to the dialogues of the middle period, like *The Republic* and *Phaedrus*. Now, in what way are these two works different? *The Sophist* is known to have, since olden times, the subtitle "A Dialogue on the Logic (*logos*) of Being (*on*)." An interpretation on this point has appeared among researchers that Plato is perhaps distinguishing in this work between "being" [*aru*] as *copula* and "being" [*aru*] as designating reality, and this has generated many disputes.[28] It is easier to state this problem in the Japanese language. In regard to the word (or expression) "*aru*" [being], there is the distinction between " . . . *de aru*" ["it is . . ."] and " . . . *ga aru*" ["there is . . ."]. "It is . . . ," in which "is" is used as a copula, is connected to the logic of linguistic expression, while "there is . . ." designates the judgment of being in regard to an object that really exists. The latter connects to the issue of "that it is" and the former links to the issue of "what is." If we proceed to think by taking this perspective, it would come to mean that this distinction was not yet made in *Parmenides*, which is a dialogue preceding *The Sophist*. That is, it means that logic and being cannot be separated. This is indeed the fundamental contention exhibited by Parmenides' philosophy.

THE PASSIVE UNDERSTANDING OF "BEING" [ARI]

Next, after Fragment Two cited above, there is a short fragment (Fragment Three), of merely one line. Let us quote Mr. Suzuki's translation: "[t]his is because the same thing is there for knowing (*noein*) and for being (*einai*)."[29]

There are also many people who translate *noein* as "to think" [as opposed to "to know"]. If we translate this phrase accordingly, we can interpret it as asserting that thinking and being are in agreement. Even though this fragment is short, it is quite well known, and there are many interpretations and disputes over it. This is reportedly because the scholars interpreted *noein* to mean, as it were, a harbinger of the epistemological paradigm; this interpretation was in turn motivated by the strong tendency, arising in modern times, to take *noein* to mean intellectual inference. In other words, this is an interpretation that expands on the agreement between consciousness and the real. Herein is concealed, it is said, the influence of modern idealism, such as from Descartes, Kant, and Hegel. The fundamental standpoint of idealistic philosophy is sometimes designated by such Latin phrases as *adequatio intellectus et rei* (the correspondence between intellect and existence), and it would seem that Parmenides' statement accords well with this statement. However, among contemporary researchers, there are many who question such a modern interpretation. Mr. Suzuki reads *noein* to carry the strong meaning of *sudden intuition*, while also weighing the views of Western scholars regarding the meaning of *noein* that appears in Fragments Two and Three. He maintains that it ought to be basically interpreted as the *intuitive understanding* of the truth of being [*sonzai (aru)*], even though he recognizes that the character of logical reasoning is added to this meaning (Suzuki, 154ff).

I also think that such an understanding may be appropriate, but what I would like to point out here is the fact that the idea of the "understanding of being," placed as a foundation of Heidegger's *Being and Time*, was triggered by this phrase of Parmenides. While there are not a few places in this book that allude to Parmenides, almost all of them are related to the above Fragment Three. For example, after mentioning Aristotle's famous phrase, "all men by nature desire to know,"[30] to indicate that it designates the origin of learning, Heidegger makes the following statements: "[t]his Greek interpretation . . . brings to an explicit understanding what is prefigured in the statement of Parmenides: 'for the same thing is there for thinking and for being.' Being is what shows itself in pure, intuitive perception [*Vernehmen*], and only this seeing [*sehen*] discovers being. Primordial and genuine truth lies in pure intuition" (sec. 36).[31] "From time immemorial, philosophy has associated truth and being. The first discovery of the being of beings [that it is] by Parmenides 'identifies' being with the perceptive understanding of being."[32] Therefore, it comes to mean that thinking and being are identical (sec. 44).[33]

As is seen, Heidegger states that the understanding of being [*sonzai (aru)*] is an activity of passive and intuitive reception prior to intellectual thinking. What then, in this case, is in any way here understood as "being" [*aru*]? It is none other than an understanding of the "being" [*aru*] concerning world, nature, or cosmos. On the basis of living in the world, human beings are always within such an understanding of being. At this point Heidegger was first thinking that the task of *Being and Time* as a fundamental ontology was to clarify the meaning of the facticity that the human being him or herself (*Dasein*) *is* in the world, and that through this a path toward a general ontology will be opened up that would clarify the meaning of "that it is" regarding all that is. What may be thought of here as the final goal of the investigation is the *meaning of the "being"* [*aru*] of the whole world. However, because he relied in *Being and Time* on the theoretical methodology of

Husserl's phenomenology of consciousness, this project in due course obliged him to make a "turn" in his methodology.

Watsuji Tetsuro saw through Heidegger's task that it was to search for the meaning of the "primordial being" of the world prior to its bifurcation into logic and being. Since this is a significant point, let me summarize. Two ways of usage may be distinguished in Japanese, regarding the word "being" [aru], Sein. One is used as the copula that is found in the form "it is ... [... de aru]," which connects the subject S with the predicate P as in "S is P." In contrast to this, "being" as in the case of "there is S [... ga aru]," designates the judgment of being in regards to the object, that is, the judgment that S exists. While this distinction between "it is ... [... de aru]" and "there is ... [... ga aru]" is clear in Japanese, it is not so easily distinguished in the Western languages. It is here where the task of logic lies, that is, to investigate, examine, and clarify, the multifarious usages of the copula that is used in the form "it is ... [... de aru]" (predicate P). In contrast, the task of traditional ontology is to classify the modes of judgments of being, "there is ... [... ga aru]" (individual subject S). What Heidegger's fundamental ontology aims at is to clarify the meaning of the primordial "being" that is common to these two usages. This is the view of Watsuji.

If we examine Heidegger's work after *Being and Time*, we find that he has taken the path that Watsuji saw. In works such as *What Is Metaphysics* and *Nietzsche*, and so on, he comes to distinguish between essential being[34] (*Was-sein, essentia* [quiddity, to ti estin]) and real being[35] (*Dass-sein, existentia* [to estin]). He has in mind the meaning of *Sein* (being [aru]) that "lies prior to the distinction of *Was* and *Dass*." What is here called real being designates "that *there is* something," that is, "being" [aru] as a real fact. And essential being designates "that *it is* something," that is, "being" [aru] as the meaning of an expression. Heidegger states that there is placed in man a passive understanding in regard to the fact that *there is the world as a whole*, prior to the distinction between "there is ..." and "it is...." The reader may feel that he or she understands what Heidegger says here, but may also feel that there is one thing that does not ring a bell. To explain the latter point with a concrete example, the following is illustrative. A newborn baby may vaguely understand that there is a world surrounding it, that is, that there is a world. This is a passive and intuitive understanding that *there is (being) the whole world*. Moreover, through the acquisition of language, the child comes to know *that there is something* there, and simultaneously comes to know *what it is*. If the child learns the word "tree," for example, it comes to understand that *there is* a tree as well as *it is* a tree. The form of expression regarding the judgment and meaning about the being of thing-events simultaneously emerges through their distinction. The former issue connects to ontology as the classification of "what is," and the latter issue develops into logic as the analysis of language (concepts).

Heidegger accordingly believed that the task of philosophy is to pursue the meaning of the primordial "being" [*ari*] of the world, understood prior to the differentiation into logic and being [*sonzai*]. However, he was thrown into a cul-de-sac, because he was dependent in *Being and Time* upon the method of phenomenology that takes logic as its foundation. It is difficult to clarify the meaning of being through intellectual inference because the understanding of the primordial "being" [*aru*] is by nature passive. For this reason, he was obliged to make a "turn" in his methodology. His later thinking moved toward the issue of aesthetic sense and the theory of art, and proceeded in a direction that attempts to comprehend affectively the being of nature and world. Concurrently, he came to show a stance of anti-science.

After *Being and Time*, he distanced himself from the trend of existential philosophy and insisted that philosophy ought to return to Greece. The idea he had in mind was the natural philosophy from about the time of Parmenides. It is to see a sacred "*divinity*" within nature as a whole, a state wherein something divine and something human are one. Although I think that such ideas of his suggest the whereabouts of a thought facing the contemporary world, I feel doubtful whether we can anticipate a future in art or anti-scientism. My view is that the significance of the problem raised by Heidegger may perhaps be in the point that it teaches us the necessity of rethinking afresh the image-thinking that emerged in the ancient world. Therein can be found the task of questioning the relationship between the total nature of being in the world and the psychological human nature by assuming a standpoint prior to logic. If I may be permitted to make a hasty observation, it may be thought that one important task for today's philosophy is to reflect upon the methodology of science, and to discover the connection between the region of the mind and the region of matter. [I will take up this issue in chapter six.] And another basic task may be to question the realm of ethics and religiosity through a reflection upon psychological human nature. The issue of image-thinking will be a stepping stone in this direction.

THE ETERNAL AND THE CHANGING

Let us return to Parmenides. In the beginning part of the longest fragment, Fragment Eight, he states the following:

> What-is is ungenerated and imperishable; Whole, of a single-kind, steadfast, and complete; Nor was [it] once, nor will [it] be, since [it] is, now, all together, One, continuous; for what coming-to-be of it will you seek? How and whence

did it grow? I shall not allow you to say nor to think [that it comes] from what-is-not; for it is not to be said or thought That [it] *is not.*[36] (trs. Hirokawa)

There is neither past nor future for *on* (being [*aru*]). It only "is" [*aru*] eternally. Parmenides says that *logos* (logic) prohibits the thinking of *me on*. In other words, he is claiming that one must not take time into consideration at all. Consequently, change must be denied. Along with it, movement would also probably have to be denied. This is a problem that his friend Zeno tackled.

Even though we may, for now, accept his contention that denies the significance of time, what made me wonder about his contention is: What was his thought on space? Following the above citation, Parmenides states the following, after repeating the claim that "[t]he same thing is that there is thought and for why there [is] thought":[37]

Since, then, there is a furthest limit, it is completed, from every direction like the bulk of a well-rounded sphere, equally balanced in every direction from the center; for it must not be somewhat larger or somewhat smaller, here or there.[38]

We can discern in this passage the image of something like a perfect spherical object. It seems that he is thinking of the "being" [*aru*] of the cosmos as something like a perfect sphere, and assumed it to be in an eternal dimension, wherein we can recognize the stance of the image-thinking of this period being still retained. We might also characterize his thinking as a transcendental cosmology that attempted to comprehend the "divinity" of nature by thoroughly pursuing the idea of intellectual logic. His stance may be feasible if we are to take as an issue the eternity that transcends the dimension of experience. However, how are we to explain the change and movement of events in the world that we experience in the dimension of the senses? This is an issue that he has not dealt with. Image-thinking is that mode of thinking that emerges at the limits of logic.

Zeno is famous for formulating an argument that denies movement. For example, he is said to have stated paradoxes such as "the arrow in locomotion is at rest,"[39] and "Achilles can never overtake the tortoise."[40] This is an argument based on mathematical thinking. While there is a deep relationship, even today, between logic and mathematics, this is probably because the basic idea of logic and pure mathematics is thought to be established without any relation to time. Mr. Ogino Hiroyuki has provided commentary upon this problem presented by Zeno, while introducing the arguments of contemporary scholars.[41] The problem he presented here is called "the paradox of division." In order to reach its goal, a flying arrow must pass through the midpoint [between it and its goal]. However, mathematically there are an infinite number of midpoints. It is impossible, then, to pass through an infinity of points within a finite amount of time. Therefore, we are led to the conclusion that there can be no motion. This is a natural conclusion because a point is defined in geometry merely as a position without any magnitude. It is for the same reason that Achilles, who has swift feet, cannot pass the slow tortoise. Although this is an explanation that emphasizes the infinite divisibility of time, it follows the same fundamentals. Bertrand Russell, the philosopher of mathematics, claimed to have solved the difficult problem by using set theory, but, according to Mr. Ogino, this is merely an argument that starts from the presupposition that Achilles had passed [the tortoise], while ignoring the procedure of dividing time into infinity that is contained within this paradox. Is it not the case that the concept of infinity is unrelated to experience, even though it is logically thinkable?

In contrast, the philosopher Bergson claimed that motion by nature is not divisible and that what can be divided is merely the trace of motion remaining [as an after-image] in space. In fact, as I currently have an interest in Bergson's theory of time, I am wondering whether this issue might not be related to time-consciousness or the issue of the cognition of time prior to becoming related to motion. Although we have in possession criteria for measuring time (i.e. hour, minute, second), how did we ever obtain them? Time itself is something that we can not see nor hear. That is, time by nature is not an object of perception (sensory organs). We can only cognize time *indirectly* through the perception of an event *in space*. Although Bergson thematized Zeno's paradox in a book of his early period, *Time and Free Will*, he later presented a kind of thought-experiment, that of pure perception, in his *Matter and Memory*, that dealt with the mind-body relationship. While this argument was ignored by the philosophers of that time, it attempted to postulate a condition wherein only perception (sensory organs) is operative without accompanying any memory at all. In such a case, we merely perceive the state of the *present moment* in regards to an event in space. Because pure perception is severed from memory, it holds no past and consequently no future. In such a state, it would be the case that "a car in motion will always be at rest," which is parallel to Zeno's paradox. This is because pure perception, which carries no memory, can perceive merely an image at rest like a frame of a movie film. (When this is viewed theoretically, what is suppressed here is the idea of infinite divisibility. The moment is time that is infinitely divided.) Because the perception of a car in motion is the *effect of an after-image*, when it is viewed from the psychological viewpoint, it is connected to the realm of memory. Bergson states that present perception operates always in connection with memory, that is, *the activity of the unconscious*, in virtue of which the cognition of time such as past-present-future, arises. This is one theme in the mind-body theory, but I will not here delve into it. [In chapter six, I will address this topic more fully.]

THE FUTURE DIRECTION OF ETHICS AND PHYSICS

A philosopher who comes up at the conclusion of the Elesian school is Democritus. It is said that he came from Abdera of Thracia, and received his teaching from Leucippus. Because it is not clearly known if Leucippus was the first to formulate the argument of the atom, his idea is regarded together with Democritus as atomism. It is reported that he also received teaching from Anaxagoras of the Milesian school, but that he was dissatisfied because Anaxagoras did not accept his claim. Although Democritus is more or less a contemporary with Socrates, and he lived longer, he is included among the pre-Socratic philosophers out of convenience. While he knew of Socrates, Socrates apparently did not know him. It is said that he was displeased with the Sophists of that time whose activity was in the pursuit of reputation. There are many episodes reporting his lively character. Although we are left with very many titles of his works, almost none of the works themselves remain. The surviving fragments left behind are something like precepts of life, and the content of his well-known atomistic theory is in fact known to us only through the accounts of ancient scholars. However, there are numerous accounts in regard to this, and a great portion of the fourth volume of the Japanese translation of Deils' and Kranz's *Die Fragmente der Vorsokratiker* is spared for Democritus. I wonder how this came about. It seems that this is due to the fact that the philosophy of Democritus influenced Epicurus greatly (342–270 BCE). Democritus was not read widely during the classical Greek period, but came to be regarded as an important philosopher only after Hellenism during the Roman period.

The idea of the atom was conceived in order to explain motion and change. The basis of this idea was to reinterpret what Parmenides called *me on* as *kenon* (void). According to Galen (second century), Democritus called the atom "thing," and void, "nothing [what is not]." The atom moves about within the void and eternally continues colliding and intertwining with other atoms. The motion of things occurs as a result of the motion of the atom attempting to fill up the void that momentarily appears around the infinite atoms. Aristotle commented on this point that Democritus deeply thought about generation and extinction and the alteration of motion. A comparison with Parmenides shows the following: while "the thing that is not," logically speaking, cannot be conceived in Parmenides, because there is no separation between logic and being, Democritus restricted the issue only to the being of nature without thinking about logic. The void is not an issue for logic.

It appears that there were various kinds of atoms that Democritus conceived of, and he explained such things as flavor (taste) and color (sight) in the form of the atom as well. Furthermore, he conceived of the soul (*psychē*) as a type of atom and called this *nous* (intellect). This soul-atom has the shape of a globe, and breath is what prevents it from going outside of the body. According to Aristotle's report, Democritus understood death to mean the departure of the soul-atom inside the body. From a modern perspective, it may be possible to interpret this view as "materialistic," treating the psychological function as if it were a material atom. However, when it is viewed from the point that the atom is something eternal, we may also interpret this view as a panpsychism that inherits the tradition of the *archē* theory of natural philosophy. The issue is how to deal with ethics when standing in such a viewpoint. It seems that Democritus preached the idea that ethical education is to transform the figure and unity of the lump of atoms that constitute the soul, into another form. Democritus' view of ethics is known, as stated above, for greatly influencing Epicurus after the period of Hellenism. That is, atomism became an idea that unites physics and ethics. There is no posture here of pursuing a transcendent and eternal dimension through logic, as in Parmenides. Although this attitude is found in the direction inherited by Plato, I feel a subtle difference here from Socrates, who had his foundation in ethics and faith.

During the Hellenistic and Roman periods, methods of psychological practice such as meditation methods became popular, and such a meditational strand becomes inherited by neo-Platonism and Christianity of the latter Roman period. I can here discern something commensurate with the ancient East. In the traditions of the East, whether of India or China, the path to the transcendent dimension necessitates psychological training such as meditation. In such cases psychology becomes the basis, and logical thought is secondary.

Translator's Note

Yuasa uses chapter two to examine the issues relating to image-thinking, while focusing on the linguistic expression of, and psychological basis for, the Western and the Eastern understandings of Being (or being). He shows that the East Asian tradition fostered image-thinking without developing any emphasis on the rationalistic understanding of Being and without relying on logic, primarily because this tradition uses pictographs. Because pictographs are like pictures, they evoke an affective inter-resonance between the embodied subject and the object pictured.

Of the many intriguing comparisons he brings up in this connection, the following point is crucial and significant in understanding the difference. Yuasa interprets the Western languages to be a "vocal language" that appeals to auditory perception, while he regards the Chinese language as a "written language" that appeals to visual perception. The point he emphasizes here is the difference that arises in attempting to cognize and express thing-events in encountering nature. He states that while this point is secondary in the Western languages because the meaning of a word is based on consensus gentium, this is primary in the Chinese language because it "places the primary importance in visual perception," enabling people to "directly encounter nature face-to-face." He draws from it the psychological implication, namely, that there is no essential distinction in the user of the Chinese language between conscious thinking and unconscious thinking, whereby "unconscious thinking" Yuasa means "intuition" and "dreaming." When he makes this observation, however, he has in mind primarily the experience that emerges in the course of meditative self-cultivation.

CHAPTER TWO

Image-Thinking and the Understanding of "Being"

The Psychological Basis of Linguistic Expression

CHINESE, JAPANESE, AND WESTERN EXPRESSIONS* FOR "BEING"

When speaking about philosophy, we can distinguish between the problem of language that is used in expressing thoughts, and the problem of lived experience or facts that the speaker attempts to grasp through expressions [of these thoughts]. The former is a problem of the form of expression; the latter is a problem of the content. Although the problem of language tends to be easily neglected, there is a grave difference in the characteristics of the languages of the East and the West, and we can see a situation where this difference [of language] comes to influence the way of thinking itself, [some instances of which I examined in chapter one.] This is particularly important [in the time] before the modern period, when there was hardly any direct interchange at the level of thought between the East and the West.

Because modern Japanese philosophy after the Meiji period (1868–1912), on the whole, was initiated by the form of the importation and acceptance of Western philosophy, its terms are imbued, at their root, with the coloration

---

* We have generally used "expression" to translate the Japanese word *hyōgen* [表現]. However, at times we have also translated *gengo* (language, 言語), and sometimes *kotoba* (word, *parole*, 言葉) as "expressions." This ambiguity in translation points out precisely the differences between Western and East Asian languages that Yuasa wishes to highlight. A character can equally be a "word," an "expression," and even a "sentence."—Trans.]

of the translated Western terms. Ordinarily, a translation into indigenous Japanese words [*yamato kotoba*, 大和言葉] did not occur; instead, neologisms were created by using Chinese characters and Chinese words.[1] If we limit our perspective to the world of professional research specialists, this does not give rise to a great deal of inconvenience; as these researchers are well versed in the content of Western philosophy. They can understand their meaning-content [*iminaiyō*, 意味内容] among themselves, even if they use translated words. However, for the average Japanese, who is not a specialist, this fact is one of the causes that makes philosophy difficult to understand. For example, because the philosophy of Heidegger uses many everyday words, Western-ers may easily understand the intended nuances of these words, but, when translated into Japanese, they end up becoming expressions that are extremely difficult to comprehend. This situation is also the same in the case of sci-ence, but because science is clear as to facts and content, even if one translates Western languages, one does not face the difficulty of understanding the con-tent. However, in the case of philosophical terms, if one does not understand, to a certain degree, the history of philosophy and the historical and cultural background that led to the use of these words, there are occasions when it is not possible to understand correctly their meaning content. This is probably one of the reasons why it is difficult for people to understand philosophy in Japanese society.

Another factor that makes the situation complicated is the use of Chi-nese characters. Many philosophical terms are compounds that were created in modern times, but there are many occasions when the meaning of these words deviates from their original sense and usage in the Chinese character or in the culture. However, since Japanese specialists in Western philosophy do not ordinarily have a very specialized knowledge of China and Japan, this fact is not brought to self-awareness on many occasions. When one thinks about philosophical problems from the viewpoint of Japan vis-à-vis the West, with the West as the standard, it causes no great inconvenience. However, when one assumes the perspective of broadly comparing the East and West, by going back to the cultural traditions of the East, it will probably become necessary to think through this point.

Putting generalities aside, I would like to take up the meaning of the word "being" ["*aru*" or "*sonzai*"].[2] This word has played an important role in the history of Western philosophy; from ancient Greece until the modern time of Descartes, the fundamental paradigm of philosophy has been placed in ontology. If we look at its substantial content, ontology is given the char-acter of metaphysics as the principle investigation of nature and the cosmos, and it carries the meaning of investigating the principle of all that is (i.e., that which exists). When we enter the modern period, the paradigm of ontology was discarded and epistemology took its place. However, after entering the twentieth century, the modes of thinking in epistemology had reached a certain kind of dead end, and phenomenology, pragmatism and other types of philosophy have arisen. In Nishida Kitarō's philosophy, which is regarded as representative of modern Japanese philosophy, there are elements that also agree with the trends of the philosophical movement of the twentieth century.[3] Out of this movement, Heidegger once again brought up ontology, but because he introduced a new distinction between "Being" (Sein) and "beings" (Seinendes), conceptual expression became extremely complicated.

We can discover even in the history of East Asian philosophy something that corresponds to metaphysics in the sense of the principle investigation of nature and the cosmos.[4] However, it did not take the form of the investigation of being [or Being]. In the history of Western philosophy, the investigation relating to being (i.e., is), gave birth to the dispute of how to see the relation between so-called essentia ("essence" or "it is . . ."), and existentia ("that it is," or "there is . . ."). Logic and ontology arose out of this distinction, [as I pointed out in chapter one]. In contrast, a discussion analogous to this has never arisen in the history of East Asian philosophy. I wondered why this was the case. Using the word "being" [sonzai, 存在] as a clue, let us approach this problem.

The Japanese word "being" (sonzai) appears to be a compound that was coined in modern times, but the actual origin of the word is still not known.[5] To speak from a Heideggerian context, the word "being" is a nominalization of the be-verb "Sein" that is a predicate, but this word [sonzai], in Chinese or Chinese characters, cannot be restricted to a predicative use due to the nature of the Chinese language. Rather, the content that the word "sonzai" expresses, shows its original figure [in language] as a noun, and its use as a verb is secondary. For this reason, one must use the expression "sonzai suru"[6] [存在する] to make a verbal expression—an expression that is not used in the everyday language; one can simply use "aru" ["to be" both in the sense of "it is . . ." and "there is . . ."] in ordinary Japanese expressions. What we need to pay attention to here is the fact that "sonzai suru" can only mean "there is . . ." [to indicate an existence] but cannot mean "it is . . ." [to indicate an essence]. Because sonzai is primarily a nominal expression, this word carries the nuance of a being, as "that it is (in a certain space)." Consequently, for example, it is ordinarily sufficient to translate the distinction between essentia and existentia as a difference between "essence" [honshitsu, 本質] and "being" ["sonzai," 存在]. If we wish to speak accurately, this distinction must be translated as the distinction between "essential being" [honshitsu sonzai, 本質存在] and "actual being" ["genjitsu sonnzai," 現実存在]. Thus, these expressions end up becoming complicated expressions that are difficult for ordinary people to understand. If we were to put these abstract philosophical terms in ordinary Japanese, this distinction [is an expression that] points to the difference in the meaning-content of *"aru"* (i.e. *that* it is) when contrasting between "it is . . ." [. . . *de aru* (である)] and "there is . . ." [. . . *ga aru* (がある)].[7]

The fundamental reason for the generation of this troublesome problem lies in the peculiar nature that Chinese characters possess. Heidegger's *Sein und Zeit* is usually translated as *Sonzai to Jikan* [存在と時間], though there are those who advocate a different opinion, insisting that *"Sein"* should be translated as *"yū"* [有] (e.g., Watsuji Tetsurō[8] and others). Insofar as *Sein* is originally a verb, this opinion is certainly appropriate, but even if it is rendered as *"yū"* this does not mean that its meaning is sufficiently conveyed.[9] When it is used in contrast to *mu* ("nonbeing" or "nothing," 無), *"yū"* comes to mean "being" or *"Sein"* but, originally, it is a word that means "to have" or "to carry" (*motsu*, 持つ), as is seen in such compounds as *sho-yū* ("to possess," 所有), *yū-yō* (lit., "to carry a use," i.e., "to be useful," 有用), *yū-eki* (lit., "to carry a benefit," i.e., "to be beneficial," 有益), and *yū-shikisha* (lit., "one who carries knowledge," i.e., "a knowledgeable person," 有識者).[10] After all, its meaning as "to be" (*aru*) is simply secondary and derivative. However, how about the words *son* [存] and *zai* [在]? *Son* [存] is a term that shows originally the condition of being *in the midst of a temporal process*, as indicated by such compounds as *ho-zon* ("to preserve," 保存), *son-bō* ("to survive or perish," 存亡), *tekishasei-zon* ("survival of the fittest," 適者生存), and *on-zon* ("to warmly preserve," 温存). The meaning of "being" is a derivative usage. As for *zai* [在], it indicates the condition of being *in a space* (either idealistically or really), as in expressions such as *zai-ke* ("being in the house," i.e., "a layman," 在家), *zai-taku* ("being at home," 在宅), *zai-ya* ("being in the field," i.e., "out of the office," 在野), and *zai-ko* ("goods in stock," 在庫). In this case as well, the meaning of "being" is simply a derivative usage.

In addition, we can mention *"ya"* [Chin., *yě*: 也] as a word that is used to mean *"aru."*[11] In Japanese, it is alternatively read as *"nari,"* and although it is understood to mean "it is . . ." (*de aru*), this word, as an auxiliary character that attaches to the end of a sentence in the Chinese language, is a word that indicates a tone of affirmation or exclamation. There are many words beside this that are utilized in a manner similar to *"ya."* For example, *"yǐ"* [矣] indicates the condition of strong affirmation and exclamation (in Japanese, it corresponds to *"kana"*). *"Kana"* [Chin., *zāi*: 哉] is used, in addition to the sense of exclamation, to indicate an interrogative or rhetorical question (corresponding respectively in Japanese to " . . . *ya*" and " . . . *kana*"). Moreover, *"ya"* [耶] is an auxiliary character that is used in interrogative and negative rhetorical questions.[12] In short, these auxiliary characters, in the writing systems of Western languages, correspond to the question mark and the exclamation mark. Though they perform the role of indicating *a psychological condition*, logically, they do not possess a special meaning. Insofar as we look at these characters logically, there is no special meaning in them. However, the highly developed expressions of these auxiliary characters show an historical and cultural background that is different from the West.

If we pursue our thinking about this point, we run into the following problems. First, as the development of these auxiliary characters indicates, in the expressions of the Chinese language the affective nature is stronger than the logical nature. Another fundamental problem we must think through is that Chinese characters were originally ideographs that appealed to visual perception. That is, they possess a characteristic that must be called "image language" [イメージ言語]. As I will deal with this later, the form of thinking that is observed in the history of Chinese philosophy is conditioned by the fact that it is an image language. Because Japanese uses the *kana* syllabary as a phonetic alphabet, and has many particles (*te, ni, wo, ha*) corresponding to inflectional endings, it has the advantage of making an easier connection with Western linguistic expressions, but in the traditional Chinese language, we may note first of all that there is no phonetic alphabet that is devoid of meaning in the words themselves. As I mentioned, it is for this reason that there is no "good fit" for translating words that are used to express "being" or "*Sein.*" In other words, in expressions that use Chinese characters, there must necessarily be, in some way, a concrete meaning-content that accompanies the characters. There is no word that shows the abstract and general meaning of "being" [the Japanese "*aru*"] without [having a] specific content. The various difficult problems surrounding the translation of *sonzai* [存在], in fact, originate here. When we think about Western philosophy, problems in ontology have a decisive significance, but the conception of this point is completely different historically between the West and East Asia. Apart from how appropriate the Sapir–Whorf hypothesis[13] may be—the hypothesis that language defines culture—we cannot deny the fact that philosophical thinking in East Asia has come to be historically brought up by means of these conditions. On the other hand, it is also clear that philosophical thinking in the West has been defined historically by the methods of expression of Western languages. At least until modern times, the philosophy of the East and the West has not gone outside of their respective historical and cultural conditions. It is probably necessary for us today to bring this fact to self-awareness and to proceed to think about these issues philosophically.

THE CHARACTERISTICS OF EXPRESSIONS IN THE CHINESE LANGUAGE

We hear the opinion from a number of scholars (e.g., Nakamura Hajime[14]) that the Chinese language is a language that lacks a logical character. It is often the case that this sort of opinion is stated with Western languages (or their cognate language systems) as a standard, but I cannot necessarily and immediately follow this view. For it is possible to think the foregoing question, "Is there not a logic unique to Chinese language and sentences, and is there not a progression of thinking unique to them?" What is important to us is to think through the characteristics of the Chinese people's way of thinking that is at the base of this phenomenon that is presumed to "lack a logical character."

The late scholar of Chinese philosophy, Professor Nishi Junzō, states that the Chinese language is a language without a [grammatical] subject.[15] Professor Nishi's discussion points out some important problematic points, but because these points do not seem to be very well known, I would like to spend some time introducing their general content. Nishi states that the lack of a subject in the Chinese language means that there are no words, based on the grammar of the expressions of Chinese sentences, that indicate noun declensions, or verb tenses, transitive, intransitive verbs, or passive [verbs]. Among these are many functions related to predicate expressions, but this "grammatical institution" (i.e., syntax) is necessary for a grammatical subject only when there is an embodied subject [shutai, 主体][16] for it, and it accordingly becomes effective.[17] Nishi points out that if there is no such syntax, it also means that there is no grammatical subject. For example, the character "rain" [雨] can designate "rain" itself (i.e., a nominative expression); it can also become the verb "to rain," and it can even be used as an adjectival expression, "like rain." From the point of view of semiotics (i.e. the usual grammatical rules of Western languages), something corresponding to syntax is originally lacking [in the Chinese language].

Nishi states that having no grammatical subject means that words alone cannot complete the meaning/thing-event [imi-jishō, 意味事象] at which the expression of words aims. However, if we take Western languages as a standard, no grammatical subject means that there is no predicate either. In Chinese, even if there is a connection in terms of some kind of meaning/thing-event among individual words, and hence a unity, there is no synthetic unity as a language. Individual words only float on the surface of meaning/thing-events, and their mutual synthetic connection is not shown in the words as linguistic expressions. The system of meaning/thing-events never appears on the surface of the [Chinese] language. Although words play the roles of various parts of speech, based on their function, these roles are not essential to the words themselves. They are variable. The character of the words themselves in the language system is, [paradoxically,] characterless. Consequently, even though there is a connection between words in terms of meaning/thing-events, formally they stand isolated, wherein all words are equal. The connective continuity of words is achieved only according to the demands of meaning/thing-events. Therefore, in the arrangement of words there is no formal necessity. The arrangement floats on the surface of the meaning/thing-events that are in the back of the language,[18] and each word interresonates with each other, and is made to echo the meaning/thing-event in terms of its meaning and content.

In such a language, which is formed according to the arrangement of individually isolated words, there is no formal system that would correspond to concrete meaning/thing-events. Despite this, that words form a definite meaning/thing-event is because expressions are gathered together into one [whole] by something *other than the language*. Consequently, there is no synthetic unity, or completion, based on language. A unity of meaning occurs in the back of the language, waiting for the primordial meaning/thing-event wherein language is produced. The connection of words is not united according to the expressed words, but, without being expressed clearly, they achieve connective continuity by a meaning that arises naturally in and of itself. There is no correspondence between individual words and meanings, and the meaning of words cannot be determined unless the meaning itself that cannot become a word participates there.

Because isolated words are characterless, they are of themselves complete and self-sufficient. They have no external determination that is added in virtue of a comparative relation with other words. Consequently, what a certain word expresses cannot be defined as to whether it is a thing with substance, or function, or mode, or abstract idea. If we write the ideograph "山" [yama], it is difficult to make *a clear distinction between the idea and the existence* based upon the expressed sentence,[19] since we can also take it to mean "there is a mountain." There is no other way to judge than according to the entire linguistic context. In short, at every juncture in the connective continuity, words recede into the world of meaning that is prior to the words themselves, by cutting themselves off [from the surface linguistic context]. Here, each word is a creation out of the meaning that lies in its background; each word returns to the primordial origin, through which meaning itself is made anew, and the succeeding word emerges in response to the meaning.

After Nishi's discussion, he has summarized the characteristics of the Chinese language as follows, while bearing in mind its comparison with Western languages. Each word in the Chinese language is a subjective-objective creation, and in this respect it is possible to say that Chinese is a temporal language. In contrast, Western languages are spatial insofar as linguistic expression is objectively established parallel to meaning and the whole meaning cannot be formed until the arrangement of words is completed. Spatiality may also be paraphrased as being intellectual. If this is the case, the temporality of the Chinese language means that it possesses an *affective* character, or rather, to be accurate, a *life-bearing* character [*semeiteki*, 生命的]. However, language is not music, and insofar as it consists of words delimited by specific modes, it shows a conceptual, spatial, and, consequently, an intellectual character. But, because this is connected with an essential, even primordial "foundation of meaning," this intellectual character is always colored by an affective and living substance that is in the background. Nishi characterizes this substance as literary: "the fact that in China a philosophy, in the sense of a systematic, conceptual, structure, did not develop, is perhaps due, at least in part, to the character of the language."[20] In the Chinese traditions, philosophy has always been literary.

Nishi's conclusion is: "the Chinese language is poor in intellectual abstraction, is insufficient in objectivity, and is a dumb language." The arrangement of words is a connection of things in which there is no connectivity. The basis of this connectivity is not in the words, but lies, going beyond words, in the midst of the meaning and thing-events, which become the background of the place wherein the words are produced. In other words, the objectivity of language, and hence its ideational character, is tacitly denied. It is said that there is a great deal of metaphor in the Chinese language, but there are many cases where this is not the literal metaphor of Western logic. Where phrase A is a [so-called] metaphor that expresses the meaning of B, if phrase A directly makes one sense the meaning of B, one cannot call this a metaphor.

I introduced Nishi's discussion at long length; but if we reflect taking into account the above discussion, we can also sense a bit of a resemblance in the function of Japanese expressions and those of the Chinese language. In Japanese, there are many cases where personal pronouns, such as the expressions "I" and "you," are deleted. If one were to use these words in everyday conversations with friends, there would arise a feeling of formality, [because] the pronouns "he" and "she" are words that have come to be used through the influence of the West. In classical Japanese, for example, in the tales of the Heian period [794–1186], important personal pronouns are almost never explicitly mentioned; they are rendered naturally comprehensible from the midst of the flow of the context. In Western languages, if "I" and "you" are lacking, conversation and explanation are probably impossible. In Greek and Latin, there are many cases of personal pronouns being deleted due to verb conjugations; but, in these cases, it is easy to identify the grammatical subject from syntactic rules. At any rate, [in the Western languages] the personal pronoun is the starting-point for describing situations where the embodied subject engages the world or the environment, whereas in Japanese this is often not clearly expressed.

Nishida Kitarō grasped Western logic that began with Aristotle as a synthetic unity via the grammatical subject, or via a grammatical subject-synthesis.

Against this, he called his own standpoint the synthetic unity of the predicate, or the predicate-synthesis. Out of this type of thinking, the so-called logic of *basho*[21] [*basho no ronri*, 場所の論理; "*basho*" means "place" or "*topos*"] was born. Nishida came up with the logic of *basho* as a method of thinking that directly overcomes the modern epistemological paradigm that divides the subjective and the objective, while placing them in opposition. It seems, at least for now, that Nishida's idea of *basho* is commensurate with the mode of expression of the Chinese language, in which Nishi pointed out that there is a place of meaning/thing-events that transcends the language [and occurs] in the back of the form of linguistic expressions. Nishi says that expressions that always arise anew from the place of meaning/thing-events are subjective-objective creations, wherein there is a dynamic flow—a flow in which the subject *qua* expressor and the object *qua* expressed are inseparably one. Expressions by means of language always acquire a meaning by returning to the place of meaning. It is often said that Nishida's "logic of *basho*" is connected with his Zen experience,[22] and I need not point out that Zen is a school of Buddhism that became very Sinicized. We can say, for now, that the characteristic of Zen thought does not lie in intellectual inference, but lies in overcoming the standpoint of intellectual logic. Does this not perhaps mean that we find ourselves in the place of Nishi's meaning/thing-events that is prior to language?

Returning to the problem of "being" [*sonzai*], as Nishi states, the objectivity [of things] and their ideational character in language are in fact denied in the Chinese language. This means that language as a system of ideas cannot become an objective system apart from reality ["*genjitsu*," 現実].[23] The predicate "being" ["*aru*" in Japanese; "to be" or "*Sein*"] is an abstract expression, devoid of all concrete content and has nothing to do with the content of individual thing-events in reality. We can probably say that the unique character of the Chinese language, whose linguistic expressions are not divorced from concrete thing-events (and, consequently, does not have a word indicating "being"), appears most clearly in this point. If we change perspective, [the Japanese word] *aru* must be the total function that permeates the whole of expressed sentences (and, therefore, the place of meaning/thing-events), wherein expressions and lived experience are not separated in regard to "*aru*" that is differentiated into "it is . . ." and "there are." In consequence, *aru* is not singled out as a predicate that is abstractly delimited, and, further, *essentia* and *existentia* are not separated as in Western languages. To borrow a Heideggerian turn of phrase, the term "Being" (*Sein*) always functions in the midst of all beings (*Seiendes*), although it never appears as itself. The later Heidegger, drawing an × through the word *Sein*, emphasized that while remaining hidden, its activity appears.[24] This way

of capturing the matter, it would seem to me, is commensurate with the
ancient Chinese mode of thinking.

THE RELATION BETWEEN LOGIC AND PSYCHOLOGY IN THE LINGUISTIC EXPRESSIONS OF THE CHINESE AND WESTERN LANGUAGES

If we turn back to look at history, writing originally began with ideograms,
which were pictographs. The hieroglyphs of ancient Egypt have taught us
this. It is also said that pictographs existed in the ancient Mayan and Incan
civilizations. The scholars and artisans of this period devised these writing
systems, and only individuals with specialized knowledge understood them.
For a long period, Chinese characters were also symbols that were unrelated to
the general populace. In contrast, it is said that the origin of phonetic writing
was in the Phoenician writing system, which had contact with Egypt. Phoe-
nicia flourished as a nation of commerce, and interacted with peoples who
spoke many different languages. For this reason, it was necessary to have an
easy writing system that was connected with auditory perception, for the general populace to understand. If we call languages, such as Western languages,
which are expressed through phonetic writing, "vocal languages" ["*onsei-
gengo*," 音声言語], we can probably also call the Chinese language, which is
expressed through ideographs, a "written language" ["*mojigengo*," 文字言語].
(Here I am not putting into consideration the issue of the simplified system
of characters that is used in contemporary China.) While the foundation of
linguistic expression in a "vocal language" is *parole*, which appeals to auditory
perception, the foundation of linguistic expression in a "written language" is
the image, which appeals to visual perception. From this perspective, let us
attempt to compare the structure of both.

In the Western languages the relation between individual words and the
objects they designate is arbitrary, and the determinate rules and structure
are found in the relations that connect words. This is the distinction that
Sausurre makes between *parole* and *langue*. If we look at this from a philosophical point of view, *parole* is related to the area of semantics. In semantics,
the relations between expressions that designate the substantial objects or
thing-events that are found synchronically in (the realistic or idealistic) space
come to be questioned. In contrast, the rules of language that controls the diachronic time of *parole* are in the syntax or grammar. This, then, becomes the
base that gives logical character to expression and thought.

However, the distinction between *parole* and *lange* in the method of
expression of the traditional Chinese language is nothing but derivative. In
the Chinese language, the characters that correspond to individual words are

pictographs, or ideographs that are combinations of pictographs, and they are both different from Western languages.[25] Hence, along with the fact that individual words always designate an image that expresses a concrete and definite content, these words are always monosyllabic. That is, in Chinese an inseparable relationship holds among character (a visual image), word, and sound. Here, we can see the relation of word = image = sound, as it were. In short, in the method of expression of the Chinese language, the fundamental means of recognition is placed in visual images, where the one sound = one word relation appealing to auditory perception is subordinate. If we look at history, the origin of pictographs goes back to the divination [practice] of the mythological age of the Yīn dynasty around 1500 BCE.

In the case of the phonetic letters of Western languages, the phonemes or syllables that make up sounds, if individually separated, have no meaning whatsoever. Because sounds are different from drawings or figures, they have no relation at all with objects;[26] the relation between one word = one sound and the object that it designates is arbitrary and a word is nothing but a mere sign for the purpose of designation. [For example,] there is no intrinsic necessity to write "dog" as "d-o-g" and to pronounce it as such. (Incidentally, the Chinese character for dog [inu, 犬] displays the image of a figure with legs firmly planted on the ground, and with ears raised at attention. Due to this connection between the character and the image, in the names of all animals it has become the custom to attach the animal radical "犭," which is derived from the character for dog.)

As is seen above, because the relation between words and the objects that they designate is arbitrary in Western languages, the necessity of rules that control linguistic expressions is found only in the syntax that connects these words. Here, we discover that the diachronic process of the unfolding of speech (parole) plays a fundamental role when attempting to cognize and express the meaning that the thing-events of the world disclose to us. Written sentences that depend on visual perception are given merely a derivative role, subordinate to the speech act. On the other hand, in the method of expression of the traditional Chinese language that gives primacy to visual perception, every character = word = sound already expresses a definite, concrete meaning and content. In other words, the essence of individual words, which are not merely signs for designation, fulfills the role of symbolic images that are just like pictures or iconographs that passively and cognitively receive the given thing-events therein. For this reason, while the individual character = word = sound carries a very concrete character in the Chinese language, as directly opposed to the Western languages, the structures and rules that connect words are not clearly indicated in the written sentences of the speech acts themselves. Words all stand in isolation from each other, and are given arbitrarily as a succession of synchronic images. The character or the word for rain [*ame*, 雨] can indicate "rain" (*ame*), and can also be used as a verb to mean "it rains" (*ame furu*). There is no other way than to judge this distinction from the context as a whole. It is not determined by *grammar*. In addition, in the case of nouns, there are no declensions (e.g., the distinction between the nominative and the objective cases). In the case of verbs, there are no distinctions of tense (if one wants to *clearly* distinguish between the past and the present tenses, it is necessary to add on a new word). If we look at the Chinese language in light of the Western way of thinking, where syntax gives the logical form to thought and expression, it can probably be regarded as a language that lacks logical character. However, we, instead, ought to recognize here a difference in the fundamental stance humans take when attempting to cognize and express thing-events, on facing them in a world filled with meanings.

I wonder which is more fundamental in the cognition of the world, auditory or visual perception? We cannot say. Visual perception relates to space, while auditory perception is related to time. Painting, which depends on visual perception, is a spatial art, whereas music, which depends on auditory perception, is a temporal art. However, one probably cannot say which is primary. If space and time are preconditions for the cognition of the world, both are necessary.

However, if we compare them from the point of view of how we view the relation between human beings and the world, a grave difference arises here. If one takes visual expressions as having primary importance, the relationship of "seeing" to "seen," found in the relation between self and world, is foundational, wherein the relationship of self to others becomes secondary. That is, the relationship where the embodied subject [*shutai*, 主体] sees the world *in the midst of silence* becomes fundamental, as in the case of Zen experience. In contrast, if one takes auditory perception as primary importance, consensus and rules [*consensus gentium*] that dominate human relationships between oneself and others become dominant (i.e., logic as *logos*). If we shift this to the relationship between human beings and nature, the stance of placing primary importance in visual perception directly encounters nature face-to-face. In contrast, the stance of taking auditory perception as primary presupposes the rules of human relationships, through which one comes to grasp nature. In short, it is perhaps correct to say that in the West, the rules of linguistic expression that have a bearing on contracts in interpersonal relationships between self and others precede written expressions, and carry the primary guiding role in these expressions. In contrast, self-expression by means of images possess the primary guiding role in China, and visual images about the natural world that envelops the human relationships of self and other expressed therein become the a priori limiting condition prior to the separation between *langue* and *parole.* Therefore, the method of thinking in traditional China, in its essential points, possesses a character that we ought to call "symbolic image-thinking" [*shōchōteki imēji shikō,* 象徴的イメージ思考].

Seen from a psychological point of view, this means that there is not an essential distinction between conscious thinking and unconscious thinking (e.g., dreams and intuitions). In dreams, images unfold one after the other, but it is difficult to judge how these are related to each other—at least based on conscious logic. Similarly, each individual word, which is presented one by one, stands in isolation in Chinese writing = Chinese language, wherein the logical form that governs the relations of these words is not indicated in the language and the sentences themselves. Judging from the given context as a whole, we reach as far as the meaning that the individual words designate. Consequently, words cannot be connected with other words unless they *return* to the world itself, latently in the background of the given images. In other words, [words are connected] by returning to *the place (basho)* from which the meaning of thing-events emerges (i.e., ultimately, the ground of the Being [*ratio essendi*] of all thing-events). This operation is commensurate with the method in which psychologists analyze dreams and make clear the meaning behind them. The *Book of Changes* [*Yijing*] is a book of divination that served as the source of Chinese philosophy. The divinatory texts of the Yīn dynasty (?–1027 BCE), which are the origins of divination in China, show the beginnings of ideographs. Psychologically, divination is a cognition based on *unconscious intuition*, which means, one might say, to totally intuit the relationship of self as a human being and the world existing (*aru*) "here-now" from their ground.

In thinking about the characteristics of philosophical thought in China, it is necessary to keep in mind the special nature of the Chinese written sentence = Chinese language, as I have previously elucidated. We can discern there a stance that attempts to accept passively the activities issuing forth from the world, by advancing forward on its own toward the world itself and becoming identified with the world disclosed as an image. At the foundation of this stance is discovered an intuitive intentionality that moves toward the ground of being (i.e., that which *is*) that holistically integrates individual thing-events. Consequently, the thought of Chinese philosophy is not merely one of intellectual cognition. Always accompanying it are will and emotions that the image necessarily arouses. Thought does not merely remain as thought, but is the action of a total personality that accompanies will, emotions, and desires. Consequently, logic cannot be separated from psychology. And at this foundation is an *intuition* that moves toward the primordial origin of being and the formless meaning of the world. Consequently, in China, philosophy is simultaneously literature and poetry. Moreover, the world is grasped as a momentary image of which the eternal movement [of the cosmos] allows us to have a glimpse in the midst of time.

Needless to say, this does not mean that Saussure was unaware of the dimension of the lived-meaning that is at the base of linguistic expressions. He distinguished between the two dimensions of "syntagmatic" and "associative" relations in linguistic expressions. Syntagmatic relations are the relations between words that are the elements that form sentences, that is, syntax that creates the linguistic context that appears on the surface. In contrast, associative relations are those relationships that might be called a latent linguistic context, which is in a deeper layer beneath the "syntagmatic" relationships. According to Saussure, in forming sentences, word groups, which have not been selected, must be considered besides the chosen words. The former points to a dimension that has not surfaced, even though it is latent in the interior of the speaker's mind. Concerning the relation between these two dimensions, Saussure says the following:

> From the associative and syntagmatic viewpoint a linguistic unit is like a fixed part of a building, e.g., a column. On the one hand, the column has a certain relation to the architrave that it supports; the arrangement of the two units in space suggests the syntagmatic relation. On the other hand, if the column is Doric, it suggests a mental comparison of this style with others (Ionic, Corinthian, etc.) although none of these elements is present in space: the relation is associative.[27]

A Doric column, being selected, appears right before one's eyes. When we see it, in our mind, we can compare and bring to mind other styles of columns, such as Ionic and Corinthian. "[I]t [i.e., the Doric column] suggests a mental comparison of this style with others," means that this relationship is connected with an *unconscious layer* of the mind, such as that lies latent at the base of linguistic expressions is the same as the dimension of the ground of being [i.e. *ratio essendi*] and meaning in the Chinese language and sentences that have a system of expressions heterogeneous to Western languages. There, a deeper region of the mind is found to be universal, which goes beyond the differences of language and is prior to the utterance of the words.[28] This mode of thinking may be connected to the issue of Chomsky's "transformational generative grammar"[29] [—particularly the deep structure of a sentence out of which the surface structure is derived].

What sort of issue does the foregoing observation present to the philosophical comparison between the East and the West? In the philosophy of the ancient and Middle Ages in the West, ontology and logic occupied an important place. The former represents the world, and the later represents the standpoint of human beings. When we come to the modern era, epistemology takes the place of logic, and the world as a being becomes an object for the ego or for subjectivity [to observe and then to manipulate]. In contrast, in East Asia, human beings and the world were not separated, nor did they oppose each other. In the ontology of Daoism and Zen Buddhism, the individual and the world always dwell in holistic and unitive relations of oneness. The cognition of these unitive relations, as I will discuss in the following, is not through logic, but through a lived experience in the field of practical self-cultivation [*shugyō*, 修行], that is, through intuitive knowing.

LOGIC AND LIVED EXPERIENCE

While keeping in mind what I have noted in the foregoing, I would like to think still further the characteristics of Eastern philosophy. In Chinese philosophy before the modern period, there was not a clearly delineated field of study that corresponded to logic as in the West. In the "Hundred Schools of Thought" during the period of "Warring States" (403 BCE–221 BCE), there was a school of thought called "the School of Names" [Chin., *Míngjiā*; Jap., *Meika*: 名家] which arose from the dialectician, Gōngsūnlóng [Jap., *Kōsonryū*: 公孫 龍], who was known for his theory that a "white horse is not a horse,"[30] but, as the authority of Confucianism established itself, this school disappeared from history. In the debates used between the "School of Names" and the "Mohists" [Chin., *mòjiā*; Jap., *bokka*: 墨家], there was an area that, in part, had a bearing on semantics (the investigation of the relation between a word and the object it designates),[31] and so these can be included in the field of logic. However, these streams of thought disappeared in due time from the stage of philosophy. The theory of the so-called rectification of names [正名論], upheld by the Confucians and the Legalists, defeated the School of Names and the Mohist school.[32] This was a debate based on the practical demands of correcting the relationship between name and substance. Therefore, the essence [of the "rectification of names"] must probably be regarded as belonging to ethics or to political science (i.e., the theory of ideologies). In other words, a characteristic of traditional thought in China, we might say, lies in the area of ethical or political thought that is based on practice, and this thought proceeded to deny and exclude logical thinking.

If we look at the history of Western philosophy, from the time of ancient Greece on [into the present], we witness the flourishing of theoretical investigation and the arts, which is related to the method of using words in oratory and dialectics (the art of dialogue) or rhetoric. Further, there is a strand in Western philosophy that developed in the Middle Ages, with logic at its center, but, in the history of Chinese philosophy there has hardly been any discussion of this kind. Even if we look at the history of Japanese thought, which developed under the influence of Chinese culture, there is no field of inquiry that corresponds to the study of logic before the modern period. Nishi made the statement that the Chinese language is "poor in intellectual abstraction and is a dumb language," and he phrased it this way so as to make the reader comprehend the problem easily. However, it is a fact that theoretical reflection and investigation did not develop regarding the connective relationships within language and in regard to the method of using words in interpersonal relationship as in oratory. This contributed to the weakening of the study of logic [in China]. As I observed in the foregoing, the foundation of Western languages is that it is a vocal language, and, consequently, phonetic letters are used. In contrast, in China, ideographs appealing to visual perception occupy [a place of] central importance for linguistic expression, and this [fact] is not unrelated to the lack of development in logic.

   If we trace their origin, ideographs are, at the root, similar to pictures; and it is difficult to determine a meaning-content univocally. It is analogous to the situation when what a picture as a work of art "says" depends on the viewer. On the one hand, while a writing system that relies on ideographs can concisely express a great deal of meaning-content, this in turn makes the content fuzzy (i.e., ambiguous). In contrast, the meaning-content can be, relatively speaking, correctly conveyed in vocal languages, as is seen in the Western languages, but there the writing becomes verbose. For example, my family name, "Yuasa" [湯浅], if written in Chinese characters, can be done with only two characters, but in the Roman alphabet five letters are necessary. This is because each character already possesses a concrete meaning-content. On the other hand, because the meaning-content of the characters is multivocal in Chinese sentences, it becomes necessary to delimit the meaning of characters by making compounds of two or more of them. It is for this reason that the Chinese character *son* [存], as I used as an example in the foregoing, is not usually used alone, but is used in the form of compounds such as *"son-zoku"* ["to continue to exist," 存続], and *"ho-zon"* ["to preserve," 保存]. Zhŭzĭ (Jap., Shushi: 朱子)[33] said about the *Book of Changes* [*Yìjīng*] that "that which can be gained through words is shallow; that which can be gained through images is deep." One could also say the same about the relationship between vocal letters and ideographs. Zhŭzĭ and Wáng Yáng-míng [Jap., Oyōmei: 王陽明],[34] two representative thinkers of neo-Confucianism, held different opinions regarding the meaning of the character *"gé"*[35] (Jan., *"kaku"*: 格), which means "to study" or "to investigate." This character appears in the phrase *"géwùshìzhī"* [Jap., *"kakubutsuchichi"*: 格物致知], that is, "the investigation of things, and then coming to knowledge." How they understood this character made for the fundamental differences in their philosophies. Their differences [of interpretation] arose from the special characteristics that Chinese characters have as ideographs. If we take the point of view of social history, Chinese civilization ruled over a large region that surpassed all of Europe put together. Because many different ethnic groups and nations were under China's control in ancient periods, a vocal language would not work for the whole of their peoples. Therefore, the writing system as a visual language became widespread probably for the purposes of political rule, such that it could be commonly understood among the intelligentsia. At any rate, to think by relying on a writing system that appeals to visual perception has the tendency of making the character of thinking imagistic. Nishi's remark that Chinese philosophy is literary or affective probably has a bearing on this point.

If we take up the case of India, which is located midway between East Asia and Europe, we can clarify further the differences in the method of thinking between East and West regarding logic. In the history of Indian philosophy, logic was extremely highly developed. The Buddhist logic that is called *inmyō* [Chin., *yīnmíng*: 因明] is just such an example.[36] (*Inmyō* means "to clarify the reasons.") Although this Buddhist logic is thought to be indigenous to Chinese and Japanese Buddhism, in actuality, it is not. It was a branch of learning in India shared in common by the various religious schools and sects, which went beyond their [sectarian] differences. *Inmyō*, furthermore, also possessed an oratorical character. Since in ancient India (as was the case with Greece) debates were widespread and became a custom among scholars of different religious schools, *inmyō* occupied a position of great significance. It was Xuánzhuàng Sānzàng[37][Jap. *Genjō sanzō*: 玄奘三蔵] who transmitted *inmyō* to China on a full scale. He participated in debates between different religious sects in India. However, *inmyō* did not occupy a position of primary importance in China. Even Xuánzhuàng's disciples are said to have disparaged it as a "trifling matter" for Buddhism.[38] This is one symbolic example that relates to the differences between the traditional cultures of East Asia and India.

Nishi says that philosophy, in the sense of a systematic conceptual structure, was not produced in China. Since logic is useful for providing a fundamental method for the purpose of erecting conceptual structures, we might say that a lack of logic entailed this consequence. However, even if there is no logic, it does not mean that a systematic conceptual structure is impossible. The Chinese took the stance of creating an intellectual, theoretical system through a method different from logic. The process of the Sinification of Buddhism makes clear the circumstances regarding this [point].

Nāgārjuna[39] established the philosophy of Mahāyāna Buddhism in India, and his method of theorization was based on logic. The fundamental proposition of Mahāyāna Buddhism is the so-called "form is emptiness" (*shiki soku zekkū*, 色即是空), [articulated in the *Prajñāpāramitā* literature]. The Chinese character *shiki* (Chin., *sè*: 色; Skrt., *rūpa*) means that which is formed, and points to the thing-events of the actual world that can be cognized with the senses. The Chinese character *kū* [Chin., *kōng*: 空; Skrt., *śūnya*] is a word that carries such meanings as "empty" and "having no content," and is an expression indicating the dimension that goes beyond actuality, that is, the transcendental dimension known through the lived experience of *nirvāṇa*. Using the terminology of Western philosophy, we can probably say that "emptiness" [*kū*] corresponds to transcendence and "form" [*shiki*] corresponds to immanence. Nāgārjuna used logic to explicate the heterogeneity of both. Sueki Takehiro elucidated Nāgārjuna's methods of argumentation using contemporary logic. The fact that this attempt was possible is because Nāgārjuna's stance of thinking has its foundation in logic. However, when Buddhism entered China, the method [of thinking] that gives primary importance to logic was not accepted. It was the third patriarch of the Tendai [Chin., *Tiāntái*] School, Zhìyì [538–597, Jap., Chigi: 智顗], who laid the foundation for the Sinification of Buddhism. In order to grasp the meaning of "form is emptiness," Zhìyì used the standpoint of practical experience, that is, the theory of self-cultivation [*shugyō*, 修行] in lieu of logic.

At the foundation of Zhìyì's theoretical structure is the so-called triple meditation [*sankan*, 三観] advocated by Tendai Buddhism along with the theory of "triple truth" [*santei*, 三諦]. The Chinese character *kan* [観] means the method of observation, that is, the meditation method. The "triple meditation" refers to: (1) "emptiness meditation" [*kūkan*, 空観], (2) "meditation on the provisional" [*kekan*, 仮観], and (3) "the right meditation of the middle way" [*chūdō shōkan*, 中道正観]. Emptiness meditation designates the process of entering the world of emptiness from the world of the provisional (*ke*, form) by overcoming desire vis-à-vis self-cultivation. This means cognizing, through lived experience, the transcendent dimension that goes beyond the sensible world. Conversely, the "meditation on the provisional" designates the standpoint of *practice* where the embodied subject [*shutai*], who has experienced emptiness, returns to the world of form [*shiki*]. This means returning once again to the standpoint of the ethics of the world after having cognized the transcendent dimension. This is a way of thinking in keeping with the Mahāyāna Buddhist idea of compassion [*jihi*, 慈悲; Skrt., *karuṇā*].

> If the Mahāyāna Buddhist practitioner overcomes his own desires by entering into the world of emptiness from the world of the provisional, he is no longer the same as ordinary people. Moreover, because the Mahāyāna practitioner saves other people from the afflictions of desires (*bonnō*) by returning from the world of emptiness to the world of the provisional [*ke*], his stance differs from the Hīnāyāna practitioner (who seeks only his own

enlightenment). Even in the midst of existence, he is not tainted by it . . . [W]ith the mind/heart [*kokoro*][40] of compassion he heals illness. Boundless is the love extending to all people. He continues his great efforts of saving people. . . . If he were to stay in the realm of emptiness, he would be of no use to sentient beings. The aspiration of the practitioner lies in saving other people. To benefit others is the meaning of "entering into the dimension of the provisional."[41]

While in Nāgārjuna's theory, primacy is placed in distinguishing [and overcoming] the two dimensions of form and emptiness through logic,[42] Zhìyì places primary importance in the fact that through the route of practical experience two dimensions come to be united as one, despite the fact that these two dimensions are separate. The third observation of "the right meditation of the middle way" means that one must not be one-sided in observing [either] emptiness or the provisional.

The first, that is, the practice of "emptiness meditation," refers to the process of self-cultivation that is centered around the methods of meditation. In contrast, the second, the practice of "meditation on the provisional," is related to ethical action toward others. When *prāxis* is thematized in Western philosophy, it usually refers to a situation where the second sense [of the triple meditation] is applicable, and the first sense of the term is lacking, that is, in the narrower sense of self-cultivation. Having said this, however, meditation methods were employed in all the philosophies of the Hellenistic Age, such as Stoicism, Epicureanism, and neo-Platonism, but these traditions disappeared from the stage of philosophy as Christianity became established. I would like to call the first sense of practice as represented in methods of meditation "inward-looking" practice as is suggested by Jung's term "introversion," and the second sense of practice, "outward-looking," as in Jung's "extroversion." (I gained a hint as to the use of these phrases from Jung's psychological theory of types. Jung said, broadly speaking, the spirituality of the East is introverted, while the spirituality of the West is extroverted.)[43] Needless to say, the custom of self-cultivation existed in the case of Indian Buddhism, and the difference in the dimensions of "emptiness" and "form" represents modes of thinking which arose based on practical experience. However, while in India *logic* was used in explicating this distinction [and overcoming it], in China *facts* in the process of *practical experience* were utilized in place of logic.

In comparing the philosophy of the East and the West, I think that it is necessary to pay attention to the issue of inward-looking practice as stated above (concretely, the experience of self-cultivation). That is, while the theory of self-cultivation is fundamentally lacking in the traditions of Western philosophy, it has been regarded as the primary experiential foundation in the East, in virtue of which philosophical thought has been erected. In this respect, India and China are in agreement. In the tradition of the philosophical thought of the West—if we take Aristotle as a standard—the stance of *theōria* (observation, theory), which makes nature an object external to the self, was placed at the foundation. In contrast, in the philosophical thought of Asia, there is a strong tendency to look toward the internal world of the self itself and its transformation through self-cultivation. In this case, the philosophical tradition of India consisted in applying logical analysis toward inner psychological experience. In the case of East Asia, one might say that it advanced philosophical thought by placing primary importance on inward experience as well as placing its foundation in the facts of practical, ethical experience without depending on logic.

THE COGNITION AND INTUITION OF LIVING NATURE

Alhough I discussed this point previously, here I would like to make one more proposal concerning philosophical terminology. The Japanese word "*shukan*" [主観] is used as the translation of the word "subject." Additionally, the word "*shutai*" [主体] is also used. Because "*shukan*" is easily connected with the meaning of *theōria*, it is an appropriate translation for the "epistemological subject" as used in epistemology.[44] In contrast, the Chinese character "*karada*" [体], which designates the body, is included in the word "*shutai*" [主体]. The body concretely shows the ways for the self itself to be. In the field of everyday experience, we think that our body is our self. The epistemological subject is the self when cognizing and observing the condition of the world outside of the self. This function is mainly based on the use of thinking and sensation (perception), for example, "understanding" and "sensibility" in Kant's epistemology. In contrast, the self as embodied subject [*shutai*, 主体] includes in its purview the body, and I would like to define embodied subject as that which expresses the self, including the affective activity that accompanies "being the body." When seen in this manner, the self as epistemological subject designates the surface layer of the activities of the embodied subject. The reason why I have distinguished the epistemological subject and the embodied subject is because I think that this distinction is necessary and useful in pointing out the special characteristics of Eastern philosophical thought. While the epistemological subject is the self that knows that which is other than itself, the embodied subject is also a self that attempts to know this as well as that which is internal, in other words, the self itself. The embodied subject is able to include the meaning of the self, which takes the standpoint of inward-looking practice.[45]

Incidentally, in comparison with the West, one of the characteristics of the traditional cultures of East Asia is to cherish a deep concern for the relations between human beings and nature. [I will take up this issue again in chapter four in connection with an analysis of the worldview upheld by the *Book of Changes (Yijing)*.] We can probably understand this well if we look to the fields of literature and the arts. For example, one should consider examples such as Chinese-style poetry, *haiku*, Zen poetry, mountain-water landscape paintings [*sansuiga*], and brush-painting [*suibokuga*], wherein one can sense the affective interchange of life between humans and nature. In the West, landscape painting made its appearance following the Renaissance, but this served simply as a background for the painting of human figures. The depiction of nature painting by the Impressionists resulted from the influence of the landscape painting of Japanese woodblock prints [*ukiyoe*].

The process of the Sinification of Buddhism that began with the Tendai school of Buddhism indicates well the issue of humans cohabiting with nature.[46] In Chinese Buddhism, it was called "mountains, rivers, blades of grass, trees, and lands becoming Buddha."[47] This mode of thinking became widely spread due to Tendai Buddhism (though, actually, this type of thinking was already present from before Tendai). This mode of thinking was absent in Indian Buddhism. In Indian thought there is a strong tendency toward transcendentalism[48] by seceding from the actual world, and, consequently, concern for the natural world is weak. Because the concern of Indian Buddhism is directed toward the reincarnation of life and any emancipation from it, this theoretical glance extends to living beings (e.g., animals) that are close to humans, but it does not show much interest in physical nature. In contrast, Chinese and Japanese people take even physical nature as a living organism, a living place, as it were, *wherein spirituality dwells in nature*.[49] In Zen, a thorough development of this type of thought can be seen.

Since I have previously cited a few examples,[50] I do not want to repeat myself here, but when Zen practitioners express the experience of satori, they favor relating it to scenes of nature in a literary manner. There, humans and nature are not opposed to each other as subject-object, based on intellectual observation. This is a state that must be regarded an affective interchange and an interresonance. Modern rationalism, which takes the standpoint of intellectual thought as its foundation, might say that this view is not the cognition of nature, and is nothing but the projection of a subjective sentiment. However, Zen insists that this is not the case. Dōgen [1200–54] states that there is a cognition of truth that transcends the cognition of nature as object.[51] How is it possible for Dōgen to say this? The epistemological subject that has its raison d'être in virtue of intellectual logic does not attempt to see the world of the mind/heart (*kokoro*) that is hidden in the background of the self itself. In order to know nature as a life phenomenon, one must direct a glance toward the mind/heart that is in the interior of the self. No answer is forthcoming if one seeks it outside of the self. By understanding the self itself, we reach cognition of a higher dimension that transcends everydayness. This is Zen's answer.

Previously, I said that in the traditions of East Asia logic is absent, or that this is a weak point. I cited as reasons for this: (1) that in East Asia there was no custom of dialogue and rhetoric as in ancient Greece or India, (2) the special characteristics of Chinese expressions, and (3) the historical and social institutions in which people who spoke a different language ruled. We can also consider this issue from a perspective specific to philosophy.

In the case of the West, Plato's theory of Ideas became the starting-point for logical thinking. In the myth of the creation of the cosmos in the *Timaeus*, Plato relates that God as the demiurge created the world while commanding a view of the heavenly, ideal world, which is the perfectly good, beautiful, [and true].[52] God [then] endowed form to matter (*hylē*) which was formless chaos, using the ideal world as a model. Here, in contrast with the perfect, eternal, and unchanging cosmos in the heavenly world, the being of all things on the earth is delimited by matter that has chaos as its essential nature. Consequently, they cannot escape imperfection and mutability. From this viewpoint, which clearly contrasts and divides the world of Ideas and the sensible world, arises the problem of how to think about the relation between the universal and the particular. Aristotle grasped this contrast as the relationship between primary substance *qua* particular and secondary substance *qua* universal.[53] The former is the individual particular that can become a subject and can never become a predicate, that is, "this particular thing" (*tode ti*).[54] Out of this also arose the so-called distinction between essence and existence. When we look at this from the viewpoint of logic, it turns out to be an issue in semantics, that is, the relationship between language (concept) and the actual object it designates. Plato gave primary importance to the transcendence of the Idea as universal, whereas Aristotle thought of the Idea as immanent in the individual particular. In epistemology, the difference between Plato and Aristotle became the origin for the separation of the positions in thought between idealism and realism (empiricism). Insofar as they recognize the dualistic distinction of matter (*hylē*) and form (*eidōs*), that is, the material and the spiritual, they are in agreement. Plato and Aristotle differ in their opinions only in respect to semantics, wherein we can probably discern the beginning of the history of the opposition between idealists and empiricists in the West.

In contrast, in the thought of East Asia, such a debate could not arise from the beginning because it took a fundamentally different viewpoint from the West concerning the relation between chaos and cosmos. In the *Zhuāngzĭ* (Jap.,

Shōshi: 荘子), there is a famous story.[55] The Emperor of the Southern Ocean and the Emperor of the Northern Ocean would go to the place of Chaos, the Emperor of the Middle, to play and were treated to meals by Chaos. However, because Chaos lacked eyes, a nose, and a mouth, it was lacking in every way. And so, having conferred between themselves, they set out with a chisel and an ax, and every day they went to open a hole in Chaos. When they had made the seventh hole, Chaos said, "No more," and died. (In ancient China, it was said that the human body had nine orifices. Chaos died because he was about to take on a human form.) This story indicates a mode of thought in which Chaos who is in an invisible heaven must not be judged by the human intellect (i.e., logic). Lǎozǐ explained as follows concerning the Dao, which is the primordial ground that nurtures all the things of the cosmos.

> There was something that is one, yet chaotic, which existed before the open-ing of the heavens and the earth. Soundless in silence, vague, and formless, it depends on nothing and cannot be changed by anything. It never stops breathing, manifesting itself in every phenomenon. It may be considered the Great Mother[56] who gives birth to this world. I do not know even her name; I will call her Dao for the time being. If forced to give her a name, should I call her Great? Because it is great, it flows and moves and flow-ing and moving, it reaches far and wide. And if it reaches far and wide, it returns to its primordial ground.[57]

That which is "soundless in silence, vague and formless"—this is nothing other than Chaos itself. Lǎozǐ states that the flowing activity issuing from Chaos as the primordial ground, named "Dao," is that which generates and changes all things of the cosmos. However, where then is the cosmos (order) that is to be contrasted with chaos? It is housed in all the things on earth.

In Confucius's commentary on the *Book of Changes* [*Yìjīng*], known as *Xìcífù* [繫辞伝], there is a famous passage that reads, "What is above form [*keijijōsha*, 形而上者]—this is called the Dao; what is under form [*keijikasha*, 形而下者]—this is called the vessel." The term "*keijijō*" [形而上] is used as the translation for Aristotle's "metaphysics" [*keijijōgaku*, 形而上学], but if we examine this in more detail, their meanings are slightly different. The *Metaphysika*, theoretically speaking, means "going beyond nature." (When Aristotle's complete works were put in order, this work was placed by chance, after the *Physica* and was accordingly given this title.[58]) Consequently, meta-physics is an ontology that treats of being in generality and in abstraction, and goes beyond the concrete and individual conditions of the being of the thing-events in nature that we experience. In contrast, "that which is above form" (*keijijōsha*), as stated in the *Book of Changes* [*Yìjīng*], means a being *prior to* form, but it does not mean a being that goes beyond form. This is seen as the Dao that is Chaos. "*Keijikasha*," which corresponds to this, means "that which is under form," that is, it designates all the things on the earth. (Additionally, the Chinese character "*ji*" [而] in "*keijijō*" [形而上] and "*keijikasha*" [形而下者] is a character that carries the two meanings of "and" as well as "but." That is, "that which is above form" [*keijijōsha*] and "that which is under form" [*keijika-sha*] hold a relationship in which each is severed from each other and yet they are connected to each other.) If we take note of the issue of the possessing or lacking of form, in Plato, there is the realm of Ideas in heaven (i.e., the cosmos of perfect forms), and the thing-events on earth housed by chaos. In other words, while the cosmos of all things of the earth, due to the limitations of matter, are imperfect, they also have an original nature that tends toward the primordial [origin] that is chaos. In short, whereas in East Asia *chaos* is in the heavens and cosmos is on the earth, in the West, the opposite is the case. The cosmos is in the heavenly realm and chaos exists immanently in all things on the earth. Here we can discern the fundamental reason for the theoretical disputes that arose in the West concerning the ideal (the universal) and the real (the particular), and the essential and the existential. That is, the univer-sal as essence is in heaven whereas the particular as the actual is on earth, and both are clearly distinguished from each other. Here, the dichotomy of mat-ter-form is the major premise. Consequently, the theoretical question neces-sarily arises as to what kind of relationship exists between them.

In East Asian thought, which sees the relation between chaos and cos-mos directly opposite that of the West, this kind of logical problem does not arise. It has been said that Confucius wrote a section of the commentary to the *Book of Changes*. However, according to contemporary research, it is said that a Confucian scholar of the early Hàn period [202 BCE–8 CE] took from the Daoists and created this commentary by incorporating material from the thought of Lǎozǐ and Zhuāngzǐ. The phrase from the commentary that defines the Dao as "that which is prior to form" [*keijijōsha*] comes from Lǎozǐ's and Zhuāngzǐ's thought that regarded the Dao as chaos that cannot be known clearly, and which is the primordial ground of the life of the cosmos and its existence. In this case, although it would have been easier theoretically to dis-tinguish the relationship between "*keijijōsha*" and "*keijikasha*" as the relation between "that which is without form" and "that which is with form," there is a reason for not doing so.[59] *Keijijōsha* (i.e., the Dao) is not a perfectly tran-scendent being, but, rather, the activity issuing from there dwells in all things, enabling them to be generated and to go through changes. "That which is above form" [*keijijōsha*] does not designate "that which transcends form," but, rather, "that which is prior to form." It is grasped as the activity generating and changing that which has form. Consequently, every thing as "that which is under form" (*keijikasha*) is called a "vessel" that receives that activity. (The Chinese character "*utsuwa*" [器] means "a tool" or "something useful.") To be concrete, "vessel" refers to the thing-events of the natural world that have form and body, such as utensils, plants, and animals, including mountains, streams, and human beings. Lǎozǐ said that the activity of the Dao pervades all of the natural world as a mother who nurtures all things. Here are the roots of the view of nature based on life, which Chinese Buddhism later developed. Another passage of [the alleged] commentary by Confucius on the *Book of Changes* [*Yìjīng*] states, "one yīn, one yáng; this is called 'Dao.'" It states that the activity that issues forth from the Dao is concretized through the interchange of the *yīn-yáng* phase change. Later, in order to indicate this activity, the term *ki* [Chin., *qi*: 氣] came to be used.[60] That is, all things are generated and go through changes in virtue of the fact that the phases of the activity of *ki*, which issues forth from the Dao, alternates between *yīn* and *yáng*. Consequently, because *keijijōsha* ("that which is above form") and *keijikasha* ("that which is under form") stand in a relationship in which they gently and mutually permeate each other, and are connected by the activity of invisible *ki*, they cannot be clearly and logically differentiated as completely separate dimensions. Thus, dualistic thinking that separates the material from the spiritual, as in the West, did not arise in East Asia.

The stance of East Asian philosophical thought, which attempts to negate logical distinctions by means of the intellect and to go beyond them, is expressed best in Zen. Further, the roots of this kind of thinking can probably be sought in this type of metaphysics. In understanding being (i.e., that which is), such distinctions as "there is …" [… *ga aru*] and "it is …" [… *de aru*]; essence and existence, objective reality and subjective logic are not separated here, as in the West. Being (to be) is the activity of invisible life that makes the totality of humans and nature to be what they are.

PART II

Translator's Note

In chapter one, Yuasa addressed image-thinking in the Greek pre-Socratic period. After Plato, however, there occurred a tendency to replace image-thinking with rationalistic thinking. This stance has continued to this day as the predominant and preferred way of defining human nature in the West. However, he has also shown that both the ancient Western and Eastern philosophies were originally engaged in a common activity of the mind in the epistemological stance they took in viewing nature. On the other hand, in chapter two, Yuasa thematically focused on image-thinking that was confined to the East Asian tradition. Because both of these observations arise from the excavation of ancient philosophies, he fears that it may give the reader the impression that such a mode of thinking must be archaic and hence even anachronistic to resurrect. The reader thus may dismiss the stance of image-thinking on the ground that it does not carry any relevance for us today.

To dispel this hasty judgment, Yuasa designs Part II to show that it also applies to contemporary peoples fostered and nurtured in the Western tradition. For example, both the visual perceptions and dreams that we experience are instances of image-experience. We may for now understand image-thinking to mean the conscious activity of the mind that incorporates a philosophical reflection on image-experience arising from the unconscious. To this end, Yuasa thematizes image-thinking in the context of Jung's theory of synchronicity. This is because synchronistic phenomena provide image-thinking with image-experience in a most pronounced way, although they may be rare for people of rationalistic persuasion for they remain unconscious to them. For this reason, Yuasa's treatment of Jung's theory may become a stumbling block for those who cling to rationalism as the only viable conceptual stance for understanding reality.

CHAPTER THREE

What Is Synchronicity?

The principle on which the use of the *Yijing* is based appears at first sight to be in complete contradiction to our [Western] scientific and causal thinking . . . [T]he Chinese did have a science whose standard text-book was the *Yijing*

C. G. Jung, "Richard Wilhelm: In Memoriam" (1930)

INTRODUCTION

In this chapter, I will discuss the issue of synchronicity. I have, in fact, been making preparations for it, as I wanted to write a book on Jung and Eastern thought for the past several years.[1] Jung himself has stated that "the understanding of synchronicity is the key which unlocks the door to the Eastern apperception of totality."[2] But this is a very difficult problem, since Jung himself has not adequately written on this. For this reason, I need to examine his letters and other writings, while also incorporating my own thoughts.

Jung made his first reference to synchronicity in a memorial lecture for Richard Wilhelm he gave in Munich in 1930. It was also around 1950, ten years before his death, that he made another reference to synchronicity. In his book, *The Psychology of Eastern Meditation*,[3] there is an essay "Yijing and the Contemporary Period," which I translated with Mr. Kuroki Mikio [into Japanese]. Jung wrote this piece as the preface (1950) to Ms. Baynes' English translation of the *Yijing* [*Book of Changes*; Jap., *Ekikyō*: 易経], which Richard Wilhelm, a Sinologist, translated into German. In this work, Jung states that the principle of synchronicity is presupposed by the *Yijing*. It appears that this piece was written around 1948, and afterwards, at a conference in Eranos in 1951, he lectured on synchronicity. The edited version of this lecture resulted in the essay "Synchronicity: An Acausal Connecting Principle."[4] This came out in a volume co-authored with the famous physicist Wolfgang Pauli.[5] Here

97

I will call this piece the "Synchronicity Essay." This is a very difficult essay, and there are different evaluations of it even among Jungians.

After writing this book up until his death, Jung wrote books such as *An Answer to Job*[6] and *Mysterium Coniunctionis*,[7] but he has not written anything on synchronicity. There is a book, *Number and Time* [*Zahl und Zeit*],[8] that Marie-Louise von Franz, one of Jung's students, wrote. This is [also] a book on synchronicity. According to von Franz's preface, although Jung was making preparations to write a more systematic work on synchronicity, he entrusted the manuscript to her two years prior to his death because he was unable to complete it. For this reason, his thought on synchronicity remained incomplete. In his later years, using the hypothesis of synchronicity as a clue, Jung posed a challenge to the principle of causality whereby modern science had been erected ever since Descartes. That is, Jung was groping for a new view of the world that would replace the modern worldview. This being the case, these two essays on synchronicity are extremely important. [However,] since the hypothesis of synchronicity has not been presented in a clear fashion, I would like to discuss this by incorporating my own interpretation.

THE OVERLAP BETWEEN THE WORLD OF SPIRIT AND THE WORLD OF OBJECTS

Jung calls synchronicity alternatively "meaningful coincidence." For example, suppose that when I am thinking in my mind of a certain friend, this person happens to visit me. In this case, the event occurring in my mind and the surrounding environment, that is, the factual event that occurred in the external world, coincide in terms of "meaning." To be more specific, the event in the mind is my thinking of that person, whereas the event that occurred in the external world is the fact that that person came to visit. Here is an example. A well-known novelist, Shiga Naoya (1883–1971), writes in an essay that one night his friend Morajes, who was already dead, appeared in his dream. Morajes used to live in Tokushima, and was a Portuguese who wrote novels about Japan. The next morning, however, a person came to visit Shiga from Tokushima and inquired about him. It appears that Shiga sometimes experienced this sort of thing, but he said that he gave up thinking about its meaning, for his mind was already senile. Of these two events, one is a psychological fact, while the other is a physical fact; these two coincide regarding the existence of this person (in other words, the "meaning" of an event in life or the information about that event). Therefore, we can state that the experience of this nature involves the coincidence of the *cognition of the meaning of information* concerning the psychological event and the physical event, or alternatively, an internal event and an external event.

Therein emerges the problem of whether such a coincidence is meaningful or meaningless.

Ordinarily, it is difficult to think about the clear relation concerning the coincidence of such events. Therefore, it would be dismissed as an accidental coincidence, that is, as a meaningless coincidence. However, in a case where it is felt that there is some meaning there, what exactly is in question? Here, what becomes an issue is the emotion we have when we encounter the coincidence. Upon encountering such a situation, for example, there occurs the feeling of astonishment. This is a subjective feeling. Although subjective feelings are ambiguous and unreliable, we need first to think carefully about the movement of the mind such as emotions (or intuitions). As counselors [and analysts] may already be informed of this, the waves of emotion that occur upon encountering a certain event, hold the key to solving the problem in an analytical session.

What significance, then, can a phenomenon such as this hold? And if there is any significance there, this will extend so far as the problem of a worldview (or expanding the scope further, a cosmology) concerning how one is to think of the relationship between human beings and the world. In many cases, even if we experience such a coincidence, we tend to forget about it as an accidental coincidence. On the other hand, in cases when we experience a psychologically critical situation, we sometimes receive the strong impression that it has some meaning. Suppose that in a dream, one sees an extremely clear image of a certain person's death, and soon afterwards one is informed of that person's actual death; one would strongly feel that the dream has some kind of meaning. Ordinarily, there are probably many occasions when it ends up only with the *feeling* that it has some meaning.

Jean Shinoda Bolen, a Jungian counselor residing in California, states the following about her grandfather.

[M]y grandfather had an uncanny way of knowing when an old friend or relative would die. The person would appear to him in a dream or in a waking vision, carrying a suitcase. In this way, he would know that they were leaving and moving on. My mother remembers his remarking on several occasions that so-and-so died—my grandfather had "seen" him on his way with the suitcase. Then, often weeks later, news would come verifying what Grandfather already knew clairvoyantly. Because he had come to American from Japan, a considerable distance separated my grandfather in New York City from relatives and many old friends. The news took a relatively long time to travel via standard means, by sea over the Pacific, by land to the East Coast. An historical event in this category is Swedenborg's "Vision of the Great Fire" in Stockholm in which he described what he "saw" to others.

Days later, the news arrived of the actual event, which had occurred at the time when he had had the vision and as he had described.[9]

In order for such a phenomenon to become a theoretical issue, or for the experience to carry some meaning rather than being accidental, one of the conditions is that the experience be repeated many times. That is, either the same person must have such an experience several times, or several different persons must have the same kind of experience. With the repetition of a number of such experiences, that person will probably think that such events must have some kind of meaning. Jung himself also had come to think of this issue on the basis of his own experiences.

There are many cases of reports in which a person nearing the end of his or her life appears before a friend or family members. This happens right at the moment of death in order to inform them of the person's immanent end, as in the case of the grandfather's experience, which Bolen cited. Let me here introduce the case of Dr. Doi Toshitada, a friend of mine, who mentions his own experience in his book. Dr. Doi is an executive officer of Sony Corporation and is also a director of its Computer Institute. As a technician, he is known as one of the co-developers of CD. But he is now known in the world as the producer of a new robot. He uses a pseudonym, Tenge Shirō, when he writes books for the general public. Dr. D, who appears below, refers to himself.

> You know, I was on my way back to Japan from a business trip. I was walking inside the San Francisco International Airport. Then suddenly, the face of Mr. Ibuka Masaru, the founder of Sony Corporation, showed up, and loomed large to my right side.[10]

As Dr. D practices meditation in his daily life, apparently it is not rare for him to see visions during meditation. However, it was the first time for him to have a vision in his waking moments while walking in an area of heavy traffic filled with noise. He says: "When I calculated the time difference, I was shocked. What a surprise it was! He passed away nine minutes after I had the vision. Unknowingly, tears fell from my face."[11] The time of Mr. Ibuka's passing was 3:39 A.M., December 19, 1997.

What needs to be noted about this report is that because Dr. Doi follows a routine of daily meditation, it is not rare for him to have visions during meditation. Various meditation methods have been transmitted in the traditions of the East such as Yoga, Esoteric Buddhism, Zen, and Daoism, and it has been [often] reported since ancient times that with the practice of meditation one begins to experience visions like the one mentioned above. These meditation methods are widely practiced today among the general public even without any specific relation to a religion. Because this kind of custom has not been followed as much in the West, it is not the usual practice to incorporate such perspectives of self-cultivation theory into the study of parapsychology.

Let us take up another kind of example Jung cites in his "Synchronicity Essay."[12] In this experience, a beetle of ancient Egypt called a scarab—usually translated as the "sacred beetle"—flies into a room when Jung is speaking with a certain female patient. This patient was extremely intelligent, and because she would not listen even when Jung was explaining his opinions, the analysis and the treatment were not going well. But, while speaking beside the window, they noticed there was a fluttering noise behind Jung; a beetle was trying to come into the room through the window. Jung opened the window and caught the beetle, and showing it to the patient, told her that this is the scarab that "you were just now talking about." There she received quite a shock. At that time while the room was dark inside and the outside was bright, the bug was fluttering trying to go from the bright outside into the dark inside, even though insects have the habit of tending toward the light. Jung says that at that point the patient felt an eerie feeling, and afterwards the treatment made smooth progress. What is important here is that she felt *uncanny* about that incident, and the movement of that emotion shattered the shell of her intellect. No doubt, this is also an example of the coincidence in meaning between the patient's inner mind and an outer event.

In the previous example of the scarab, Jung interpreted the event to mean that the patient faced the need to undergo a rebirth of mind. That is because, in ancient Egypt, the scarab was made a symbol of the metamorphosis or rebirth of the soul. Therefore, the patient's having the dream of a scarab was interpreted to mean that the unconscious was demanding from her consciousness a transformation and rebirth of mind. (We might say that this is an example of what Jung calls the compensatory function of the unconscious.) It is certain that the dream was suggesting some problem that carries great significance for her past. A skillful analyst will not overlook such clues.

I will cite one more example that Jung mentions in his biography. This is an experience involving the suicide of a patient suffering from depression.[13] While traveling, Jung woke up suddenly in his hotel in the middle of the night. Because he felt as if someone had come into the room, he turned the light on, but there was nothing unusual. He then became aware that upon awakening he felt an intense pain in the forehead and at the anterior of the head. The next day he was informed that this patient had killed himself with a pistol, and moreover the bullet had pierced through his forehead to stop at the anterior of his head. When a rapport develops between the analyst and the patient, whereby a strong [psychological] connection is established in the unconscious dimension, it is easy for this sort of phenomenon to occur.

Aside from this case, many other examples may be mentioned, but it appears that Jung often had this sort of unique experience. In his biography, he calls this type of experience, "synchronistic phenomenon ... observed in connection with an archetypal situation."[14] "Archetypal situation" in this case refers to a situation with great meaning for the person experiencing it, for example, the death of Jung's patient. In these situations the phenomena of such natures are easily observed. He observes, in connection with this, that the collective unconscious is common to everyone, which may also be regarded as "transpersonal unconscious." We will discuss this later. At any rate, on the basis of his long personal experience, it appears that Jung came to hold the conviction that there is such a phenomenon as "meaningful coincidence."

These phenomena alone, however, cannot be dealt with as a theoretical issue. One of the important points of which Jung took note is the conditions under which they can occur at all. He focused on whether meaningful coincidences can occur under definite conditions more frequently than chance-occurrences beyond the level of expected chance. Even though we ordinarily stop with a subjective emotion concerning whether there is meaning or not, it is necessary to proceed to the question regarding the *conditions* of these occurrences. This is the reason why Jung came to concern himself with the problem of synchronicity.

To give my current thought on this, these paranormal experiences mean that psychological information is transmitted in the field of the transpersonal unconscious, which is deeper than, and transcends, the dimension of the personal unconscious thematized by Freud. This may be exemplified by an analogy. Take an example of icebergs floating in the ocean separated from each other. It is analogous to a condition in which they are connected as one beneath the surface of the ocean. A spiritual network connects oneself with an intimate family member or a friend in the transpersonal unconscious field. I think that each of us, like a broadcasting station, is unconsciously transmitting a message to a family member or friend. A deep experience of this kind, with one's self at its center, has been generated through "encounters" we have had with many people throughout our life. And I think that a spiritual network, fostered by each of us, latently exists. Human society is set up with the numerous spiritual networks intertwined within it. It is a network connected by mutual love. However, I might note that there is not only a relationship of this kind, but probably there are networks connected by hostility and hatred. The object of this kind of paranormal "encounter" includes not only the human, but the physical environment, as well. Clairvoyance is such an example.

Now, if we examine Jung's "Synchronicity Essay" from a theoretical point of view, we find roughly three issues of concern. One is the relation to the

Yijing, that is, [generally] the relation to Eastern thought. The second is the relation to Rhine's parapsychology, and the third is the relation to contemporary physics. I would like to discuss these three points next.

DIVINATION OF THE *YIJING* AND ITS WORLDVIEW

First, concerning the relation with Eastern thought, as I mentioned previously, although Jung began to speak about synchronicity in his commentary to the *Yijing*, he already had an interest in the *Yijing* dating back to his younger days. He started to fully engage the *Yijing* after meeting the Sinologist Richard Wilhelm in 1920. Even prior to this date, during his struggling years of the 1910s when he had parted from Freud, he experimented with the *Yijing*'s divination in Bollingen's villa, using yarrow sticks made out of reeds. Jung took up the *Yijing* from an experiential and an experimental concern, rather than a philological concern. He said that his interest lay in whether the *Yijing*'s method of divination *was actually effective or not*. He writes that according to his experiments:[15]

> [Divination] indicated a higher probability than can be considered accidental coincidence. Thus I am critical of the idea that the divination of the *Yijing* is merely by chance. It can be understood that the number of clearly correct predictions that I experienced achieved a percentage far beyond mere chance contingencies. In short I believe without a doubt that what is the issue of the *Yijing* is not chance but regularity.

Afterwards, in 1920, Jung met Wilhelm who came back from China, and he invited him to Zürich in 1922. At that time, Jung asked him to experiment with divination at the Psychology Club. Wilhelm lived in China for over twenty years, had translated many Chinese classics, and had seriously studied the *Yijing*'s [art of] divination under a Daoist practitioner. At that time Jung asked him to divine about a certain case he himself was familiar with, though he purposefully did not inform Wilhelm of the details. However, the response Wilhelm came up with in front of the audience through divination exactly coincided with the situation of that case. That is not all. Jung says that Wilhelm made a prediction about the future of that patient, and two years later that prediction actualized without any room for doubt.[16] Through these experiences, Jung seemed to gradually deepen his conviction.

Many say that divination is a matter of "hit or miss." While there are some who believe, there are others who disbelieve. Even if we amateurs tried, it is unlikely for us to succeed. If one is serious about it, one would have to formally study its method under a teacher, and become familiar with the study of the [Chinese] classics in order to learn how to interpret them. This also depends on the person's innate dispositions. In this respect, it is similar to counseling [and psychoanalysis]. I think that Jung, to begin with, already had the innate disposition of a so-called psychic or had [some] paranormal abilities. Moreover, he had the long experience of being a clinician. Psychologically speaking, this is due to what Jung calls recognition by means of the intuitive function of the unconscious.

We will leave the question of whether divination is accurate or not to the reader's own opinion. If divination under a certain condition does hit the bull's-eye, the issue of meaningful coincidence emerges. What becomes an important point here is that usually we get carried away by that occurrence, and thus we end up focusing our concern solely on the event, that is, the aspect of hit or miss. However, what is important here [to note] is that *one's self* who is observing the event is incorporated into the event as a whole. In other words, we are not observing phenomena from the outside. This is the point that radically differs from the way of thinking accepted by modern science. According to the Galilean or Newtonian view of science, that is, the worldview of classical mechanics, things happen following objective, causal relations. In other words, they occur independently of our human mind that is the epistemological subject, but when we problematize divination, the *psychological condition* that surrounds oneself as the observing subject enters the picture. Because the *Yijing* always considers the activity of the subject's mind, while taking into account the connection between inner condition and outer condition, we must take note of these psychological conditions from the side of the subject. This is the reason why Jung later takes up its connection to the "problem of measurement" in contemporary physics [—an issue I will address again briefly in chapter five and extensively in chapter six.] And herein lies one of the points that collides with the hitherto held idea of modern science. Generally speaking, this difference concerns whether to view world-events as objectively occurring independently of the human subject, or to view them as occurring in an inseparable relation to the subject. Depending on the view one takes, the relationship of human beings and nature alters fundamentally.

However, as mentioned earlier, even though he performed divination since his youth, Jung has kept this a secret for a long time. The first time he touched upon this topic was [as I mentioned in the Preface] in 1930 at a lecture, held in Munich, that eulogized Wilhelm's death. While mentioning in this lecture that the worldview of the *Yijing* is in accordance with the synchronistic principle (*das synchronistische Prinzip*), he provides no explanation for it. Thus, he had not, after all, spoken about this for twenty years after the incident, while all along retaining this idea in his mind. Even in his lecture on synchronicity, Jung himself states that "[i]n writing this paper I have, so to speak, made good a promise which for many years I lacked the courage to fulfill."[17] In other words, Jung was taking precaution because he thought that this idea would be criticized by society as unscientific superstition for the reason that this type of thinking involves a content contradicting the modern scientific worldview.

Concerning the relation with the East, Jung writes, in a preface to a work by an Orientalist, that to understand synchronicity is the key to opening the door to thinking about the Eastern concept of "wholeness" (*ganzheitliche Tendenz*) that appears mystical to us.[18] The modern way of thinking as represented by science first analyzes the phenomenon into various elements, and then reconstructs it by gathering those elements together. That is, the whole is understood as the sum of its parts. By contrast, the Eastern way of thinking grasps the whole from the start. Jung remarks that synchronicity is the key to understanding such an Eastern way of thinking, while maintaining that this has to do with the issue of the unconscious.

Now, I will briefly explain the meaning of the worldview of the *Yijing* [although I will provide a more detailed explanation of the *Yijing* in chapter four.] The reading of the *Yijing* is divided into sixty-four [hexagrams]. Jung interprets these readings as projections out of the unconscious psychological state in a definite situation, whether of the diviner or of the person for which the divination is performed. In other words, the *Yijing*'s readings, divided into sixty-four, are patterns of the analogical classifications for the psychological condition surrounding that person. They accompany the human psychological condition when a person faces a serious problem. However, even though we speak of the psychological condition, this is hidden within the unconscious, and the person concerned is not sufficiently aware of the condition of the *psyche*. The act of divining externalizes it. That is, divination enables one to become aware by bringing the condition to a possible form for consciousness to cognize.

Here, the idea seems to be presupposed that the unconscious (or the *psyche*) holds an intuitive function. The human being always unconsciously feels something about [one's] destiny in the situation in which one is placed, even though one does not consciously understand it.[19] That is, through intuition the unconscious feels something about the situation that places one's self in this world. Divination is what expresses this feeling in a form that consciousness can cognize. In this case one of the characteristics of the *Yijing*'s divination is its extremely strong future orientation. In the *Yijing* there is always a "succeeding line" [変爻].[20] The reading does not only show the present situation, but also teaches what situation will ensue in connection to the reading that is divined and how one should deal with that situation. Therefore, divination is not simply an objective prediction, but considers the importance of how one would cope with one's future in that situation. In the tradition of the *Yijing*, there is a proverb: "the *Yijing* is the way for the morally superior person [君子] to cope with worries and concerns." This proverb, I think, discloses well the meaning of the *Yijing*'s divination. People go to the *Yijing* when they stand at a crossroad in their life and are unable to make a decision. This maxim points out a paradoxical situation, namely, that when this occurs, the inquirer is in turn questioned by the *Yijing* as to the height of his or her personality. A story relates that Confucius received an incorrect response from the *Yijing* only once in his lifetime.

When Socrates was indicted in the Athenian court, he first thought about how to defend himself. No sooner had he thought about it, then the *daimon* told him not to do anything like that.[21] The *daimon* always prohibits actions, but never commands him to take action. This is because Socrates alone should decide. This is the meaning of knowing one's mind (soul), wherein human freedom is found. The fundamental spirit of the *Yijing* is the same as this. This is the reason why the *Yijing* is considered in Chinese philosophy to be a classic of ethics.

The fundamental concern of the *Yijing* centers on what decision to make when one stands at the crossroad of destiny that would determine one's future. The future situation that is divined does not necessarily mean determined. Knowing that it is probable that such a situation might occur in one's future, it is left to the individual to decide. In that case, how one accepts one's responsibility with an ethical or moral attitude determines the depth of one's personality (whether one is a morally superior person or not). In this sense, the nature of the *Yijing* lies in the issue of value regarding the decision of one's attitude toward good and bad throughout life. In the history of Chinese philosophy, the *Yijing* is considered a classic of ethics. It is said that Confucius took the *Yijing* very seriously, such that the *Ten Wings*, which is a foundational commentary of the *Yijing*, has since ancient times been believed to be written by him. From the point of view of Confucian ethics, divination of the *Yijing* designates an act of knowing the mind/heart of Heaven that controls the cosmos. One may also take it to mean knowing the divine will. In the human society of the mythological age, the custom of oracles existed in various forms in each of the cultural spheres, and the *Yijing*'s divination, we might say, is its Chinese version. It was transmitted to later ages in the form of a kind of technical book on psychology. Consequently, a psychology of faith is accepted as a presupposition in the divination of the *Yijing*, and it is said that unless one asks the *Yijing* with an ethically right attitude of mind, no correct answer comes forth. There are many cases left in Chinese history books in which are recorded the failures of powerful people, who relied on the *Yijing*. This does not mean that the

Yijing's divination did not hit the bull's-eye, but rather that when the *Yijing* is consulted for an ethically wrong purpose, the response emerging from it is meaningless. Therefore, the *Yijing* stands on a presupposition that is fundamentally different from the scientific prediction of the future. Because scientific predictions deal only with issues of fact, it does not include the issue of value and meaning in life.

Although this is a digression, depth psychology in its origin is historically related to divination. As it is known, the starting point for Freud's psychoanalysis was a book called *The Interpretation of Dreams (Traumdeutung)*.[22] This German term *"Traumdeutung"* initially had the meaning of "dream divination." The divination of dreams that the Gypsy women were practicing since medieval Europe was called *Traumdeutung*. The verb *deuten* has the meaning of suggesting, divining, judging, and so on. Freud was well aware of this and entitled his book *Traumdeutung*. That is why he frequently cited examples from the Old Testament, such as the dream of Joseph. Those people who are counselors [and analysts], as it were, are descendents of the "dream diviners." Therefore, disciplines such as depth psychology and clinical psychology, while they are important disciplines today, can be said to hold a reservoir of knowledge with an extremely ancient history and tradition, as well as deep understanding.

However, between Freud and Jung there is a significant difference in their stances concerning divination. Freud interpreted dreams in light of *causal relationships* that flow from the past to the present. Therefore in Freud's interpretation, there is no [direct concern for] future predictions. On the other hand, the divination in the *Yijing* regards the future as extremely important. That is, when one thinks of time according to the *Yijing*, one does not look at the present from the point of view of the past, as is done in science, with a view to predicting the future. Instead, one learns about the situation wherein one is placed in the present to apprehend one's future. In this case it is important to take note of the characteristic of living time (i.e., *chairos*). [See chapter four.] This is where Freud and Jung greatly differ in their thinking.

This point has a deep bearing on Jung's way of viewing the unconscious. He says that the unconscious has a compensatory function. When consciousness is steeped in a one-sided attitude, the unconscious, becoming aware of it, sends a message to consciousness in the form of a dream. The unconscious delivers to consciousness a warning that it must change [its attitude] because such a one-sided attitude would be unhealthy. (The dream of the scarab mentioned earlier is an example of this.) Accordingly, Jung's method of interpreting the dream differs from that of Freud. To put this theoretically, that the compensatory function is equipped in the unconscious means that a *teleological* activity is latent. Although the term "teleological" may sound difficult to understand, the function of compensation that Jung speaks of is an operation of the mind that would correspond to the natural healing power of the body. This means that there is activity latent in the human mind-body that teaches a direction appropriate for the purposes of living. In other words, this is an act originally endowed in the interior of the *psychē* that is unconscious, which informs us of taking the attitude appropriate for the ways the human being (or life[23]) lives.

This fact suggests that depth psychology stands on a principle that is fundamentally different from the viewpoint of modern science. This is one of the points that is important for the investigation of synchronicity. Modern science has its foundation in the research of objective, causal relations that occur independently of us human beings who are the epistemological subjects. To put it differently, because the basis of modern science is founded on the mechanistic theory (i.e., the cause–effect relationship), teleology is regarded as unscientific. It regards as important the method of thinking that appeals to casual reductionism, and claims to explain everything, including the structure of life and consciousness, by means of physical and/or chemical causal relations. However, depth psychology has clarified that teleological activity is endowed within the inner world of the unconscious, namely "the region of *psychē*." The dispute between mechanistic theory and teleology has long existed in the field of biology (or the life sciences), but, in modern times, mechanistic thinking has become predominant. [For example,] the idea of vitalism that life holds an imminent *telos* was dismissed during the nineteenth century. However, while the mechanism of the living organism that is observed from the outside can be explained, after a fashion, by causal relations, teleology is a fundamental principle of the interior world, that is, the region of the mind, the unconscious, and the soul. It is here, therefore, from which the great task of overcoming the modern worldview arises.

If we recognize a worldview based on this way of thinking, we would be led to think about the corresponding relationship between psychological phenomena, life phenomena, and physical phenomena, between the inner world and the outer world, or, to use broader categories, between the human *qua* microcosm and [nature *qua*] the macrocosm. Although Jung mentions that there was a precedence of this type of thought in Western Europe as well, as is seen in Leibniz and others, Eastern thought, he notes, has its original foundation upon this sort of thinking. (Leibniz was a philosopher who had a long abiding interest in Eastern thought.) What becomes an issue arising here is that we ourselves who are observers are simultaneously the participants in the phenomena, and the teleological region irreducible to causality is hidden in the depths of the living organism. This point collides with the view of nature upheld by modern science.

PARAPSYCHOLOGY AND ITS MEANING

Next, I would like to [briefly] discuss the connection with parapsychology, [although I intend to give a fuller explanation of it in chapter five]. The field of research that is today called parapsychology begins with Joseph Banks Rhine, who was a professor of psychology at Duke University. The first work I ever read by Jung was thirty years ago, and it was the "Synchronicity Essay," which included a detailed introduction to Rhine's parapsychological research. At that time I was studying at the Institute of Psychology of Religion, which Dr. Motoyama Hiroshi established. I translated Professor Rhine's work into Japanese as I received a request from Professor Rhine by way of Dr. Motoyama.[24] I think that this was the first time that parapsychology was introduced to Japan. Professor Pratt (of the University of Virginia), who was the collaborator of J. B. Rhine, visited the institute twice, and taught me the method of research in parapsychology. (Dr. Motoyama is now president of the California Institute for Human Sciences [CIHS] in California.) Professor Rhine passed away several years ago. In his "Synchronicity Essay," Jung writes: "decisive evidence for the existence of acausal combinations of events [i.e., synchronicity, meaningful coincidence] has been furnished with adequate scientific safeguards, only very recently, mainly through the experiments of J. B. Rhine and his fellow-workers."[25] However, he also added a remark that they were not sufficiently aware of the far-reaching conclusion that can be derived from these experiments, [on which I will elaborate in chapters five and six.]

Jung highly regarded Rhine's research, and in a letter addressed to a certain person he wrote that if a Nobel Prize for the humanities was created, Rhine's research should be the first to be awarded the prize. Nevertheless, he also held a critical opinion of Rhine's method of parapsychological research, and this is related to its methodological presuppositions or worldview.

If we broadly classify Rhine's research, it can be divided into ESP and PK. ESP (extrasensory perception) is translated [in Japanese] as "transsensory perception" [超感覚]. Since clairvoyance and telepathy are perceptions that do not rely on sensory means, they are examples of ESP. PK (psychokinesis) has various translations, but one that is easily understandable refers to the phenomenon called [in Japanese] the "power of [image-]thinking" [念力].[26] Psychokinesis is a function of the mind that influences a state of matter with psychic power (without physical contact). (In addition, there is another phenomenon, precognition, that is to be distinguished from ESP and PK.)[27]

First, concerning the relationship between Jung and Rhine, the two had corresponded for over twenty years before Jung wrote his "Synchronicity Essay." Since they were sending their works to one another, each knew the content of the other's research and they exchanged opinions in their letters. If one reads the collection of Jung's letters, one can well understand his way of thinking. The first time Rhine sent a letter to Jung was in 1934. After reading a certain work[28] by Jung, Rhine sent to him a book he wrote, *Extra Sensory Perception*.[29] In the accompanying letter, after stating that he is now thinking of a new experiment on the mind's capacity of externalization, Rhine asks a question about a certain experience from Jung's youth.

This experience refers to an incident that occurred in relation to Helene Preiswerk, Jung's maternal cousin. She is the woman who became the experimental subject for Jung's doctoral dissertation.[30] This event was also related in his autobiography. It happened when Jung was conducting experiments on Helene for his doctoral dissertation, which he eventually submitted to the medical department of Zürich University. At the time Jung was twenty-four years old and Helene was sixteen years old. One day a breadknife that was kept in a drawer in a sideboard of Jung's house broke, when the sideboard suddenly exploded. At first, not knowing where the sound came from, he looked diligently, here and there, for its source, until he found, in a basket in the drawer, the knife that had split into four pieces. In answer to Rhine's request, Jung sent him a written account of this event. He also provided an account concerning the fracture of a hard oak table with a sudden explosion. Those who have read his biography are no doubt familiar with these accounts.[31]

The reason why Rhine was aware of these occurrences, it would seem, was that he had heard about them from his own teacher, a professor named William McDougal. When he was young, McDougal studied abroad in [continental] Europe and associated with Freud and Jung, and did research with them. After going to America, McDougal became a professor of psychology at Duke University and spread psychoanalysis in America. Rhine was his student. Having heard about Jung from his teacher McDougal, he sent a letter to Jung. Along with his reply, Jung also sent a photograph of the fractured knife, to Rhine.

Now, what Jung says in his reply is as follows:[32]

> I am highly interested in all questions concerning the peculiar character of the *psychē* with reference to time and space, that is, the apparent annihilation of these categories in certain mental activities.

The limitation of time and space appears to be negated in such paranormal phenomena. To put differently, if we think about the nature of such parapsychological phenomena, it may be that things such as temporal gap or spatial distance no longer hold meaning. That is, could it be that time as well as space becomes zero? Jung felt, it seems, that the explosions of the breadknife and of the oak table had some connection to the psychological state of Helene at that time. For example, in a letter to Rhine, Jung reports that at the time Helene shared a deep interest in his experiments, and was very enthused about them. Moreover, even though she lived very far (about four kilometers) from Jung's home, she often caused a rapping sound (the sound of hitting something, a result of what is called a poltergeist in psychical research) on the furniture of Jung's house. These are the kinds of incidents he wrote about.

If these events were related to Helene's psychological condition at the time, the occurrence in her mind and the physical event that took place in the external world were synchronized and in correspondence, as if telepathically. Their coincidence shows some "meaning" (e.g., Helene's affection toward Jung) concerning the circumstance that is suggestive of the relationship between Helene and Jung. In this respect, this event shows an instance of "meaningful coincidence," that is, synchronicity. In this case, what is ordinarily thought of as a causal relation is not present at all between Helene's psychological state and the sound of explosion. If that is the case, then it would mean that the sound of explosion does not follow the law of the transmission of energy that is delimited by time and space (as in the cases of radio waves or sound waves). This is the meaning of his phrase: "the apparent annihilation of these categories in certain mental activities." What is important here is the possibility that the psychological function and the *physical* phenomenon are connected. If such a possibility can exist, it is necessary to assume, in dealing with such phenomena, a principle and methodological stance that are completely different from the study of objective, causal relations, which does not take into account the conditions of the subject's mind. Here is the point that collides head-on with mind-body dualism since Descartes (i.e., the modern way of thinking that regards the mind and the body as unrelated).

This letter was the first exchange between Jung and Rhine. Since then Rhine often sent a letter to which Jung would write a reply.[33] One time in 1938 when Jung visited America, the two met in New York. However, this was the only time that they had any direct contact. In his letters Rhine also frequently requested Jung to make his personal experiences public. However, Jung consistently refused these requests. In one letter, Jung states that he is not so optimistic as are Americans, and that he has learned to remain reticent, for if he openly discussed such experiences he would be regarded not sane in Europe.

In 1942, Rhine raises the question whether all science begins first from the inquiry of a phenomenon difficult to explain. In response, Jung answers that this is indeed the case. Jung replies that if we were able to obtain all of the facts, this would probably bring about completely new views about the human being and the world for science.

In a letter of 1949 addressed to Jung, Rhine asks Jung to express his thought systematically and consistently. In reply, Jung states that his observation is clinical, and therefore the inclusion of a certain degree of subjectivity is unavoidable. Consequently, even if one were to collect the anecdotes, no scientific treatment is possible. For such phenomena to be convincing, it is necessary to provide a detailed explanation concerning the person who directly experiences it and the surrounding circumstances of the time. And yet an explanation that would convince a third party is impossible. He states that this is why he has not made his opinions public [concerning this].

Another letter, exchanged in 1945, is important. In this letter Jung asks Rhine to send him a questionnaire concerning topics of his interest. In response, Rhine sent him a questionnaire with five headings, to which Jung replied. To summarize, the first point is that parapsychology ought to be treated theoretically as one field (or a supplement) of the psychology of the unconscious. The next point is that there are cases when the unconscious can influence matter, or can receive information about a thing without any bodily contact. Accordingly, the third point is that the phenomena of ESP or PK cannot be explained without presupposing the relativity of time and space. Jung states that Newtonian absolute space is limited to the macro-standpoint, that is, the gross realm that our everyday consciousness and sensations know, whereas from the micro-standpoint, that is, the subtle realm that cannot be immediately grasped by sensory perception, the limitation of time and space is not absolute. This means that ultimately materialistic causality is relative and not absolute. Moreover, when the world of the mind pertains to the latent domain, physical causation also becomes relativized because the mind influences the activity of matter: the deep layers of the unconscious transcend causal limitations that are framed by time and space. To transcend the limitation of time means that no time is involved in the communication of information. While it usually takes a definite period of time for information to spatially travel from one place to another, this becomes zero.

Moreover, he states that the collective unconscious is something transpersonal—he also calls this the objective *psychē*—and that the collective unconscious is *one* unconscious for the plurality of human beings. That is to say, the unconscious found in the collective dimension is merely a single unconscious, not separated into the many individual bodies. It follows that the collective unconscious is the same in every *place* and all *time*. For since it is something that is not limited to the individual, it is not limited to the individual's body [either]. Moreover, it is expressed in all environmental conditions transcending not only human beings, but simultaneously the multiplicity of the biological and physical environments. In this connection, he asks Rhine to think about the divination of the *Yijing*. To put it simply, the collective unconscious has an objective character transcending the individual, which may also be called the cosmic unconscious. Just as the physical external world is one world common to us (multiple individuals), so the collective unconscious is a "one world" common to us as well. While the world of the unconscious latently encompasses such a cosmic expanse, it is also the case that all events do not occur diachronically, and that the differences of spatial distance come to hold no meaning at all. The basis here is that an event possesses a kind of simultaneity, namely it occurs simultaneously at any place and any time. He explains that he chose the term *synchronicity* on the basis of the simultaneity possessed by such phenomena.

After the publication of his "Synchronicity Essay" in 1952, people from all over the world sent letters to Jung to inquire about this issue. (Among them is also contained a letter from Hans Bender, who is currently a professor at Freiburg University.) To cite one of the inquiries, there is a letter from A. D. Cornell of the Parapsychological Research Association at Cambridge University. In a letter addressed to him, Jung says the following. Even though Rhine calls the cause that triggers this kind of phenomenon, "*psi*-capacity" (popularly called paranormal ability), Jung states that "this is not a capacity." In other words, even if one cites *psi*-capacity as the cause of paranormal phenomena, since this term simply means "the capacity to cause paranormal events," this alone would not explain anything. Jung states that such a phenomenon is fundamentally one kind of spontaneously occurring phenomena, which occurs, by accompanying the emotion in an archetypal situation, to those who have a dispositionally low threshold to enter the collective unconscious, or even to normal people when in an extreme state of shock. Moreover, in reply to a scholar named Abraham, he states that, in such a case, we are not the mover, that is, the subject who moves such phenomena, but rather we are the moved object. He writes that this is where the modern scientific method of thinking reaches its limit.

If I were to give my interpretation, this means that this method of thinking presupposes a certain power endowed on the subject, and this ability as the cause triggers, and is capable of "catching," such a phenomenon. It proceeds to the idea that there is [first] paranormal ability or *psi*-capacity in the subject, and that it then [methodologically] separates subject and environment, or subject and object, which parapsychology came to accept after Rhine, who followed the methods of modern science. Jung says this will not do. To put it differently, our mind-body is a potentially open system, and it must be thought of as a being that can never be separable from the movement of the cosmos as a whole and/or from its connection with other minds. While in ego-consciousness, there is an original propensity to become independent of, and isolated from, the world, the human being is nothing but a passive being at the root dimension of the unconscious (that is, a being that is made to live) that is firmly connected with the cosmos and other living organisms. This kind of view of the human being is different from that of the modern view, and is close, instead, to the view that has been traditionally espoused in the East.

In the *Mysterium Conjunctum*, Jung calls the collective unconscious, "one world" (*unus mundus*), using the terminology of alchemy. Just as the world of objects is "one cosmos" that can be commonly cognized by people, so the *unus mundus* is a hidden, though different, "one cosmos," a fragment of which can be glimpsed from the interior of the mind (*psychē*). In other words, the cosmos and the human being as a whole are connected by an order that transcends the individual, and is common not only in respect to matter but also in respect to mind. This means that we, as individuals, are nothing more than merely one object that is moved by the power of such a world. Therefore, he frequently expressed a critical view toward the method of parapsychological research; as long as we think only of the consequences, it does not depart, methodologically speaking, from the hitherto-held scientific worldview. What is important in the investigation of paranormal phenomena concerns the question of what kind of new views of the human being and world will emerge from it. Consequently, it becomes necessary to reexamine the previously held view of science.

The previously held method of research in parapsychology has focused solely on the fact that ESP and PK exist, namely, that such physical events do occur, without sufficiently analyzing what kind of psychological conditions (e.g., the movement of emotion) can be found there. Put differently, contemporary parapsychological research conducts its research on paranormal phenomena basically by borrowing the method of experimental science. In contrast, Jung states that paranormal phenomena fundamentally suggest the necessity to revise such a method along with the views of the world and the human being based on that method. He states that it is from there that a change will occur in the views of the world and of the human being after modernity.

In the final analysis, Jung's point is that what is important for parapsychological research is to concern itself not with the existence of such phenomena, but rather with the conditions under which such phenomena occur, and whatever meaning these conditions may teach us regarding the being of the human and the world. Accordingly, it is based on this inquiry, he maintains, that we must rethink the method of modern science and the modern paradigm of knowledge.

SYNCHRONICITY AND CONTEMPORARY PHYSICS

Now, we come to the third point, that is, the issue of the connection between synchronicity and contemporary physics. In a reply addressed to Rhine, Jung had already stated that causality belongs to the way of thinking espoused by Newtonian macro-physics, while synchronicity approaches the way of thinking advanced by contemporary micro-physics.

In a letter of 1948 to Rhine, Jung writes how, having read Rhine's newly published book, he is recommending it to physicists of his area who are interested in parapsychology. He probably had Pauli and associates in mind. (Pauli was a colleague of Jung at the Swiss Federal Institute of Technology in Zürich, and was a very famous and great scholar who had received a Nobel Prize in physics.) In this letter he writes:[34]

> Your experiments have established the fact of the relativity of time, space, and mind with reference to the *psychē* beyond any doubt. The experimental proof is particularly valuable to me, because I am constantly observing facts that are along the same line. My chief concern is the theoretical problem of the connection between the *psychē* and the time-space-continuum of microphysics. We have some discussions over here with physicists concerning this matter.

The space-time continuum refers to Einstein's theory of relativity (i.e., the special theory of relativity). According to the theory of relativity, we must think of a micro-phenomenon as occurring in the four-dimensional field (i.e., space-time continuum) unifying the three spatial dimensions and the temporal dimension because the temporal definition of phenomena changes depending on the change of their spatial location. Jung was probably thinking that paranormal phenomena entail a reform in the concept of space-time. [I will return to this topic in chapter six.]

Such statements can also be found in the preface to the *Yijīng*, which I mentioned earlier. He states that the way the spirit observed the cosmos in ancient China can be compared to the view of contemporary physics, and that contemporary physics deals with a certain kind of "psychophysical" problem.[35] It seems that this observation is made in association with Heisenberg's "indeterminacy principle," that is, with the so-called problem of measurement in mind.

As this is an important topic, I will first explain, in the order of discussion, the latter, the problem of measurement. In the macro-world that we can experience and conceive through sensory perception, namely, the world of everyday experience, the laws of physics are thought to be established independently of states of the epistemological subject. For example, the movement of the celestial bodies occurs objectively according to the universal law of gravitation, independently of our act of observation. This is the picture of the world presented by Galilean–Newtonian classical mechanics that is based on causality. However, to measure the subatomic micro-world, the correlative relationship between the state of the epistemological subject and the state of the object becomes an issue. Heisenberg showed how the indeterminacy principle is at work amongst micro-elementary particles such as protons and electrons. The proton is viewed as having a position and a mass of energy, but we must cast light upon it in order to measure it. However, when we determine the position of the proton through measurement, the mass of energy becomes indeterminable. On the other hand, if we try to determine the mass of energy, the position is altered. This means that the act of measurement alters the state of the object, and we cannot understand the state of the elementary particle existing prior to measurement. This is the problem known as the "problem of measurement." Put differently, at the level of micro-physics, there is a mutually dependent, correlative relationship between the epistemological subject and the state of the object, and we cannot think of a state of the object existing independently of the epistemological subject. This is what Jung referred to as a kind of "psychophysical" problem.

However, the view concerning this problem of measurement, that is, its epistemological stance, is understood in various ways, and the opinion of physicists concerning this is not necessarily in accord. The perspective initiated by a well-known physicist, Niels Bohr of Denmark, has exercised great influence and is called the Copenhagen School. Bohr's stance is called phenomenalistic or idealistic, namely, that physics must stop at the description of phenomena observed by the epistemological subject, beyond which one can say nothing more. This stance of thinking maintains that there is no method to go beyond the wall to the other side. This is opposed to the stance of Newtonian objectivism (realism), namely that the task of physics is to pursue the real that is independent of the epistemological subject. [I will elaborate on this point in chapter six.]

Let us here touch briefly on the connection with Eastern thought. Bohr advocates a principle called complementarity. It means that the elementary particle has the characteristic of both being a particle and a wave, and that both are correct views concerning it. Because in the macro-world, an ocean wave, for example, involves molecular movements of water, it is founded on the particle-nature, and what appears to be a wave is in fact reduced to the movement of particles. However, at the micro-level, it cannot be determined which is more fundamental. In order to render this principle of complementarity readily understandable, Bohr uses the example of the [polar] concepts of *yin* and *yáng* in the *Yìjīng*. In the *Yìjīng* there is a famous proverb: "With the division of the Great Ultimate two poles emerge."[36] The "Great Ultimate" refers to the Dao, namely, the ultimate reality that is the foundation of all phenomena in the cosmos. This is something metaphysical insofar as it cannot be seen (i.e., something transcending sensible material phenomena). In contrast to this, "two poles" designate the activity of *ki*-energy in the "*yīn* and *yáng*" phases. This is a principle that signifies the condition of the physical (namely, the material) dimension that we can experience. In other words, Bohr took the symbol of the Great Ultimate (Figure 3.1) as designating his own philosophical worldview because the principle of complementarity is commensurate with the idea that two experiential conditions become separated out from the ultimate, invisible Dao. Moreover, Heisenberg, who was very close to Bohr, states that Bohr, having talked to Tagore, a famous poet of India—a poet who was the first to be awarded the Nobel Prize for literature in Asia—was deeply impressed with the resemblance of ideas between the Eastern view of the cosmos and contemporary physics.

Now, let us discuss the relationship between Pauli and Jung, which is the main focus of this section. Although Jung's "Synchronicity Essay" was published together with Pauli's essay, which dealt with Kepler's cosmology, Pauli's essay had no direct bearing on synchronicity or parapsychology, since it was a study of the history of science. Later in 1955, Pauli contributes the essay "Ideas of the Unconscious from the Standpoint of Natural Science and Epistemology" to an anthology commemorating Jung's eightieth birthday.[37] This essay makes a contention that there is an essential resemblance in regard to the method of cognition between the problem of measurement in contemporary physics and depth psychology. I think that this essay of Pauli raises an extremely important issue.

Pauli states in this essay that cognition concerning the unconscious involves the same kind of paradox as the problem of measurement. To cognize the unconscious means to bring it to consciousness. To cite the case of

Figure 3.1.

dreams as an example, a dream is the state when the activity of x, which is the unconscious, is brought to consciousness, but it does not mean that the unconscious itself (x) is brought to consciousness. Pauli calls this situation a paradox in terms of the method of cognition that is the same as the problem of measurement. That is, when we measure a micro-phenomenon such as an elementary particle, that act of measurement itself generates a disturbance in the state of the object. If light is applied to an elementary particle, its state is disturbed. The physicist can only cognize the disturbed state, and it does not mean that they can grasp the state of the matter-in-itself (x) independent of the epistemological subject. This is the same situation as when the psychologist cognizes the unconscious. Therefore, Pauli says that the phenomena of depth psychology and the phenomena of micro-physics are similar in regards to the fundamental nature of their method of cognition.

Pauli's point refers to the following situation. Depth psychology confronts the unconscious that in itself is impossible to be cognized, namely, the *psychē* in itself (*psychē an sich*), and we can only analyze its image when it becomes observable for consciousness (e.g., dreams). In the same way, contemporary micro-physics confronts something like matter in itself, which is mysterious and impossible to be cognized in itself (what Kant calls the "thing-in-itself," *Ding an sich*), and can only analyze the state when it becomes observable for the epistemological subject (i.e., the disturbed state of the elementary particle). This is an explanation very appropriate to the Copenhagen School.

The foregoing can be schematized as in Figure 3.2. While our consciousness perceives material phenomena in the external world, beyond that perceived image, there is concealed the mysterious thing-in-itself (x_1). And, on its interior side, consciousness experiences the image (e.g., dreams and hallucinations) flowing from the unconscious. Beyond the psychological phenomena experienced as images, there is concealed the soul in itself (x_2). The idea of synchronicity implies that between x_1 and x_2, there is a latent corresponding relation, namely, a relationship of preestablished harmony, though consciousness cannot understand it.

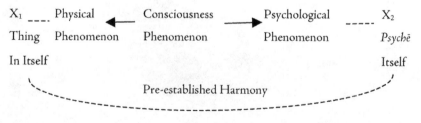

Figure 3.2.

NATURE'S PSYCHOID NATURE

[Although I made the following point in the Preface, I will reiterate it here.] According to Pauli, after making contact with Rhine's parapsychological research, Jung came to engage in a methodological reflection on the concepts of psychology that he had used up to that time. "Jung incorporated a drastic change in the concepts he had thus far used in order to deal with various fundamental issues. He made this change particularly taking into consideration the extra-sensory phenomena."[38] What Pauli is calling here "various fundamental issues" refers to such epistemological issues as the relationship between spirit (mind) and matter, and the role of an observer in cognizing nature. Pauli states that the concept of archetype of which Jung speaks was originally called "primordial image," and it has the strong connotation of an image in the mind, but by using a new concept "psychoid" (i.e., like the mind), Jung attempted to incorporate material activity into the realm of the unconscious. In other words, the sharp demarcation between the physical and the psychological is a consequence of the conscious intellectual judgment and does not mean that nature itself contains such a distinction. Nature that is purely material or physical, which scientific cognition grasps, is a consequence of observation and measurement based on definite presuppositions and methods.

To view the essence of nature as psychoid in this manner, when put from a different point of view for the purpose of an easier understanding, is *to grasp space as the field of unconscious activity that is universal transcending the individual.* The ESP experience is related to this. For example, clairvoyance is to see with the mind's eye, and telepathy is to hear with the mind's ear. At the moment when such ESP experiences occur, spatial distance that can be quantitatively calculated disappears. In other words, space as a whole is imbued with a psychoid nature. When we assume such a standpoint, we can say that the synchronistic experience shows us a "face" of nature prior to the distinction between mind and matter. This means in light of Figure 3.2 that x_1 and x_2 coincide.

Having said this, however, Pauli is not merely referring to the resemblance in epistemological methodology between psychology and physics. While having an interest in parapsychology under the influence of Jung, he was wondering whether such phenomena have bearing on *the teleological characteristics of the living organism.* Pauli states that, when dealing with such phenomena, it would be necessary, for example, to consider the psychophysiological interconnection we experience in our daily life, that is, the relationship between the mind and the brain. In other words, while Jung, in turning his attention to parapsychology, tries to relate the psychological function immediately to the physical phenomena, Pauli considers it necessary to focus upon the mech-anism of *life-phenomena* that is the intermediary between them.

Pauli asserts that it is not appropriate to limit and grasp the notion of the unconscious merely from the standpoint of psychotherapy. He claims that it would be more decisive for psychotherapy to join the phenomena of the unconscious with the general profile of the natural sciences that deal with life-phenomena. In other words, the unconscious cannot be lodged as an issue of psychology, but must be connected to the way of thinking of the natural sciences in general that deal with life (e.g., medicine or biology). In that case, doesn't the characteristic nature unique to that which has life, such as *teleo-logical* nature and teleological intentionality, perhaps also become an issue in physics? I think this is what Pauli claims.

SYNCHRONICITY AND THE MOVEMENT OF NEW AGE SCIENCE

Up to this point we have explained three issues that are related to synchron-icity. I think that Jung's remark captures well the essence of the issues regard-ing [both] the first point that is related to the worldview of the *Yijīng* and the second point that is concerned with the relation with parapsychology. However, I get the impression that his idea concerning the third point that has bearing on contemporary physics has not been sufficiently developed. The connection with contemporary physics is an issue that entered his inter-est around 1950 when he wrote his "Synchronicity Essay," after he became familiar with Rhine's research. While his interest in Eastern thought and parapsychology, as mentioned earlier, was already existent in Jung's youth, the issue of physics came later. Since it appears that Jung had not really thought through the latter point, I think this point should be taken afresh as an issue today.

Recently the term "New Age Science" has become popular. Fritjof Capra spread the movement of New Age Science to the populace. In his recently translated book,[39] comparing Freud and Jung, Capra states that their differ-ence corresponds to the difference between classical physics and contemporary physics, or between a mechanistic paradigm and a holistic paradigm. More-over, science journalists who belong to the school of New Age Science, such as Lyall Watson and Arthur Koestler, also view Jung's psychology, particularly the idea of synchronicity, as one kind of precursor to New Age Science, while treating parapsychology as a significant part of New Age Science.[40]

Here I would like to introduce the thought of David Bohm who is con-sidered the most representative theoretician of New Age Science, while exam-ining its relation with the worldview upheld by synchronicity.[41] David Bohm was a professor of theoretical physics at the University of London, who made a great contribution to quantum mechanics. He states that behind the micro-world that we can measure there lies a hidden dimension. He calls this the "implicate order."[42] The implicate order is the order hidden from the observer, the realm of the invisible. In contrast, Bohm calls the dimension of experiences that we can measure, the "explicate order."[43] The explicate order is, so to speak, the order that appears to the observer. Bohm believes that beyond the order that can be cognized through measurement, there is a hidden order that is latent. In other words, he thinks that the world has the dual structure of explicate-implicate order.

It would seem Bohm's idea interestingly approaches Pauli's idea that I introduced earlier. Pauli claimed that physics cannot cognize the thing-in-itself, *Ding an sich*, and that we can only know the state disturbed (i.e., the measured state) by the epistemological subject, wherein he discovered a cognition resembling that of depth psychology. Pauli stopped inquiry there, but Bohm, taking note of that point, tries to think about what is on the other side of the observed state, that is, the state on the other side of the wall.

According to Bohm, the explicate world can be explained through the relations between various elements. In other words, it can be described by the causal relationship between the elements or their probabilistic relation as an extension of their causal relationship. In contrast, he says that the implicate order is an order that does not conform to the view that reduces it to sensation or the elements. Bohm also characterizes the implicate order as "a holo-movement of a whirlpool of continuous energy."[44] The term "holo-movement" comes from the principle of so-called holography. Since it would take too long to explain this in detail, I will make this brief. Holography is a kind of photography without a lens. This is a system in which information about the whole is contained in its parts. In an ordinary photograph, the relationship seen between the object and the image is a one-to-one correspondence between the point of the object and the point of the picture. On the other hand, on the dry plate of a hologram, the relationship is that within each point there is contained the information concerning the whole of its object. Bohm used this as a metaphorical model. In other words, "holographic" means that the part of a given phenomenon contains information concerning its whole. In this model, whatever part may be selected, the information concerning the whole will still be included. We may describe this as "part *qua* whole," "one *qua* many," or "one *qua* all" (as is exemplified in the Huáyán [Jap.; Kegon] way of thinking contained in the *Huáyánsūtra*). Therefore, these cases show that it is in vain to explain the whole by reconstructing it vis-à-vis an analysis of the whole into its elements. We might say that this is a development of Pauli's idea of wholeness (*Ganzheit*).

At any rate, Bohm's view attempts to explain, by borrowing the model of holography, the structure of the implicate order, wherein, he states, there is no longer any restriction of time and space insofar as communication of information is concerned. In other words, when the implicate order is seen in terms of space, the distinction between parts and the whole comes to have no meaning; and when it is seen in terms of time, the cognition of information is not diachronic but synchronic. That is, according to this model the distinctions of past-present-future disappear. Using this model of holography, Bohm explains the characteristic of what he calls the implicate order.

Furthermore, Bohm takes up the relationship of the implicate order and consciousness. Consciousness in this case has a broad meaning that includes the unconscious. He states that the implicate order is the realm that becomes the common potential ground where consciousness (mind) is related to matter. Moreover, he says that there is a dual structure of an "explicate-implicate" order in the world of consciousness (mind) as in the case of measurement of matter. This idea parallels Pauli's view concerning depth psychology, as I introduced earlier. In other words, even though the sensible image belongs to the observable explicate order, at its bottom there is the ground that is the unconscious in-itself (x_2) and that cannot be completely cognized. This ground is filled with extremely vast potential information. He goes so far as to say that in the final analysis, the implicate order, which is the invisible world, is more fundamental for us human beings (or for life).

It appears that Bohm's idea was acquired through a suggestion from Eastern thought, and he himself confirms this in our interview with him.[45] Bohm was very close to the Indian philosopher Krishnamurti (who was one of the leaders of Theosophy when he was young, and after Gandhi's death served as an advisor to Prime Minister Nehru). Moreover, he responded that he met with the Dalai Lama twice and asked him his opinion about the model of the implicate order. In other words, the implicate order relates to the domain that has a bearing on the psychology of meditation. Therefore, there is a methodological limitation to the measurement seen from the standpoint of physics, for scientific measurement is incapable of grasping the psychological function.

In short, the basis of Bohm's thinking presents the kind of picture of a dual world that divides and contrasts the two orders of explicate-implicate, and it comes to remarkably resemble Jung's view that distinguishes the two principles of causality and synchronicity. They share the same idea insofar as the hidden potential order (implicate order or synchronicity) possesses characteristics that transcend temporal and spatial restrictions.

In his "Synchronicity Essay," Jung states that in the order controlled by synchronicity, the dualistic distinction between spirit and matter disappears, and a reality called psychoid (mind-like, or resembling mind)—a reality wherein spirit and matter are not separated—will be discovered. This view as well can be said to be close to that of Bohm. In 1984 we held a symposium, "Scientific Technology and the Spiritual World," which was co-sponsored by French National Radio and the University of Tsukuba. ([I will introduce more about this conference at the end of this chapter as well as in the final chapter.]) At this conference, French and Japanese scholars discussed ideas and methods related to New Age Science. Because I was in charge of the planning and execution of this conference, I sent an interviewer to London prior to the conference with the task of asking Bohm a few questions. The main points were to clarify Bohm's idea concerning the problem of measurement, and to inquire if there is something in his idea commensurate with the view of nature upheld in the East. In response to the second question, he clearly answered in the affirmative. He made the following statement. If thing and mind were together within the implicate order, the two may be thought to stand in a *soma*-meaning relationship or conversely a meaning-*soma* relationship. "*Soma*" is a Greek word that designates matter or material of the body, and "meaning" is psychological information that connects matter with the human mind. Therefore, there is a mutual, passive-active function between the domain of mind and the domain of matter. In other words, he maintains that material energy and psychological information operate as one in the implicate order. Furthermore, in answer to a question about the relationship between his theoretical model and Eastern thought, he answers in the following manner by citing the examples of Indian and Chinese methods of meditation:[46]

> In my opinion, the fundamental idea of the East is in the ultimate reality of the immeasurable, and more attention has been paid to this issue. Measurement, as it were, is given a secondary significance. While the Sanskrit term *māyā* (illusion) is derived from *measure*, in India *māyā* has the meaning of a phantasm or something superficial, and does not designate the essence of reality. I think that the idea of the implicate order is commensurate with such an Eastern perspective. That is to say, if we enter into the theory of the implicate order, then it comes to the idea of the totality of movements. The movement is something that cannot be characterized in any way, and it is from there that all things including space, time, as well as matter, unfold. This may be similar to some of the Indian ways of thinking. Furthermore I also think that this is close to Chinese ideas concerning energy. We may here think of "meaning" mentioned previously. If we suppose that body and mind carries in their interior a formless energy, meaning [namely psychological information] gives form to energy. And we can see that this gives form not only to psychic energy, but also to the body, namely physical

energy. It is here that you might say I am approaching Chinese thought. I
believe that you will probably call this "*ki.*"

Bohm's idea reminded me of the famous parable of the cave in Plato's *Republic*. The state of thing-events, accessible by means of sensory perception, is
like shadows reflected on the wall deep in the cave, and the true reality that
produces the shadows exists in the world of ideas that transcends the sensible world. This seems to resonate with the view of nature based on *ki*-energy
that has traditionally been nurtured in the East. Bohm and Jung have a com-
monality as well in that they both approach the Eastern view of nature and
the human being. I find it deeply interesting that Bohm here took note of the
Chinese idea of *ki*-energy.

Nevertheless, Bohm's idea should be considered a philosophical hypothesis, and it cannot be verified yet by experiment whether it is correct. In short,
Bohm contends that modern science needs a metaphysics that goes beyond
the limitations of physics. In order for science to deal with the mind or spiritual phenomena, it is in turn necessary to approach it from the standpoint
that transcends science.

SUMMARY

What I attempted to communicate in this chapter was that the idea of synchronicity raised by Jung is being reconsidered today, and its meaning questioned anew.

An important point here in understanding Jung's theory is how to grasp
the collective unconscious. According to the previously held view of Jung's
psychology, the collective unconscious has been defined in light of temporality. That is, it has been described, in a certain sense, as the psychic inheritance of meaning, a crystallized pattern of species-memory that goes beyond
Freud's individual unconscious. In other words, it has been understood as the
accumulation or patternment of an ancestral experience going back prior to
the birth of the individual.

That is certainly the case in Jung's published works. However, if we consider his ideas of synchronicity as seen in his biography and correspondence,
we can understand that Jung also considered the collective unconscious in
light of *spatiality*. That is, the collective unconscious designates what we may
call a transpersonal, singular cosmic consciousness that is common to more
than two individuals who are spatially separated. When it is viewed from the
human perspective, that is, from the point of view of consciousness, it means
that the collective unconscious designates a spatiality. From this standpoint,
the transmission of information occurs between spatially distinct experiences

(synchronistically or nonlocally), ignoring the difference in location in space because our consciousness or body is incorporated into space. Therefore, the order of the collective unconscious equally controls us who are spatially separate, and creates an invisible mesh by means of the connection established between mind and mind.[47]

As mentioned in the beginning, synchronicity poses a new question regarding the relationship between psychological phenomena and physical phenomena, between the world of mind and the world of matter, or between the world of inner events and the world of outer events. In the Cartesian picture of the world, these two are in principle rendered unrelated. However, according to Jung's view, we human beings (or broadly speaking, living organisms) are connected to an objective order that is the cosmic unconscious discovered externally beyond each individual, just as the world of matter externally exists objectively to each individual. That is, we are [standing] at the tangential point between two vast spheres of matter and *psychē* (soul). This applies to each and every human being. Let us say that on the one hand there is a gigantic sphere that is the realm of matter, and on the other hand there is another gigantic sphere that is the realm of spirit. The point at which the two spheres overlap is the ego of each one of us. If we draw this in a diagram, it can be represented as in Figure 3.3. We can fold the two spheres in the middle and they overlap upon one another. The order of the cosmic unconscious on the right becomes the world-behind, hidden from the consciousness of individuals, as in Jung's synchronicity or Bohm's implicate order. Behind the world of perceived things, there is the invisible world of potential information and potential energy. In the surface world, we live in the realm of matter, but latent behind it is the world in which there is no distinction between matter and mind. I think that this image enables us to understand the idea of an overlap between psychological phenomenon and physical phenomenon, between the world of mind and the world of matter, or between the world of inner events and the world of outer events. Standing on the tangential point of these two worlds is the "I" of each of us. The collective unconscious can be comprehended in this way by expanding it to the cosmos. This hidden order is what Jung, borrowing the terminology of alchemy, calls the *unus mundus*, the "one world." If we view this broadly, I think that this connects to the view that the cosmos has life and mind.

Lastly, I would like to add my personal opinion. What Jung took as a problem in synchronicity, in the final analysis, is the relationship between psychological phenomena and physical phenomena. As Pauli also recognized, this problem, as a matter of fact, relates to the issue of the living organism. The issue of life-science is lacking in the composition of Jung's thoughts. This is due to the fact that, in Jung's time, research had not yet progressed much

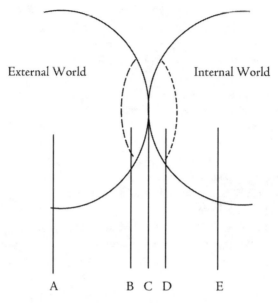

External World   Internal World

A   B C D   E

A: Thing-in-Itself
B: External World as Sensible Image
C: Ego-Consciousness
D: Personal Unconscious
E: Cosmic Unconscious

Figure 3.3. External World and Internal World

in that direction. Moreover, Bohm as well, while thinking of the relationship between psychological phenomena and physical phenomena, has not adequately considered the issue of the living organism, namely, teleology. But in fact the issue of the living organism's peculiar mechanism and teleology inevitably intervenes within the intermediary region between physical phenomena and psychological phenomena. I think that this may hereafter become a serious issue that we need to think through from now on. For such reasons I am today interested in the problems of psychosomatic medicine and "*ki*-energy" in Eastern medicine.[48] This is because the issue of *ki*-energy is believed to be involved in paranormal phenomena as dealt with by parapsychology, in addition to being related to the particular mechanism of mind-body correlativity unique to the living organism. I tend to think that, by using this as a breakthrough point, a path may open up to approach the idea of synchronicity by means of [empirical] verification.

(Kansai Lecture, Association of Japan Jung Club, November 17, 1985.)

POSTSCRIPT (APRIL 2003)

Chinese Somatic Science: How Is Ki-*Energy Understood in Somatic Science?*

In 1984, when the Japan-France symposium was held, scholars of religion, medicine, and psychology were gathered from both sides, and they engaged in discussion in order to promote the movement of New Age Science. I included a suggestion, made from the Japanese side, involving presentations on traditional chinese medicine (TCM), parapsychology, Eastern martial arts, and their demonstrations. In the martial arts demonstration there was included the performance of a technique in which a master martial artist, by emitting *ki*-energy, makes opponents, who are spatially distanced from him, fall down. This technique is called "distant hitting" [*tōate*, 遠当て], and it became a conversation piece, attracting people's attention. As a result, many *qìgōng* masters came to visit me. I studied their techniques, and experienced *ki*-energy as a subject of their *qìgōng* techniques. Afterwards, I went to China to learn about its actual situation. While I was staying in Beijing in 1997, the Chinese Society for Somatic Science (CSSS) was established. The leaders of this society came to see me with a request to make efforts to propagate *qìgōng* in Japan. In the following year, I invited scholars and *qìgōng* masters from China and held a symposium "*Ki* and Human Science" in Tokyo.[49] At about this time, a *qìgōng* boom was being generated. After this conference, I went to China many times to investigate and study *qìgōng*. I will introduce its fundamental ideas, while incorporating my own opinion.

Chinese somatic science focuses on the three fields of traditional Chinese medicine, *qìgōng*, and special abilities as its main objects of research. "Special abilities" refer to what parapsychology calls *psi*-ability (paranormal ability). A central focus in each of these fields is *ki*-energy as the object of research. Traditional Chinese medicine understands the fundamentals of the human body's organization by means of the network of meridians. Meridians are channels of the energy that circulates in the interior of the human body. However, they are an *invisible* system that cannot be discovered by dissecting a corpse. In other words, they are a system unique to the body that is active while it is alive. I am taking this to mean, for now, a system that organizes the subject-body (i.e., the lived body) of which Merleau-Ponty speaks. An important point, when it is seen from a theoretical point of view, is that the meridians are a system that does not agree with the mind-body dichotomization established since Descartes. That is, *ki*-energy is conceived to be a life-energy that has *both physical and psychological characteristics*. The fundamental principle of needle therapy used in traditional Chinese medicine lies in activating the circulation of *ki*-energy within the human body by infusing fresh *ki*-energy into the human body, while eliminating the stagnant and inferior flow of *ki*-energy.

Next is *qìgōng*. *Qìgōng* teaches us that the activity of *ki*-energy can be heightened through repeated training. Consequently, we can understand that *qìgōng*, theoretically speaking, has a characteristic commensurate with the training in martial arts. It is a bodily technique with a tradition stretching from ancient times. In the case of medical therapy, a mature *qìgōng* doctor guides patients to train themselves and practice *qìgōng* on their own. Here we can discern a methodology different from the therapeutic method of modern medical science. While modern medical therapy leaves patients to assume a passive standpoint of simply receiving doctor's treatment, *qìgōng* lets them assume an active standpoint of training themselves. The point of this training lies in activating the natural healing power latent in the interior of one's own body. *Ki*-energy is thought to be the energy that controls the foundations of life-activity. The training involves promoting and purifying the activity of *ki*-energy inside of one's own body, and transforming it to the *ki*-energy of a better and higher quality. Therefore, it is a therapeutic method as well as a method of maintaining and promoting health. That is, it can become a method of maintaining health by continually training oneself daily, while it is not limited to times of sickness.

Qìgōng is divided into internal and external *qìgōng* for the purpose of convenience. The training a patient performs after receiving guidance belongs to the inner *qìgōng*, while the outer *qìgōng* refers to cases in which a mature *qìgōng* master performs therapy on a patient or subject. In these cases, the *qìgōng* master usually touches the patient's body with his hand, but there are cases in which a *qìgōng* master, distancing himself from the patient, performs a therapeutic technique without making contact. It is probably safe to think that it is based on the same principle as the technique of therapeutic touch, which in recent years is beginning to spread in America.

The third field that is called "special ability" in China, overlaps with the research of what is referred to in the West and Japan as parapsychology. On numerous occasions, I met with *qìgōng* masters in China who have paranormal ability and observed their technique, while engaging them in dialogue. I encountered people who can demonstrate a wonderful technique, not to mention clairvoyance and psychokinesis, which Rhine's research problematized. Insofar as my research can confirm, there are cases of people who innately possess these abilities, and cases of people who have acquired them through training. If these abilities are used in the field of medicine, they can fulfill the same role as the external *qìgōng*. Moreover, there are cases among master martial artists who can demonstrate this kind of ability, though its number is limited. One impression I have received when encountering these people is that there is a great difference between the East and the West in the foundational idea when dealing with this kind of issue. While in the East this kind of issue has been dealt with as part of the issue related to self-cultivation, which traditionally has a cultural and religious background, there was no such historical and cultural background in the West. Consequently, parapsychological research in the West is preceded by an interest and concern from a theoretical viewpoints. This brings in the background of contemporary scholarly research in which there is no concern for its relationship to daily activity. By contrast, in China's case the practical purpose, as in the case of *qìgōng*, looms in the purview of research. This kind of stance is based on the traditional ethos found in the history of science and technology in China. (Modern technology of the West emerged as an application of theory, where theoretical research does not take into account the relationship it has with the practical, daily activity of human beings.) When we examine it from a broader perspective, this kind of tendency is rooted in the philosophical tradition of the East that highly values the practical standpoint.

However, there is a tradition in the East that admonishes people, as they are prone to fall into an ethically wrong tendency regarding paranormal phenomena. The tradition of East Asia such as that of China and Japan maintains that the bodily technique must conform to an ethical standpoint. Although I could hardly see such a spiritualistic stance in the contemporary situation in China and Japan, there were occasions when I met persons with such a stance, especially among the masters of martial arts, who live among [the common] people, but are not related to universities or academic institutions. In the tradition of Buddhism, this kind of "special ability" has been called "*siddhi*" [*jintsūriki*, 神通力] and is considered a kind of a by-product that naturally emerges in the course of self-cultivation. Buddhism has persistently maintained that self-cultivation should not aim at acquiring this as its goal. For example, Dōgen, a famous Japanese medieval Zen monk, teaches in the chapter of "*Jintsū*" [Divine Power, i.e., paranormal power] in *Shōbōgenzō* that although Buddhism recognizes this kind of *siddhi*, it is a "small" *siddhi*, and the true "great" *siddhi* exists in the midst of such everyday activities as drinking tea and eating a meal. This reminds me of Yang Xin, a *qìgōng* master, who is now actively promoting *qìgōng* in America. When I saw him in Beijing some time ago, he told me that he was now studying "distant *qìgōng*" [Chin., *yuǎgéqìgōng*; Jap., *enkaku kikō*: 遠隔気功]. He was accompanied by a twelve-year-old girl, who was his experimental subject. I asked him why he was conducting such an experiment. He replied: "I am not trying to become famous by showing off this kind of technique. As I read a description in a classic on the method of self-cultivation that one can perform this kind of technique, I just wanted to know if it is true or not." Then he wrote on a piece of paper "大

道無言" [Chin., *dàdàowúyán*; Jap., *daidōmugon*]. This phrase means that "The Great Dao remains silent and does not speak."

Herein lies, it would seem, a difference in the traditional ethos between the Eastern martial arts and Western sports. The historical origin of Western sports goes back to the Olympian events in ancient Greece. They emerged, based on demands of the battlefield such as physical strength, stamina, running, throwing, and the handling technique of a horsedrawn cart. We might say that the custom of the modern Olympics in which the record is valued more than anything else inherits this traditional idea. By contrast, in the tradition of the martial arts in the East runs an idea that emphasizes spirituality, even though the martial arts developed, like those of ancient Greece, through techniques used on the battlefield. The history of the Chinese and Japanese martial arts was nurtured through the influence of Buddhism and Shintoism. It came to develop the idea that training in the martial arts has the significance of enhancing one's ethical personality. Consequently, the stance of respecting the opponent's personality and capacity was sought in performing techniques. For example, Mr. Ueshiba Morihei, the founder of Aikidō, states that "Martial art is love." The ultimate goal of martial arts is not to win by defeating the opponent, but to harmonize with the opponent such that people can love each other under "that which is great" transcending humans. It would seem that "research on prayer," which has been recently initiated in America, incorporates this kind of spiritual idea.

Incidentally, I came to realize in the course of investigating the Chinese somatic sciences that the standpoint of psychology was lacking. In modern China, which used Marxist materialism as its guiding principle for establishing the nation, psychology was not studied until the time of the Cultural Revolution, as antithetical to materialism. Even *qìgōng* was an object of suppression. Today, however, the study of psychology is recognized to be legitimate, and exchange with Japan is making an advance. I have practiced meditation since my youth, and have continued to research and study it. Meditation methods in the Chinese traditions were called "quiet *qìgōng*" and stand in a pairing relationship with the usual "moving *qìgōng*" that mobilizes the body. However, almost no meditation methods are practiced in contemporary China. This is probably due to the fact that meditation methods such as those of Buddhism and Daoism were developed within the traditions of religious culture, and declined as a consequence of persecution after the modern period. When somatic science was established in Japan in 1991, we used for its English designation the Society for Mind-Body Science (SMBS), as I felt the importance of psychology.

The fundamentals of meditation lie, after all, in promoting the circulation of *ki*-energy. When it is seen from the point of view of psychology, *ki*-energy designates libido. It is life-energy equipped in the unconscious and the body. The foundational idea that is placed in *The Secret of the Golden Flower*, a meditation text of Daoism, is to transform and sublimate *ki*-energy from the state of libido (Chin., *jīng*; Jap., *sei*: 精) to the state of "divine subtle energy" (Chin., *shén*; Jap., *shin*: 神). *Ki*-energy changes into spiritual energy when the instinct and desire in one's unconscious region are purified. Freud insisted that neurosis develops when conscience suppresses the activity of libido, while Jung claimed that libido is an energy related to religiosity. When one touches the activity from the dimension of primal origin, the love of others is transformed from the eros of flesh to spiritual love.

To summarize, *ki*-energy is an energy that controls the whole of psychology, medicine, and bodily technique, including the relationship between the environment and the human body. The philosophical guideline that comprehensively includes all of these fields is sought in the idea of the *yīn-yáng* exchange of *ki*-energy that has its origin in the *Yìjīng*. According to its conceptual paradigm, nature as the environment is endowed with life, and is fostered to grow by means of the activity of *ki*-energy issuing from the Dao that exists in the ultimate dimension. Human beings, along with other life activities, are receptive of this energy and are made to live. Purifying it to a sublime level brings about an enhancement of ethical personality.

Translator's Note

As a further attempt to articulate the two goals Yuasa set up for clarification, namely, (1) to provide a theoretical explanation for the phenomenon of synchronicity, and (2) to develop a worldview that is *holistic, he moves to thematize in chapter four the Yijīng views "life and space-time," while relating it to "synchronicity and the psychology of the Yijīng." He focuses on the analysis of time and space unique to the Yijīng. Through his analysis, the reader will learn of a fuller picture of the Yijīng's views of nature and the human being. This chapter and the subsequent two chapters serve as a preparation for Yuasa to advance in chapter six the thesis of space-time and mind-body integration.*

CHAPTER FOUR

Life and Space-Time

Synchronicity and the Psychology of the Yìjīng

INTRODUCTION

The Book of Changes, the *Yìjīng*, is a classic that points to the original source of Chinese philosophy. It presents a proto-image of Chinese thinking prior to the emergence of competing strands of Confucianism and Daoism. Jung states that his idea of synchronicity is based on the thought of the *Yìjīng* [Jap., *Ekikyō*: 易経].[1] Being curious about his assertion, I became interested in this classic. He claims that this ancient Chinese classic has a significant meaning and value for the various contemporary scholarly disciplines, beginning with psychology, which is seemingly unrelated to Sinology or the study of the [Chinese] classics. Even though his view may be taken to be "outrageous" from the viewpoint of academic common sense that values specialization, Jung contends that the issue of synchronicity carries important significance and value for the various contemporary scholarly disciplines, including natural science. What is his reason for making such assertions?

In preparation for this inquiry in mind, I attempted to examine the history of Chinese philosophical thought, from the point of view of the body, in a recently published work covering the mythical ages to the modern period.[2] To state its conclusion, we can discover therein a coherent stance that regards as important the correlativity between the macrocosm and the microcosm (i.e., the human being as mind-body integration). In this chapter, I would like to think through, from a contemporary standpoint, the theoretical issue that the *Yìjīng* presents on the basis of such a preparatory investigation of Chinese intellectual history.

TIIE DIVINATION OF THE *YÌJĪNG* AND THE
MIND-BODY RELATION

For the sake of readers who have no preliminary knowledge of the *Yìjīng*, let us start with an elementary explanation. Legend has it that the *Yìjīng* originated in the mythical ages when the Emperor Fāxī [Jap.: Fugi] set eight triagrams of divining sticks (although these triagrams are sometimes read as "*ke*" in Japanese following the *Wú* reading, the official, formal pronunciation is "*ka*" [*quà*, 卦] in Japanese following the *Hàn* reading). The triagram is made up of a combination of three lines, a horizontal straight line expressing *yáng* "—" and a horizontal broken line expressing *yīn*, "--." Each line is called a "*kǒ*" in Japanese [*yáo*, 爻]. Because when placing three "*kǒ*'s" together, for example, "☰," it produces eight combinations of *yīn* and *yáng*, they are called the eight triagrams. They are respectively represented as: ☰, "*gān*" [Jap., *ken*: 乾]; ☷, "*kūn*" [Jap., *kon*: 坤]; ☳, "*zhèn*" [Jap., *shin*: 震]; ☴, "*xùn*" [Jap., *son*: 巽]; ☵, "*kǎn*" [Jap., *kan*: 坎]; ☲, "*lí*" [Jap., *ri*: 離]; ☶, "*gěn*" [Jap., *kon*: 艮]; and ☱, "*duì*" [Jap., *da*: 兌]. Furthermore, if we multiply the eight triagrams of *ka*, by doubling it to two groups of an upper part and a lower part, eight times eight gives us sixty-four hexagrams. On these hexagrams, King Wén of the Zhōu dynasty (?–256 BCE) stipulated the "Judgments on the Hexagrams" [*quàcí*; Jap., *kaji*: 卦辞] to explain the triagrams (*quà*), and the Duke of Zhōu, his collaborator, stipulated the "Judgments on the Lines" [*yáocí*; Jap., *kōji*: 爻辞] to explain each line (*yáo*). These constitute the main text of the *Yìjīng*. In addition, there is a philosophical commentary called the *Ten Wings* [*Shíyì*; Jap., *Jyūyoku*: 十翼] that Confucius is said to have added to this text. This includes: two chapters of "Commentary on the Decision" [*Tuan-zhuàn*; Jap., *Tanden*: 彖伝], two chapters of "Commentary on the Images" [*Xiàngzhuàn*; Jap., *Shōden*: 象伝], one chapter of "Commentary on the Words of the Text" [*Wényánzhuàn*; Jap., *Mongenden*: 文言伝], two chapters of "Commentary on the Appended Judgments" [*Xìcízhuàn*; Jap., *keijiden*: 繋辞伝], one chapter of "Discussion of the Triagrams" [*Shuìquàzhuàn*; Jap., *Sekkaden*: 説卦伝], one chapter of "Sequence of the Hexagrams" [*Xùquà-zhuàn*; Jap., *Jyokaden*: 序卦伝], and one chapter of "Miscellaneous Notes on the Hexagrams" [*Záquàzhuàn*; Jap., *Zakkaden*: 雑卦伝]. In total, there are seven headings and ten chapters. Of these, the "Commentary on the Decision" is a commentary on "the Judgments on the Hexagrams" as a whole. The rest deals with the philosophical thought of the *Yìjīng*. The preceding is the legend regarding the compilation of the *Yìjīng*. But today it is regarded that a Confucian scholar wrote, long after Confucius, the *Ten Wings* in the beginning part of the Hàn dynasty (202 BCE–8 CE), by incorporating the thoughts of *Lǎozǐ* and *Zhūangzǐ*.

Needless to say, the *Yijing* deals with the principle of divination. What then does it mean to "divine"? For now, we may say that it is to know the *future*. Having said this, however, knowing the past is also included as, for example, when the diviner reads [a customer's] palms. Therefore, the point of the *Yijing*'s divination can be defined as knowing the *past* and the *future* from the temporal point of the present. The meaning of the *Yijing* in this respect can be said that it is a method and technique for one type of cognizing the world that has a bearing on time.

In what way are the past and the future known in such a case? This is a difficult problem striking at the root of the *Yijing*. In my judgment, it involves an issue related to a theory of the body (i.e., a mind-body theory). When one thinks about this, just as the philosopher Bergson had already stated, the sensory organs of the human body, considered in themselves, are such that they can only know the present, [with which I will deal in more detail in chapter six]. The five senses that the body is equipped with (i.e., sight, hearing, smell, taste, and touch), whether eye or ear or skin—if we tentatively separate the body from the mind—are functions that operate at the very *moment* when each of these organs receives physical stimulus from the outside world (e.g., light, sound, scent, etc.). That is, they are the faculty of cognizing *in the present* the condition of spatial thing-events (i.e., generally speaking, matter) that are within the parameter of the body. In other words, the sensory organs alone will not enable us to know the past or the future. Regarding this point, Bergson says that pure perception is a mechanical reaction that has a bearing on space.[3] While this may sound difficult, it means the following.

"Pure," as in pure perception, refers to the thinking of the body as separate from the mind. (Perception refers collectively to the five senses.) Namely, pure perception [*junnsui chikaku*, 純粋知覚] is the sensory perception in a *pure* condition that can be theoretically postulated. A condition close to such a perception can be found in primitive organisms for which sight or hearing is undeveloped, for example, mollusks such as sea urchins, sea cucumbers, and chordates like ascidians. They primarily respond only to the spatial stimulus of the *present* by tactile sensation. Needless to say, insofar as they are living organisms, they cannot be without some kind of memory of the past or anticipation of the future. Nonetheless, in comparison to the higher animals, their perception is "purer." Bergson states that pure perception in extreme conditions can be found in inorganic matter, though therein is discovered only a mechanical reaction of the present in response to a function coming from the outside.

In a word, bodily organs, once isolated to that extent, are aware of only the spatial *condition* of the *present*, and are not organized to have knowledge of time. This shows that human knowledge of the past and future is a working of the mind. The past is *recollected* from *memory* and reproduced in the mind. Moreover, the future, too, is in the *anticipation* and *imagination* of the mind. Consequently, in order to principally investigate the human cognition of time, it becomes necessary to take up a mind-body theory.

Incidentally, when we cognize a condition of spatial thing-events while relying on perception and thinking, and, based on it, intellectually infer the states of the past or the future, we assume the standpoint of observing the world on the basis of the principle of causality. For example, when a meteorologist attempts to predict tomorrow's weather, he or she directly or indirectly (through a measuring device) examines the observed data of the past through sensory cognition, infers accordingly, and makes a prediction about the future. In such a case, we think that because there is a definite objective *cause* in the past, the future will happen as its *effect*. In this way, the causal mode of thinking deduces its effect by setting up a definite cause. This is the principle whereby modern science is established.

By contrast, divination does not mean to infer a future state from data obtained by sensory cognition. Needless to say, some sort of experiential data is given at the time of divination. For example, when one is undecided about something and has a diviner tell one's fortune, one must provide the diviner (i.e., fortune-teller) with information about one's present situation. However, to tell the future is not to infer a future state merely from such experiential data. For now, we can take this to mean knowing the future through intuition.

In that case, where in the body can we find such a function of intuition— if indeed there is such a function? Of course, it cannot be in the sensory organs. Nor can we find it within consciousness that engages itself in intellectual judgment. When psychologically viewed, the functions of perception and judgment belong to the realm of *consciousness* that has surfaced in the mind. By contrast, there is the unconscious part in the realm of the mind that ordinarily does not appear on the surface. The reason why we can remember the past is because we can call up a memory "stored" in the realm of the unconscious. In this regard, the unconscious is a deep layer in the realm of the mind, distinguished from the body. We cannot seek the origin of intuition anywhere else than this. We can define "divination," psychologically speaking, to mean the knowledge of the state of spatial thing-events in the future (or the past) by means of intuition arising from the unconscious.

In this case, the divination of the *Yijing* depends on the sixty-four classifications of the hexagrams. What does this mean psychologically? In the second chapter of the "Commentary on the Appended Judgments" [*Xìcízhuàn*; Jap., keijiden: 繫辞伝], it is stated that "Change *is* a sign [象]. A sign is an image [像]." "Sign" has the meaning of shape, but the Sinologist Miura Kunio translated it to mean symbol.[4] Certainly to explain all events from the mere combination of a solid horizontal line "—" and a divided horizontal line "--" is nothing but symbolic. On the other hand, "shape" designates the image when a form gives an impression to people. That is, the triagram [yáo; Jap., kō: 爻] classifies the nature of a future event or state into sixty-four types vis-à-vis the form of a sign or image that usefully serves as a symbol.

The function that emerges from out of the unconscious usually appears by taking the form of an image. For example, a dream appears in the form of an image. In this respect, we can say that a dream contains *information* that the unconscious sends to consciousness in the form of symbolic images. That the information is received in the form of symbolic images, and that the reception of that information is related to the unconscious—in regards to these two points, divination and dreams psychologically share the same characteristic. This is the reason why Freud was interested in the dream interpretation of ancient times as seen, for example, in the Old Testament in the Bible, and the title of his first work on psychoanalysis, *Traumdeutung* [*Interpretation of Dreams*], which originally meant "dream divination." The custom of such divination can be widely seen in the premodern world, regardless of East and West. However, what draws our attention in the case of China is not only that divination was spread as a popular folk custom, but also that the idea embraced in it had deeply penetrated the philosophical thought of intellectuals. Perhaps the reason for this may be sought in the fact that the nature of the *Yijing*, to put it in contemporary terms, is a kind of semiology. It is an attempt to know the symbolic image [quà; Jap., kō: 爻] as "that which signifies (signifier)," that is, *signifiant*, and to know what is behind it as "that which is signified (signified)," that is, *signifié*. In this sense, the *Yijing* is a work that points to the origin of the image-thinking represented by the Chinese culture that is based on ideographs [as I elucidated in chapter two]. The "signified" is the meaning of thing-events that is discernible in their existence in the world, and, in this case, the "significance" is whatever the diviner may learn as a human being from out of the situation encountered in the course of living his or her life. [As I discussed in chapters one and two, this "image-thinking" is an important topic in understanding "being."]

Incidentally, many dreams, as Freud thought, are the manifestation of desires repressed below consciousness. Each takes on the form of an image. In such cases, the content of the dream-image expresses the past. In contrast to this, Jung proposes that a dream contains something of a different nature. He classifies dreams into such categories as foretelling dreams, warning dreams, diagnostic dreams, and perspectival dreams. [For example,] a foretelling dream refers to a dream that intuitively knows future circumstances. If we were to follow Jung, the past and future are enfolded within the present. To be more precise, as I mentioned previously, the present is a state in which consciousness is joined with the *body*, while past and future exist latently within the unconscious at its bottom.

When Jung was thinking about the divination of the *Yìjīng*, he had another issue in mind, which had to do with the parapsychological research that began with Rhine. If there are cases such as foretelling dreams, we might surmise that the capacity, which parapsychology identifies as clairvoyance or telepathy, exists latently in the realm of the unconscious and becomes activated through some trigger on a certain occasion. In this regard, we may say that paranormal phenomena such as clairvoyance and telepathy are some of the capacities belonging to the intuition of the unconscious. Consequently, Jung was led to think that the *Yìjīng*'s divination is related to parapsychology. This issue would be considered a stumbling block for contemporary intellectuals. For the modern person disciplined in rationalistic thinking, this phenomenon of paranormal ability that parapsychology treats will appear somewhat dubious. This suspicion has something in common with the feeling felt by the intellectual in regards to the *Yìjīng*'s divination. Leaving this issue for the next chapter, I would next like to think about the *Yìjīng*'s theory of time.

THE *YÌJĪNG*'S THEORY OF TIME

In order to discuss Jung's [idea of] synchronicity, it is necessary to think about the nature and meaning of what time is. According to the *Yìjīng*, each hexagram, classified into sixty-four types, is endowed with its own indigenous "time." The "time" referred to in this case means "timing" or the "situation" of that temporal condition. The *Zhōujīzhézhōng* [Jap., *Shūekisecchū*: 周易折中], composed during the Qīng dynasty (1616–1912), divides "time" into four kinds. In order to understand the *Yìjīng*'s theory of time, let us next discuss some concrete examples.[5]

According to the *Zhōujīzhézhōng*, "time" refers to the change of phases between *yīn* and *yáng* that demonstrates a given situation from moment to moment. For example, if we look at the hexagram of "Peace," ䷊ [*tài*; Jap., *tai*: 泰], the text explains that "[t]he small departs . . . the great approaches."[6] The "Commentary on the Decision" provides an interpretation of that phrase as follows: "This means that as the *yáng-qì* of the heavens descends, and the *yīn-qì* of the earth rises and unites with *yáng-qì*, all things enter upon union and fulfillment."[7] It then judges that this corresponds to the season of January. The meaning is interpreted through the application of this hexagram to the change of seasons. Furthermore, if we follow the original thought of the "Commentary on the Decision," the hexagram of the *Yìjīng* is applicable to nature as well as human affairs. While the text of "the Judgments on the Hexagrams," that is [*Guàcí*; Jap., kaji: 卦辞] states concerning the hexagram of "Peace," ䷊, [*tài*; Jap., *tai*, 泰] that "[T]he small departs … [t]he great approaches," it explains that when this hexagram is applied to human affairs, its reading discloses a situation wherein when the aspiration of [both] the ruler and the retainers are unified, the designs of inferior people are in decline. Therefore, the *Zhōujìzhézhōng* [Jap., *Shūekisecchū*: 周易折中] cites temporal change in the condition of the natural world, as the first basic quality of "time" endowed in each hexagram. As hexagrams interpreted as belonging chiefly to this category, the following hexagrams are mentioned: "Standstill," ䷋ [*pǐ*; Jap., *hi*: 否] (July); "Splitting Apart," ䷖ [*bō*; Jap., *haku*: 剥] (September); "Return," ䷗ [*fù*; Jap., *fuku*: 復] (November), and so on.

Although the explications of the hexagram are in this way applicable to nature as well as human affairs, many signify timing in human affairs. In the *Zhōujìzhézhōng*, the following are cited as the second category: "Conflict," ䷅ [*sòng*; Jap., *shō*: 訟], which is interpreted, according to the explanation of the "Commentary on the Decision," as referring to the time when one should not fight to the end in a trial, that is, the time to avoid conflict at every turn; "the Army," ䷆ [*shī*; Jap., *shi*: 師], which refers to the time that divides victory from loss in war; "Biting Through," ䷔ [*shìkè*; Jap., *zeikō*: 噬嗑], which is a reference to the time when penalty is pronounced; "the Corners of the Mouth," ䷚ [*yí*; Jap., *i*: 頤],[8] which refers to the times such as when one eats together with others. This category is, so to speak, a hexagram relating to the mode of conduct in a situation that mobilizes a group.

As the third kind, there is the hexagram signifying the principle for individuals to make a decision to advance or retreat. [For example,] the followings are cited: "Treading," ䷉ [*lǚ*; Jap., *ri*: 履], which is the time when things move favorably; "Modesty," ䷎ [*qiān*; Jap., *ken*: 謙], which is the time when success is obtained with humility; "Influence," ䷞ [*xián*; Jap., *kan*: 咸], which is the time when one ought to be in interresonance; "Duration," ䷟ [*héng*; Jap., *kō*: 恒], which is the time when one escapes misfortune.

As the fourth kind, there is the hexagram entrusting the image of a certain thing. For example, "the Well," ䷯ [*jǐng*; Jap., *sei*: 井] symbolizes a well, and "the Caldron," ䷱ [*dǐng*; Jap., *tei*: 鼎] symbolizes a cauldron. But these are hexagrams that proscribe *a person* to wait for the [right] time like a wise man, rather than acting carelessly. (The explanations that followed each hexagram above summarize the gist of these hexagrams from the main text and the "Commentary on the Decision," but the explanations are [in fact] much more detailed and complicated. Moreover, when one actually performs divination, the explication becomes far more complex, because only one of the six divining sticks is taken to provide the main answer.)

If we look at these explanations, we can see that the *Yijing*'s divination, while designating the character of each and every situation surrounding human beings (whether as an individual or as a group), also explains how one ought to act in such a situation. In a word, divination is for the purpose of being able to appropriately act, without mistaking the timing, by knowing the circumstances in which one is currently placed.

In order to see how the *Yijing*'s divination actually works, let us cite a real example. When Jung was asked to write the preface to the English translation of his Sinologist friend Wilhelm's German translation of the *Yijing*, he posed the question of what the value of the *Yijing* may be and attempted to divine the answer by relying on the *Yijing*.[9] That is, by regarding the *Yijing* as a wise old man, he asked, "What do you think of me now?" The hexagram he obtained was "the Caldron," ䷱ [*dǐng*: 鼎]. As I briefly explained earlier, this hexagram teaches, by entrusting the image of a valuable cauldron for food, that a wise man ought to wait for the opportune moment and ought not to act haphazardly at this time. That is, the *Yijing* states that although the *Yijing* has value, this value is not yet well known, and thus one must proceed with prudence. This was, so to speak, *Yijing*'s response to Jung. In addition, prior to completing his preface, Jung asked the *Yijing* what it thought of Jung writing its preface. The *Yijing*'s response was the hexagram of "the Abysmal," ䷜ [*kǎn*; Jap., *kan*: 坎]. This hexagram entrusts the image of a deep pit, and signifies an abyss. At this time, an emphasis was placed on the third line [*quà*; Jap., *ke*: 爻], and the lesson was that: "Looking forward and backward, an abysmal pit continues one after the other. In the midst of such danger, stand and wait. Otherwise, you will fall into each further abysmal depth within the pit. You must not do this." However, in this case a continuation called a "succeeding line" [*biànquà*; Jap., *henkō*: 変爻] was added that explains future alterations. This is linked to the hexagram of "the Well," ䷯ [*jǐng*; Jap., *sei*: 井]. This is the lesson that while at present the well is filled with dirt, making its water undrinkable, a spring of life, if restored, is concealed there. The wise old man, Master *Yijing*, was warning that Jung's endeavor to inform the world of its value would plunge him into danger; that the situation was better if he would keep still. At the same time, it was answering that although at present no one knew of the value of the *Yijing*, with effort, the time would come when it would exert a significant value. Content with this response, Jung organized his preface according to its intended meaning.

The preceding will enable one to understand even in approximation how the *Yijing* thinks of "time." What is at issue for us, in this case, is how time is grasped. In the explanation of the "Judgments on the Hexagrams" [*Quàcí*, 卦辞] that is found in the "Commentary on the Decision," words that praise "time", such as "how great the time of . . . is," are frequently added at the end of a sentence. Upon examination we find that in each "Commentary on the Decision" is found, one after another, phrases emphasizing the greatness of the value of time, for example: 16 "Enthusiasm" [yù; Jap., yo: 豫], 27 "the Corners of the Mouth" [yí; Jap., i: 頤], 28 "the Great Error" [dàiguò; Jap., taika: 大過], 33 "Retreat" [dùn; Jap., ton: 遯], 38 "Opposition" [kuí; Jap., kei: 睽], 39 "Obstruction" [jiǎn; Jap., ken: 蹇], 40 "Deliverance" [xiè; Jap., kai: 解], 44 "Coming to Meet" [hòu; Jap., kō: 姤], 49 "Revolution" [gé; Jap., kaku: 革], 56 "The Wanderer" [lǚ; Jap., ryo: 旅]. Take the hexagram "Revolution," as an example, wherein water is signified by ☱ [duì; Jap., da: 兌] in the upper triagram and ☲ [lí; Jap., ri: 離] signifying fire in the lower triagram, they are explained to assail one another to give birth to reform. For this reason it is called "renovation." The old saying that "with the restoration of peace, people will be happy and become obedient" signifies that, after reform, the people will eventually become obedient with trust. The reformist has a civilizing[10] virtue, ☲ [fire; Chin., huǒ; Jap., hi: 火], and the public is happily made to become obedient, ☱ [water; Chin., shuǐ; Jap., mizu: 水]. In this way, since reform is supported by the hearts of the people, there is no regret. With reform under Heaven (i.e., on earth), the four seasons run smoothly. The reforms by King Tāng and King Wǔ responded to the hearts of the people without rebelling against the mandate of the heavens. After these statements are made, it is pronounced as a concluding remark, "how great is the time of 'reform'." The phrase, "how great is the time of . . . ," is a typical formalized phrase and gets repeated in the same way at the end of each hexagram in the "Commentary on the Decision," as mentioned earlier.

If I were to add a contemporary interpretation, we can probably say that this hexagram of "Revolution," [gé; Jap., kaku: 革] signifies the state of mass psychology that dominates over a situation of social unrest such as a revolution or civil strife. The populace always holds the psychological tendency "to become happy and obedient once peace is restored." To state it in Jungian terms, this is one characteristic endowed in the collective unconscious that transcends the individual. And if put in Hegelian terms, we can also state that it is one quality provided by the Zeitgeist [spirit of the times]. The author of the "Commentary on the Decision" is exclaiming in admiration what a great significance the "time" of "reform" has that knows in advance the situation of social change.

As has been seen, the author of this "Commentary on the Decision" emphasizes what a grave role time plays in the Yìjīng. We can see that in this case, time manifests the quality and the timing of the action that the subject ought to take under a given situation. This is how the Yìjīng conceives of time, that is, its theory of time.

One of the important points in this case is the rule by which the Yìjīng prohibits performing divination twice over the same matter. Time in the

Yijing relates to the issue of making a decision in each specific temporal situation, when one is living through one's life. This is qualitatively different from
scientific prediction. Divination is not established upon causal determinism.
Instead, determination is left to that person's free decision. In other words,
the issues of *historicity* and *ethicality* enter in here.

THE THEORY OF TIME AND THE VIEW OF NATURE

Now, what sort of a cosmology or view of nature would relate to such a theory
of time as seen in the *Yijing*? And would this teach something meaningful and
important for us today? There are two points of issue. One concerns how the
relationship between time and space is grasped, and the other deals with how
to view the relationship of human affairs and nature, that is, the human world
and the natural world. As I stated in the foregoing, this is because the hexagrams of the *Yijing* originally possess the fundamental character of divining
both human affairs and nature.

     Let us start with the time-space relationship. It has become known, due
[in part] to the [efforts of] theologian Paul Tillich, that there were two different views concerning time in ancient Greece. One is *chronos*, while the other
is *chairos*. *Chronos* refers to objective time in the usual sense of the term, that
is, physical time. (In Greek mythology, *Chronos* is the god of agriculture who
administers the seasonal changes.) When we attempt to tell time, we take
changes in the physical state of the external world as a clue. For instance, we
come to know how much time has passed by observing the situation where
spatial thing-events are known through the senses, such as the direction the
clock's hand presently points to, or the degree of change in the sun's position.
This is the measuring of the quantity of time (i.e., the length of time that can
be expressed quantitatively). When science attempts to know the characteristics or laws of natural phenomena, it employs such objective time. Bergson
states that such time is "spatialized time." He said this because the time that
flows through past-present-future is originally what the mind apprehends
through the use of memory and imagination. In this regard, the past and
future are distinctions that we human beings set up, and insofar as we think
while separating mind and matter, we are led to think that time is not something within the matter in itself of the external world. As stated earlier, this
is because we cannot know the past or future simply by relying on the body's
sensory organs.

     In this case, Bergson postulates "pure perception" as the extreme condi-
tion of the being of a body that is separated from the mind, but he postulates
in turn "pure duration" (*durée pure*) as the extreme condition of the being of
the mind that is separated from the body. This is the time (of the mind) that

flows, wherein the past and future are woven into its present. This is, when viewed psychologically, the same conscious-unconscious structure that Jung was thinking of.

Our cognition occurs where the mind as "pure duration" encounters matter as "pure perception"—that is, where the flow of time is spatialized. Bergson says that cognition, put differently, occurs when the remembered image is connected with the sensory stimulus. As this issue deals with the relationship between epistemology and the theory of the body, I will omit a detailed explanation here.[11] Stated simply, when we play the piano or type on the word processor, for example, we look at the keys and touch them (i.e., visual and tactile sensation). But when we look at the keys, we play or type while remembering (*souvenir*) the meanings of the words or notes "stored" in the subconscious (i.e., mind). In other words, cognition means the joining of perception and the recollection of memory (i.e. a function of the unconscious). While modern epistemology and science consider cognition (i.e., to know) only as a joining of perception and thinking, that is to say, an issue belonging to the conscious functions, Bergson claims that at the foundation of cognition, the function of the unconscious plays a significant role. When we take note of this point, cognition (i.e., to know) means the joining of perception and memory (i.e., the unconscious). This means objectification by extending the flow of time that is woven within the conscious-unconscious, toward external space (e.g., thing).

Although I will later address Bergson's theory of time in further details [see chapter six], I want to make a remark concerning its relation to science. Bergson once criticized Einstein's theory of relativity based on the ideas presented above. Because this critique was based on his misunderstanding of the theory of relativity, Bergson later retracted his criticism. However, there was one preconception on the side of Einstein as well. While Bergson's critique made the point that physical time is nothing but the spatialized time, Einstein was thinking the same thing from the opposing standpoint. He felt that the time that is distinguished into past, present, and future holds no meaning for science, and that time in this sense is nothing but a kind of illusion. [see the section titled "Is Time an Illusion?" in chapter six.] Because the distinction between past and future belongs to the problem of the mind, and has no bearing on the laws governing matter, he considered that this view of time is not an issue for science.

At any rate, it would seem that time is teaching us something important in thinking about the relationship between body and mind, and hence, more broadly, the relationship between matter and spirit regarding the scientific method of thinking and the unconscious that is the seat of memory and intuition. This is the issue for human beings concerning the connection between the external world and the internal world. In other words, when we assume the standpoint of the unconscious, might it not be possible to view the world from a perspective different from the scientific standpoint that has previously been assumed regarding time? This is the issue, namely, of changing the paradigm concerning the view of nature.

Now, what is the significance of the other time, *chairos*, that Tillich took up? If we consult the dictionary, although this word has meanings such as the appropriate measure or the proper ratio, it also has many usages related to time, for example, a favorable season, the proper time to act, a decisive moment, the arising of an opportunity, and so on. In short, the term signifies the quality of *timing* for the subject to act under a certain situation. While the time of *chronos* is a numerical time, quantified in light of matter, the time of *chairos* is qualitative and cannot be quantified. It is the time apprehended *in the mind* by the subject. For now, we may also call it psychological time. However, it probably cannot be reduced to a time that is merely psychological. This is because, from the traditional viewpoint of Chinese medicine, the workings of the mind and body—as long as one is alive—cannot be separated from one another. Therefore, the psychological time that the subject apprehends is connected with life-time.[12] Moreover, because such psychological life-time is the *quality of the "time"* apprehended in the *surrounding situation*, wherein a person is placed in the present, it is also connected with environmental conditions. Consequently, in this case, what becomes an issue is how the environment, such as the world or nature, is grasped.

It is evident that the *Yijing*'s theory of time is based on the time of *chairos* discussed above. As a consequence, there arises the question of how the view of time, grasped in this manner, is connected to the view of nature. This issue relates to the fundamentals of the ancient Chinese view of nature.

It is an issue requiring the examination of the intellectual history regarding Chinese philosophy. As a Chinese proverb states, "a person is a small heaven-and-earth," the primary form of the human being lies where the human being as a microcosm lives in harmony with the activity of the macrocosm. The *Yijing* assumes the view that the human being lives passively in reception of nature's *activity*, while being within the *interior* of nature. In other words, divination is possible because the human is a being that *is made to live*, while existing in nature, by receiving its activity.

Now, it is necessary for us to think through the meaning of time from the theoretical aspects of nature and human beings. There is a famous saying in the first volume of the "Commentary on the Appended Judgments" of the *Yijing* [*xìcízhuàn*, 繫辞伝]: "What is above form is called *Dào* [way; 道]; what is under form is called tool."[13] "What is above form" signifies that which is prior to form, and it is named "*Dào*," which they regarded as the source of the function that reigns over all things, in contrast to all things of the earth that are endowed with a certain form. The idea is that this source precedes material form. On the other hand, "that which is under form" signifies that which is shaped, that is, all things on earth or the world. Although this is called the "tool," it signifies a utensil. Now, what is "that which is above form" (i.e., *Dào*) related to "that which is under form (i.e., tool)"? In the same first volume of the "Commentary on the Appended Judgments," it is stated "one *yīn*, one *yáng* is called the *Dào*." "One *yīn*, one *yáng*"[14] designates the change and interchange through the *yīn-yáng* activity that sets nature in motion. The "*Dào*" is the source of this activity and the "tool" is what becomes a utensil by accepting its activity. That is, all things primordially hold the fundamental quality of being a passive receptacle that receives the activity of the "*Dào*." In order to express the *activity* of this *yīn-yáng* exchange of the "*Dào*," the word "*qì*" [Jap., *ki*: 氣] came to be used during the Hàn dynasty. In other words, the activity issuing from the primordial "*Dào*" refers to "*qì*" and by the change of phases in terms of *yīn* and *yáng*, the state of all things that are receptive to this activity constantly undergoes transformation. Because human beings are one among all things, and are consequently a receptacle for the activity of "*qì*," we come to apprehend the *Dào* by coming to know the activity of "*qì*" issuing from all things.

This sort of a view of nature is a mode of thinking that recognizes superiority on the side of nature when viewing the relationship between human beings and nature. It is diametrically opposed to the Western (especially contemporary Western) view of nature. Herein lies a view of life according to which human beings, no different from animals and plants, live in virtue of the fact that they are made to live by the activity of nature. In short, the point is that nature is fundamentally not reduced to merely matter but is a being endowed with life; a person cannot live and cannot exist here and now, unless he or she receives the activity of this life-energy. If we were to assume this view of nature, the time of the *Yìjīng* would not merely be psychological time but simultaneously would possess the characteristics of *life-time*.[15] Now, what sort of characteristic does life-time possess?

[In this connection, I would like to examine the German word, *Zeit*, although I plan to deal with it in further details in reference to Heidegger's theory of time in chapter six.] Time in German is called *Zeit*, and the adjective *zeitig* and the verb *zeitigen* are derived from it. *Zeitig* means "opportune," "well-timed," "in time," and is equivalent to "timely" in English. This refers to the time of *chairos*. The use of the verb *zeitigen* is unique to German, and has the meaning of "to ripen," "to mature," and as a medical terminology is used with the meaning of "to inflame." The noun-form of this verb, *Zeitigung*, posseses the meaning of "maturation." The living organism is born, grows with time, matures, and in due course declines and reaches death. This time is a qualitative time that *constantly changes its characterstics*, and is not merely a physical time that is quantitative and possesses homogeneity. The ancient Chinese viewed time, in this sense, as life-time.

THE TRADITIONAL VIEWS OF NATURE OF THE EAST AND THE WEST; ARE SPACE AND TIME SEPARABLE?

It seems that when Tillich divided time into two categories, he had in mind the contrast between the mythological view of time and the Christian view of time.[16] According to him, mythological time is like a closed circle without beginning or end, and is based on the worldview in which the world eternally repeats the same states. This is because human beings of mythical ages believed in various primordial powers symbolized by the "Great Earth," and was psychologically tied to them. What he means by the "various primordial powers" probably refers to the nurturing power of nature *qua* life that gives birth to all things.

In the *Lǎozǐ*, it is stated that the *"Dào"* is like a mother who fosters and nurtures all things. If we borrow the terminology from mythology, this has the image of the Mother Earth, the Goddess, who symbolizes the maternal Great Earth. The ancient Chinese view of nature has a flavor that has refined the mythological view of nature into a philosophical theory. While the time of *chairos* is the time in which life is born, matures, and declines, there is no beginning or end in this sort of mythological time. Events of the world eternally repeat in the same way.

Christianity destroys this cyclic nature of time that has no beginning or end. It claims that the world began from God's creation out of nothing [*creatio ex nihilo*], and that the world will come, in due time, to the *eschaton* at the end of time, and will receive God's "last judgment." (The idea of eschatology that the world will reach its end first appeared in the later period of Judaism, and Jesus believed in this idea as well. And the doctrine of "creation out of nothing" was started by the Christian Church fathers during the second to fourth centuries CE.) If the world has a beginning and an end in this way, time would not be considered a closed circle but rather would possess the characterstics of a beginning point and a terminating point. If we see the world in light of this view of time, the meaning of the events of the world would come to be known only in terms of the linear progression of time. The idea of causality that attempts to clarify the meaning of phenomena in terms of the cause–effect relationship also presupposes this sort of time. This is because the cause is that which is temporally prior, while the effect is that which is temporally posterior. The view of nature of modern science presupposes this theory of time. If we view this in light of intellectual history, it would seem that Christianity and modern science stood in what may be called a relationship of incestuous hatred, as the modern scientific view of nature emerged from repeated violent confrontations with Christianity. We can see therein the common idea that linear time controls the movement of the cosmos. We may say that modern science was born from a development of this view of time in the West. In this respect, we can state that the Christian view of nature is what gave birth to modern science.

What is important here is that God is placed *above* the world. The God of Christianity is called the "Creator" and, in distinction from this, the world by contrast is regarded as "creature," that is, something that is created by God. This means that God made the world from above the world, or, in a word, from where there is nothing. Consequently, God *transcends* the world and exists outside of it. Moreover, it is held in Christianity that the human being "was made in the image of God" (*imago dei*), and is considered to be closer to God than are plants and animals, and matter. (This is a doctrine based on the myth of Genesis, according to which God made Adam out of earth.) Consequently, the human being, like God, is able to stand *outside* of the world in order to observe it and theorize it. The modern scientific view of nature thrives where there is such a connection between the view of humanity and the idea of what is called in Greek philosophy *"theōria"* (i.e., theory, or observation). Here, the human being becomes the epistemological subject who observes nature, whereas nature is objectified as its object. When seen in this manner, the human being becomes a being who stands above nature. [Accordingly, the human being comes to be defined as a "being-above or outside-of-nature."] The modern Western view of nature gradually formed in such a way.

The ancient Chinese view of nature is the exact opposite. The human being as the incarnate subject who views the world, is *within* nature, and is a *passive being* who is made to live by nature's life-power. [It is conceived to be a "being-in-nature."] Time, in this case, is the time of *chairos*. Now, in what way is this sort of time related to nature?

There is a strong tendency amongst Sinologists to think that there is no pure theory of time in Chinese thought. "Pure" in this case may alternatively be called "abstract." In short, it means that there is no attitude for *logically* thinking about time, separate from all experience.[17] To take a concrete example, what Newton calls "absolute time" and "absolute space" are forms without any content; they are, as it were, an empty time and an empty space. Although it may sound strange to speak of "empty time," it is a contentless time that is thought in the same way as the [absolute] space is thought without anything. Newtonian physics views nature first by presupposing this sort of time and space. Based on Newton's idea, Kant stated that time and space are a priori forms of cognition. The point is that when cognizing nature as object, there is such a necessity to think of time and space beforehand, prior to any experience. This was the starting point for the modern scientific way of thinking.

However, in China there never was a mode of thinking since ancient times that grasped time and space as such contentless forms. Time meant the "time" (timing) that bears the life-psychological characteristics as shown in the theory of time of the *Yijing*. Thus, space is also a space that bears definite life characteristics, that is, it is given the characteristic of "maturation," *Zeitigen*. If this is so, it does not mean that the world originally existed in the midst of a time and space where there is nothing, but rather must be grasped as being filled with all things from the [beginningless] beginning. In other words, the essence of time and space must be grasped from the perspective of the total *activity* found within the interior of the world. Time-space is the life-activity that exists behind all that is formed in the world as a whole. And by descending into the bottom of the unconscious, a person as an incarnate subject can have an intuitive lived- experience of that activity.

If we think of the relationship of time and space in this way, we can no longer think of them as being separate. Time and space are bound together as one in this *activity*. What Jung calls synchronicity is predicated on this view of space-time. By receiving a hint from Einstein's theory of relativity, he came to call it the space-time continuum. He thinks that the *Yijing*'s view of nature sees nature as the field of the unitary function of the space-time that is inseparable.

To be a little more exact, he received a hint regarding the space-time relationship previously stated from the special theory of relativity (the relationship of energy and mass designated by the well-known formula $E = mc^2$). Herein is discovered "space-time" as the four-dimensional energy system in which the one dimension of time and the three dimensions of space are unified. However, if we were to contrast this with Einstein's view of nature, the general theory of relativity that expands the idea of four-dimensional space-time into a cosmology is probably more appropriate than the special theory of relativity. Cosmic space generates a warp in this four-dimensional space-time through the existence of matter and its activity, and the movement of time becomes slow.

Although it may seem very strange, this view of the cosmos agrees remarkably well with the traditional Chinese view of the cosmos. According to the idea of the gravitational field in the general theory of relativity, when there is an object within it, space becomes warped. However, if it is fundamentally unthinkable to conceive of space where there is no matter existing in its interior, time and space must be unified in their *activity* as one. Put differently, time and space immanently carry some sort of energy-like activity within their interior. In regard to time, the Chinese thought that there is a life-power for "maturation" latently existing in life. Moreover, they believed that space is that which is filled with all things and is where they grow in virtue of that power. This is the relationship between "that which is above form" and "that which is under form," as the *Yìjīng* sees it.

What accurately expresses ancient Chinese cosmology is the Chinese character for "cosmos" [*yǔzhòu*; Jap., *uchū*: 宇宙]. The Chinese characters were a product of the intuitive image-thinking which the ancient Chinese embraced. Now, what sort of image was it that served as the source for the word "cosmos"?[18] In a fragment of a book called *Shīzǐ* [Jap., *Shishi*: 尸子] that was written during the Warring States period (fourth century BCE), it is stated: "the four directions, up and down, are called *yǔ* [宇] and coming and going, old and new, is called *zhòu* [宙]." That is, *yǔ* signifies space and *zhòu* [宙] signifies time. We can find even in the *Wénzǐ* [Jap., *Monji*: 文子] that is said to be produced before the Táng dynasty (seventh century) the statement: "Lǎozǐ says, coming and going, old and new, this is *zhòu* [宙], the four directions, up and down, are called *yǔ* [宇]." From this we can tell that the expression of *yǔzhòu*, indicating an integration of time and space, was already generally accepted from antiquity. In other words, from ancient times the Chinese had held the image of the cosmos as a space-time continuum. (The term "cosmos" [*yǔzhòu*; Jap., *uchū*: 宇宙], can already be seen, for example, in the *Zhuāngzǐ*.)

To be more concrete, the character for *yǔ*, according to the dictionary called the *Shuōyánxièzì* [Jap., *Setsumonkaiji*: 説文解字] of the later Hàn dynasty (first to second century), means the eaves of a house and refers to "the four pillars supporting a roof." In the *Yìjīng*, it is stated that "by putting up the ridge-pole above, and putting down the rafter below, wind and rain are avoided." That is, space was expressed by the character *yǔ* [宇], signifying the situation in which the eaves extend to the outside beneath the ridge-pole supporting the roof of the house. And the character *zhòu* [宙] is explained as "the place where boats and carts travel in undulation," but this carries a meaning with an image in which vehicles, such as boats and carts, move to and fro, going here and there, and going round and round. The point is that time is discovered in the midst of incessantly repeating *movement*.

To add one more comment, the terms that designate the structure of the world by means of "time" and "space" are modern ones. "Time" originally had the meaning of the "four seasons" (spring, summer, fall, and winter), and "space" derives from the character signifying "pit" [穴], that is, the caves or the interior of huts with dirt floors where ancient people dwelled. Spring, summer, fall, and winter, designate the operations of nature, and the cave is the place that the human species, after evolving from apes, made into a dwelling place. In short, the Chinese have considered nature and the human being as unified by its energy-activity since ancient times, rather than thinking of time and space by conceptually separating them.

SPACE AND THE ENERGY IMMANENT IN TIME

Now, as I mentioned earlier, the *Yìjīng*'s divination does not mean that it infers the future by observing events of the external world through the senses. It is the project of attaining a feeling-apprehension of the future state through intuition arising from the unconscious. That is, divination attempts to know the characteristics of the operation of time that mobilizes all things, changes them, and brings them to maturation. Accordingly, in this case, time stores within it a certain energy or power, which brings maturation to living organisms and changes them. The activity of this energy has been called "*qì*" [Jap., *ki*: 氣]. And all that is in space, by receiving this activity, changes while growing, becoming mature, and waning. Divination is possible because one oneself is the vessel of such activity, and because it receives (i.e., in the region of the body and the unconscious) the *qì*-energy issuing from the cosmos. In this case, time is the *activity* that generates change, while space that is filled with all things stands in relation with time, in virtue of which changes occur and all things go through generation. The philosopher Spinoza thought that nature is where the two dimensions of productive nature (i.e., *natura naturans*) and produced nature (i.e., *natura naturata*) become one. If we borrow these terminologies, we may consider the activity of time as productive nature, and the field of space as the produced nature that moves all things.

At this point, we need to think about nature from the side of space. Because all thing-events that are in space are alive on the basis of the activity of the "*qì*" that issues from the primordial "*Dào*," it means that all the thing-events of the world receive *qì*-energy with fundamentally the same quality at a certain point in time or in a time-zone. While *qì* constantly changes its phase, within a certain time-zone, it preserves a definite quality. Therefore, all things are tied together as qualitatively one with one another by way of the energy of *qì*, in the space of that definite time-zone. That is, an energy of the same quality that ties all things together as one in the same time-zone, permeates, and is active throughout the whole of space. Therefore, an invisible power operates within space that makes even thing-events appearing far and distant from one another resonate and synchronize with one another. Jung called the standpoint that views nature from such a relationship "synchronicity."

In synchronized swimming, [ideally] the hands and feet of two or more swimmers are synchronized and move simultaneously without the slightest discrepancy. We may call such a state simultaneous synchronization. The perspective of synchronicity is such that it grasps such a state as a synchronization of time and space—on the basis of the relation of the function to its field. Here, an invisible energy penetrates space as a whole, and its power is working even among things separated far from one another. The divination of the *Yijing* is the feeling-apprehension of such a state, as the world changes via the intuitive cognition of the working of an invisible power. To use historical terminology, this designates the thought of the "correlativity between Heaven and humans" that emerged during the Hàn dynasty. This is the idea in which the relationship between nature and the human being (i.e., the human body) is inherently endowed with [the power of] interresonance and harmonization.

What concretely demonstrates such an idea is the custom of naming an era, invented by the Chinese. Although the institution of naming eras was begun during the period of Emperor Wǔ during the Hàn dynasty (second century CE), in Japan it was institutionalized starting from the Taika Reformation (645 CE) to the Nara period (710 CE–784 CE). If we look at the names of eras of this period, we find that many names bear the name of rare animals or natural phenomena such as the red bird or white phoenix, white pheasant, divine tortoise, and auspicious cloud. Such names of eras were based on a divination technique called "*yīnyángdào*" [Jap., *inyōdō*: 陰陽道] and unusual natural phenomena were considered to be auspicious signs. The belief of that period held that when politics are being conducted rightfully, Heaven made these auspicious signs appear as a commendation. Accordingly, when politics are being conducted wrongfully, Heaven passes misfortune and punishes the sovereign. As is seen, the name of an era is a symbolic expression for showing in this way what state the world is in as a whole in the present time-zone. In this case, the important point that matters is that there is an invisible power operative among spatially separated thing-events. Despite the fact that a red bird or a white pheasant appeared far away from the capital where the emperor resides, Heaven made them appear in order to praise his political conduct. This [was taken to] mean that an invisible power that interresonates and harmonizes with human conduct is operative throughout space as a whole.

What sort of a view of space-time is at the foundation of the custom of naming the eras? Alvin Toffler says that the concept of time varies in accordance with culture. However, the social sciences have not yet come up with such a theory of time. He claims that in order to think of the future of history such a theory of time is necessary, and he advocates the idea of "durational expectancies." This refers to the culturally based assumptions concerning the extent of how long we may think a process will last.[19] This [also] signifies the time-zone in which history and society come to maturation, and change. Naming eras is determined on the basis of such a viewpoint.

In history, there are times of peace and security when nothing changes, and there are periods when the state of the world changes at once. Revolutions and wars are examples of this. In such times, the entire world feverishly falls into a state of madness. This is a state where the psychological and vital energy latent within the group has exploded. Jung repeatedly had a dream around the time right before the First World War began, in which Europe sinks into a deluge, and crumbles and disappears. He came to realize afterwards that those dreams were foretelling the occurrence of the war. Our unconscious intuitively *knows* the future toward which the world moves, even though consciousness may not be aware of it.

This sort of idea resembles what Hegel called *Zeitgeist*. It is an activity like that of a great spirit that resides at the bottom of the period as a whole moving the world. The thing-events of space are moved by this invisible power and, disregarding the will of each individual, move in a definite direction and go on to change. From the standpoint of psychology, Jung called the foundation out of which such a function emerges the collective unconscious.

To summarize in a word what I have stated above, the time of the *Yijing* is life-time and it expands to a cosmic dimension. And such a view is commensurate with the view held by the cutting edge of contemporary science. Although this may sound quite odd, this is what Jung believed. However there [still] remains in the end, an *aporia*. That is, does the *Yijing*'s divination succeed or not?[20] Since this issue parts from the content of the *Yijing*, I would like to investigate it in the next chapter.

Translator's Note

In the preceding two chapters, Yuasa's examination of synchronicity was concerned with theoretically articulating how it occurs. In the following chapter (chapter five) he examines synchronicity and spiritualism. Behind Yuasa's account of this topic is the concern to respond to the practical question of whether there is such a thing as the prediction of a future event. This question strikes at the root of the issues surrounding Jung's theory of synchronicity and paranormal phenomena.

CHAPTER FIVE

Synchronicity and Spiritualism

THE BIRTH OF THE THEORY OF SYNCHRONICITY

In advocating the idea of synchronicity, Jung also thematized topics besides the *Yijing*, such as astrology and parapsychology, that deal with paranormal phenomena (so-called paranormal abilities). If there is such a thing as paranormal phenomena, or if astrological divination can accurately foretell a future event,[1] perhaps the *Yijing*'s divination may also be said to do the same. But can this really be? When we proceed to think about Jung's proposal, we cannot avoid encountering this difficult issue.

An interpretation of the *Yijing* clarifies the theoretical aspect regarding synchronicity. What we dealt with in the last chapter was primarily this issue. In contrast, he took up parapsychology and astrology as material in order to explain the idea of synchronicity from the aspect of empirical fact. Because they belong to the field of research that has hitherto been placed outside of academic scholarship, there were not only a few occasions when researchers, even among Jungians, placed a question mark upon them. While holding a negative opinion about astrology, I have come to think that there is a necessity to take up parapsychology.

It would seem that the following two points are the main reasons why parapsychology has a difficult time in being accepted in the academic world. One point is that it has a close association with occultism. It was the American psychologist Joseph B. Rhine (1895–1980) who first attempted to study paranormal phenomena by means of the scientific method. And the one who inspired Rhine's interest in paranormal phenomena was his teacher, William McDougal, [as I mentioned in chapter three]. [There I noted that] when studying in continental Europe, the young McDougal was in contact with Freud and Jung. He became interested in psychic research, which was at the time fashionable in Europe, and he even worked for a while as the president of the [British] Society for Psychical Research. After coming to the United States, he lectured on psychology at Harvard University and spread psychoanalysis in America.[2] Rhine was his student of that period. Later McDougal transferred to Duke University (North Carolina), taking Rhine with him, and founded the Parapsychology Laboratory.[3] This was the start of parapsychology in America.

As the above fact shows, parapsychology undoubtedly has an history of emerging from the womb of psychic research. However, Rhine suspended any judgment concerning issues such as the continual subsistence of the soul after death, which psychic research had advocated, and he assumed the attitude of neither affirming nor denying it. This theme is an issue fundamentally different in nature from academic research. It is a matter of concern that belongs to the individual's faith or conviction. Although it is the case that the general public, unable to adequately comprehend such distinctions, vaguely superimpose parapsychology and occultism, it is a mistake, theoretically speaking, to think of it in that way. The appropriateness of parapsychology is an issue that ought to be considered apart from the evaluation of occultism.

The other reason for academia's rejection of parapsychology may be that it triggers a feeling of resistance from modern people who are raised with the rationalistic way of thinking. If we inquire historically after the ground [of this resistance], it will lead us to Descartes. Ever since the separation of mind and matter in Descartes' mind-matter dualism, that separation has become regarded as a matter of fact. Since then it has become dominant in scientific research to think that research must proceed according to the model of natural science, which studies material phenomena. It was on the basis of such a stance that a strong opposition was initially voiced, even against Freudianism and psychosomatic medicine, which recognizes the uniqueness of the activity of the mind. However, while these fields deal with the relationship between mind and body (generally speaking, the realm of the living organism), parapsychology claims that there can be, in some sense, a direct relationship between psychological function and physical function. In this respect, it may be said that parapsychology accompanies a movement that attempts to directly alter, from its root, the major premise, that is, mind-body dualism, that stands at the foundation of modern empirical science and philosophy, which has established a long tradition since Descartes. Herein lies, it would seem, the theoretical reason why modern intellectuals resist parapsychology.

I would like to omit an explanation on the contemporary situation of Rhinean parapsychology.[4] Although he recognizes that there is an important significance in Rhine's research, Jung held a critical attitude toward its method and its premise. Let us first take note of the process whereby Jung came to accept the idea of synchronicity.

While Rhine's research began in the 1930s, Jung was already in contact with Rhine from this period through the exchange of letters, and was quite familiar with his research content[5] [as was already mentioned in chapter three]. Although Jung continued to decline Rhine's request that he publicize his opinion concerning paranormal phenomena, in his private correspondence with Rhine, Jung variously expressed his ideas in response to Rhine's questions. In a letter of November 1947, he approximately states the following[6]: (1) Parapsychology belongs to the psychology of the unconscious. (2) The psychology of the unconscious has to do with mind-body correlativity. One such example is the case of psychic phenomena wherein the mind exercises an influence upon matter. (3) Parapsychology demonstrates that the *psychē* (consciousness-unconscious as a whole) involves the aspect of the relativity of time and space. (4) Although there is no useful relationship between parapsychology and psychopathology, it is a significant issue. Paranormal phenomena often occur in the initial stages of psychosis, but they stop appearing as the disease advances. (5) The relativity of time and space means that it has, to a certain extent, escaped the dominance of causality. Precognition does not mean a denial of freedom. And ESP (i.e., extra-sensory perception) emerges with the collective unconscious as its field.

Jung's reason why he did not publicize his opinion on paranormal phenomena is that, if he discussed such things, he would be considered crazy. However, [as I observed in chapter three] in his later years, he changed his mind, and published an essay that praises Rhine's research along with his hypothesis on synchronicity.[7] The background that led Jung to make his ideas about parapsychology public was the encouragement he received from the physicist Pauli, the recipient of the 1945 Nobel Prize in physics. Having gone through severe neurotic state due to his mother's suicide and a divorce, he was treated by Jung at one time. Part one of Jung's *Psychology and Alchemy* was devoted to a dream analysis of a patient who was an intellectual, and it is now known that this patient was Pauli.[8] After he received treatment and recovered, Pauli, with an interest in Jung's psychology, repeatedly engaged in discussions with him. This is the reason why Jung's essay on synchronicity was published in collaboration with Pauli.

In an essay contributed to an [aforementioned] anthology commemorating Jung's eightieth birthday, published in 1954, Pauli states: "Now it seems to me very remarkable that the most recent tendency in the psychology of the unconscious, namely that represented by C. G. Jung, has developed in the direction of *recognizing the nonpsychical in connection with the problem of psycho-physical unity*."[9] What he says here is that psychology is coming to acknowledge and accept something "nonpsychological" and that it has taken up the "integration of the psychological and the physical" as an issue. This refers to paranormal phenomena. Pauli states that Jung takes the issue of ESP (e.g., clairvoyance, telepathy, etc.) into consideration, and he came to make a "decisive change," since 1946, on his idea of the archetype (the collective unconscious). What is the meaning of all this?

Up to that time, Jung considered what he called the collective unconscious in light of time. That is, this is the idea that at the base of the individual's unconscious, there resides a structure that we may call psychic inheritance. Taking the individual as a starting point, each person has ancestors, and is endowed with a definite disposition by means of the inheritance of psychological characteristics. As the saying "a frog's child is a frog" goes, a child at some point takes over the parents' characteristics. (Because the scientific study of genes is based upon causality, there is a tendency to think in terms of deterministic causal relationships with a sense of necessity, but this is not the case with psychological inheritance.) If we expand such psychological inheritance from the individual to the group, it would become, for example, the psychological characteristics of a racial group as a whole. The characteristics of race indicate such a phenomenon. In this case, the psychological characteristics that are historically inherited, beyond the individual, are called the collective unconscious. That is, the collective unconscious, when viewed in light of time, may be called the *historical* unconscious.

What Pauli calls Jung's "decisive change" is this expansion of such an idea of the collective unconscious into *space*. The collective unconscious is, as it were, a deep and immense unconscious that spreads beyond the confines of the individual being (i.e., mind and body). Jung's "decisive change" is that he proceeded to think of it not only in light of time, but also in light of space.

[Although I made the following point in chapter three, Let me reiterate it here.] If the field of the unconscious functions spreads out in space, that means that even among persons who are mutually distant from one another, there is an invisible power connecting them at the unconscious level. Such a function, it would be surmised, is strongly operative among persons who are psychologically close to each other, such as parents and children, husband and wife, friends, or doctor and patient, and so forth. Jung had frequently experienced paranormal phenomena such as clairvoyance, telepathy, and foretelling dreams, and these were mostly cases involving situations such as a patient's death, his children being in a state of danger, his mother's death, etc. According to the research of parapsychologists, intuitive cognition as in these cases is known to become activated even amongst ordinary people in such critical situations. This means that even though consciousness may not be aware of it, *the unconscious sends information* to the surrounding world and, moreover, receives information that is sent. If such a network of information is latent in the unconscious domain, we theoretically have an explanation, after a fashion, for the reason why paranormal phenomena occur.

However, the issue is not so simple. In the aforementioned essay that he contributed to the anthology commemorating Jung's eightieth birthday, Pauli expresses one reservation, while highly praising Jung's "decision." The point is that the issue of the living organism that is positioned between psychology and physics has not been taken into consideration. He states as follows: "the dream ... is ... a psychophysical process, insofar as physiological processes in the brain necessarily accompany it."[10] If the brain is a life-phenomenon consisting of matter and if the psychological process accompanies it, perhaps we may be able to progress one step further by considering the issue of life [-phenomena] in regard to the relationship between psychology and physics. Because this is a point that both Jung and Rhine overlooked, it is a point worthy of our attention. Furthermore, concerning life[-phenomena], Pauli says the following. If the characteristic of "moving toward a goal" comes to play a significant role, which is the feature of the living organism, that is, teleology and wholeness (i.e., the characteristic of defying segmentation into parts), we physicists would sufficiently feel our inadequacy in understanding even the events that stand upon material foundation. Neils Bhor inferred that when we add the condition that a living organism must retain its state while sustaining its life, the repeatability and applicability of laws of quantum physics related to the inorganic matter, have, in principle, a limitation in cases when the laws of quantum physics take a measurement in connection to the living organism. Although Bhor's remark is circumlocutory, a simpler statement would probably be as follows: if the measured object happens to be a living organism, there can be no perfect objectivity belonging to the detected data (i.e., a numerical value derived from the repeatability of an experiment that is based on the materialistic stance). Here Pauli touches on purposiveness, that is, the idea of teleology that is contrasted with [mechanistic] causality. Teleology is a principle that has been expelled from modern science.

In investigating the relationship between the idea of synchronicity and science, I anticipate that henceforth this will probably become the most significant theoretical issue. However, for this to occur, it will probably become necessary to conduct further detailed research and investigation regarding the theory of the body and of life science.

Another task is the factual issue of how to *prove* the existence of paranormal phenomena as insisted by parapsychology. Jung himself was convinced that the *Yijīng*'s divination is accurate. Although it was [only] after he met Richard Wilhelm in 1920 that Jung became earnestly interested in the *Yijīng*, even prior to this meeting, Jung was already grappling with the practical technique of *Yijing*'s divination with help from Legge's old English translation. He reportedly practiced divination of the *Yijing* in 1920 through the course of one summer by cutting a bundle of reeds in lieu of yarrow stalks. "My only concern was whether the *Yijing*'s method of divination is actually applicable, and whether it is effective."[11] On the basis of his own experiments, Jung found that the *Yijing*'s divination indicated a higher probability of success than can be thought of as resulting from mere coincidence.

> Thus I am critical of the thought that the success of the *Yijing*'s divination is a mere fluke. It seems that the apparent number of hit-marks I experienced is way beyond the probability based on chance. In short, I believe and do not doubt that what becomes an issue in the *Yijing* is not *coincidence but regularity*.[12] [emphasis added]

Jung states that the rate of hit-marks in divination is beyond "probability based on chance." While we may say that this is a fact experienced by himself, can such a conviction, as that of Jung, really be universalized? Rhine developed the method of ESP experiments and attempted to demonstrate the existence of paranormal phenomena on the basis of the theory of probability. However, Jung's view is that this problem cannot be solved by appealing to this method. This is because reliance on the theory of probability would be to take the stance of causality that forms the foundation of hitherto held scientific thought. In his 1930 memorial lecture for Wilhelm, he mentioned the translation and commentary of the *Yijing* as Wilhelm's greatest scholarly contribution. In addition to stating that a certain type of principle of "science" may be discerned in the *Yijing*'s worldview, Jung states that this does not rest upon the principle of causality but rather on an undiscovered principle that he calls "the synchronistic principle" (*das synchronistische Prinzip*).

> My occupation with the psychology of unconscious processes long ago necessitated my casting around for another explanatory principle, because the causality principle seemed to me inadequate for the explanation of certain remarkable phenomena of the unconscious. Thus I found that there are psychic parallelisms which cannot be related to each other causally, but which must stand in another sort of connectedness. This connection seemed to me to lie mainly in the relative simultaneity of the events, therefore the expression "synchronistic." It seems, indeed, as though time, far from being an abstraction, is a concrete continuum which contains qualities or basic conditions manifesting themselves simultaneously in various places in a way not to be explained by causal parallelism, as, for example, in cases of the coincident appearance of identical thoughts, symbols, or psychic states.[13]

As he received encouragement from Pauli in this way, Jung made public in his later years (around 1950), his hypothesis of synchronicity, which he had been hesitant to do while holding it in his mind for a long time. Therein is embedded his thought for the succeeding age to come.

A REEXAMINATION OF THE
PARAPSYCHOLOGICAL DISPUTES

Jung evaluated as extremely significant the fact that Rhine insisted on the existence of paranormal phenomena and presented this as an object of academic research. However, he did not follow Rhine's thought, but took a critical stance toward it. Where does this kind of attitude of Jung's come from? In order to think about this point, it is necessary to examine Rhinean parapsychology anew.

Rhinean parapsychology assumes the stance of proving the existence of paranormal phenomena by following the methodology of previously held experimental science. One criticism about their proof is that the experimental result lacks repeatability. According to the formerly held standpoint of science, a scientific experiment must always yield the same result regardless of who and where it is conducted. However, no such stable results obtain in the experiments of parapsychology. Even though others attempt to conduct the same experiment suggestive of a high degree of causal relationship, the same result is not yielded. In other words, the follow-up experiment is incapable of ascertaining whether or not the hypothesis was valid.

Careful thought would reveal that this is naturally the case. The Rhinean method assumes the standpoint of postulating that the person on whom the experiment is conducted (i.e., the subject) possesses a certain psychological capacities (i.e., paranormal abilities). And with this as a cause, it assumes that such a subject can produce results that can be objectively cognizable via sensory perception, such as ESP (e.g., clairvoyance, telepathy, etc.) and PK (e.g., pscyhokinesis). Because anyone is conceived to potentially possess, to a certain degree, such abilities, it is difficult to exclude the possibility of the psychological function not only of the subject but also of the experimenter or the observer coming into play in the course of the experiment. Moreover, such psychological functions include portions of the unconscious. In other words, unless the conscious-unconscious psychological functions of all participants are sufficiently controlled, the result of parapsychological experiments cannot but be unstable. Therefore, we must say that as long as we observe the previously held standpoint and methodology of experimental science that assumes the standpoint of causality, proof of the existence of paranormal phenomena is theoretically nothing but uncertain.

Another issue surrounding the proof of the existence of paranormal phenomena is the so-called hypothesis of fraud propounded by those who deny it, that is, the claim that the experiments of paranormal abilities involve a sleight of hand. This claim is based on the idea that there are cases wherein experiments were conducted fraudulently, or that the same result can be obtained through trickery. This claim clearly contains a leap of logic. In order to sufficiently verify the hypothesis of fraud as the basis of the opposition, it must be demonstrated that *all* experiments in parapsychology performed up to now have been conducted under fraudulent means. However, this is impossible. Because the hypothesis of fraud presupposes that "there may have been foul play," no matter how rigorously the experiment is controlled by those who affirm it, since all that is required is to raise a new hypothesis of fraud, the opposition can do so as much as they want. There is no necessity to prove the hypothesis of fraud itself. In other words, this dispute carries the characteristic of an argument that can never be brought to a closure. While such disputes regarding the existence or nonexistence of paranormal phenomena have been repeated for the last hundred years, no progress has been made in the content of the argument regardless of the number of disputes conducted. At present, a great number of people, in fact, seem to hold the opinion that ESP (i.e. clairvoyance) may be acknowledged. However, the opposition also tenaciously remains.

In short, although many positive results are obtained when researchers recognizing the existence of paranormal phenomena conduct experiments, there always remains something theoretically ambiguous when seen from the perspective of a person holding a negative standpoint. This was noted early on by the psychologist William James who had researched paranormal phenomena, and Colin Wilson half-jokingly called this the "law of William James."[14]

Borrowing the terminology of the philosophy of science, this means that a paranormal phenomenon has the characteristic of being a phenomenon that is unable to yield to crucial experiments. A crucial experiment is an experiment that determines whether a certain hypothesis is correct or not, true or false. The theories of natural science are fundamentally built on the accumulation of crucial experiments. (For example, Einstein's hypothesis of the gravitational field was determined to be correct by measuring the curvature of light passing by the moon during a solar eclipse.) That the results of parapsychological experiments are unstable signifies the situation that, when the function of the mind participates in material phenomena, a crucial experiment itself becomes impossible.

From a different viewpoint, this means that there exist phenomena with the characteristic that does not yield decisive answers, as long as we follow the standpoint and method of experimental science. In the philosophy of science, the theory-ladenness is advocated. This means that in the standpoint of scientific research, there are certain theoretical conditions as premises, and we can observe and interpret the phenomena only on the basis of that paradigm. The method of today's experimental science stands on the premise of judging on the basis of the either–or logic of "either truth or false," "either this or that." The contemporary science of logic insists that logic describe the truth–falsity of a proposition. In contrast, paranormal phenomena show that there are phenomena with characteristics that cannot be accommodated by such a paradigm. If that is so, we probably need to approach them from a standpoint different from the previously held paradigm. There is no special necessity for mounting a rebuttal against the claims of those who deny paranormal ability. Because each of the theories of pros and cons, is disputing one another within the paradigm of hitherto held scientific thought, we can probably take up this issue from a perspective that is fundamentally different from them. Jung thinks that there is the necessity for such a new approach.

"MEANINGFUL COINCIDENCE" AND HUMAN LIFE

Jung's conception of synchronicity was so named in contrast to causality. Causality is the principle that indicates the rationalistic mode of thinking that is in agreement with the previously held standpoint of science. In other words, Jung, in advocating his idea of synchronicity, is insisting that it is possible to hold a view of human beings and a cognition of the world different from the previously maintained paradigms of science and modern rationalistic thinking.

Since Jung himself had directly experienced paranormal phenomena such as clairvoyance and telepathy, he knew that such phenomena exist. However, rather than demonstrating that such phenomena exist, he was more interested in the type of mechanism that allows for the occurrence of such phenomena. Thereby he thought, by taking note of the unconscious, that the field of the unconscious functions extends beyond the individual both temporally and spatially. He thought of the paranormal phenomenon as *one instance* of the various phenomena that occur within the field of such a spatial expanse of the unconscious. Synchronicity signifies the coincidence in meaning-content of information in regard to events occurring in spatially separate places within a definite time-zone or in consecutive points in time. For example, cognition via telepathy means the knowledge of an event occurring in a place spatially separate [from one's own place] (without relying upon any physical means of transmission of information) almost simultaneously [to its occurrence].

Consequently, the idea of synchronicity is not always applied to merely paranormal phenomena. For example, the phenomenon of mind-body correlativity is one instance wherein synchronicity is operative as well. Needless to say, pathological conditions of psychological nature are recognized to trigger physical pathological conditions by means of certain psychological conditions as the cause (e.g., stress). However, even in such a case, it is possible to see that in regard to the mind-body relationship *as a whole*, there occurs the simultaneous synchronistic function between mind and body, between psychological function and physiological function, with the unconscious as its field. Moreover, the idea of synchronicity can be grasped at the level of society. During a certain period (e.g., the contemporary period), unrelated people, living in different places here and there without having any connection whatsoever, begin to entertain ideas that are alike. Such psychological conditions of society, or grand movements as the spirit of the times, can also be seen as expressions of synchronicity. Accordingly, it has a bearing on the mind-body relationship that medicine addresses at the individual level, through issues of social phenomena, all the way to issues concerning the view of human beings and the view of nature. This is the reason why Jung questioned Rhine's idea that adheres to the paradigm of causality. In other words, he thought that rather than assuming a narrow perspective that seeks recognition from the academic world for the research in paranormal phenomena as a branch of experimental psychology, it is necessary to deal with it as a larger issue that has a bearing on the revolution of how to view human beings and nature, including such domains as medicine, history, society, physics, and religion.

In this case, because [the issue of] paranormal phenomena relates directly to the relationship between psychological phenomena and physical phenomena, it plays the role of a "frontline soldier" that seeks to modify the hitherto held view concerning the whole relationship between human beings and nature. In this sense, this issue carries a grave significance. It plays the role of, as it were, an explosive trigger for changing the paradigm of this period. This is probably all the more the reason that resistance to it is so strong. In short, the domain of influence that it exercises goes far beyond the domain that the psychologist guards. The significance of this issue is glimpsed by the fact that today interest in paranormal phenomena is gradually spreading amongst physicists, engineers, and medical doctors.

Rhine utilized the method of probability computation to prove the existence of paranormal phenomena. For example, when one conducts ESP experiments on psychics, this method of demonstration contends that ESP exists because of the high rate of hit results such that they cannot be considered as mere accidental coincidence (flukes). By contrast, Jung thought it possible to distinguish that coincidence by chance into meaningless coincidence and meaningful coincidence. This is not an issue of quantity but one of quality. The previously held scientific method of thought maintains that a rational explanation of the observed phenomena is established by reducing those phenomena to data that can be quantitatively calculated. However, among the phenomena human beings experience, there are cases that cannot be explained by quantitative calculations. An historical event would be an example. Accordingly, for investigating these kinds of phenomena, it is necessary to ask what characteristic belongs to that phenomenon. It is for this reason that there is the necessity to distinguish between "meaningless coincidence" (fluke) and "meaningful coincidence." How can these two be distinguished?

We might refer to a lecture that the philosopher Bergson gave in 1913 in London at the [British] Society for Psychical Research, and the ensuing discussion provides us with a good example of those problematical points included within such disputes.[15] Bergson tells us that at a certain conference that he was attending, paranormal phenomena became the topic of discussion. A famous doctor who was attending the conference then stood up and spoke. He used the example of a report by a female intellectual concerning her experience of a visual "hallucination." He asked how one ought to consider [such a] paranormal phenomenon, in which the woman saw the scene of her husband's death on the battlefield and, according to her investigation, that "hallucinatory" vision matched fact. This doctor continued with the following statement:

> You may perhaps conclude from that, as she herself did, that it was a case of clairvoyance or of telepathy. You forget one thing, however, and this is that it has happened many times that a wife has dreamed that her husband was dead or dying, when he was quite well. We notice cases in which the vision turns out to be true, but take no count of the others. Were we to make the full return, we should see that the coincidence is the work of chance.[16]

At the end of the conference a certain young woman came to Bergson and related as follows: "It seems to me that the doctor argued wrongly just now. I do not see what the fallacy in his argument was, but there must have been a fallacy."[17]

Bergson thinks that this woman's intuition is far more correct than the doctor's rationalistic assertion. What matters here is the fact that the woman had a "hallucinatory" experience that was real for her. Bergson states the following in regard to the fact that she vividly had a "hallucinatory" vision,

> if this were proved to me, ... then, even if it should be proved to me that there had been thousands of false visions, and even though there had never been a veridical hallucination except this one, I should hold the reality of telepathy ... to be strictly and unquestionably established.[18]

Furthermore, in regard to such rationalistic crititicism as exemplified by the doctor, he says the following.

> Arrange for the fact to be produced in a laboratory, they will receive it gladly; till then, they hold it suspect. Just because "psychical research" cannot proceed like physics and chemistry, they conclude it is not scientific; and as the "psychical phenomenon" has not yet taken that simple and *abstract* form which opens to a fact access to the laboratory, they are pleased to declare it unreal. Such, I think, is the "subconscious" reasoning of some men of science.[19]

The argument that because of one trick (i.e., fraudulent conduct), paranormal abilities [generally] are based on trickery assumes the fundamentally identical idea and way of thinking as the method of argumentation by which the doctor critiqued Bergson. That is, because there may be chance coincidences, all of them are inferred to be by chance, and concluded to be so. We can see this method being used consistently, from past to present, in all criticisms of paranormal abilities. And modern rationalistic thinking is based on the same mode of inference.

Jung's "meaningless coincidence" refers to the numerous instances like those the doctor cited in the preceding story. [By contrast,] a "meaningful coincidence" would be a case such as what Bergson was thinking of. The "hallucinatory" vision that the woman experienced, indicates an event that for her carried great significance, that is, the death of her husband. This was an event of great significance *for her life*. What is meant here by the "meaning" of an event, refers to the *historical* event with an important value for the person insofar as that individual is living his or her life.

Bergon states that if one can be convinced of the reality of the woman's experience of "hallucinatory" vision as true, we can accordingly say that the phenomenon of clairvoyance or telepathy exists. That is, when considering paranormal phenomena, we must regard as important the reality of the subjective experience belonging to the person in question who experienced it (e.g., intuitive emotions such as surprise or fear). This is the important point. Rationalism dismisses such factors. It would say that this is a mere subjective emotion and has no relation to objective fact.

Let us take up one more example, a case investigated by Ian Stevenson (professor of psychiatry) of the University of Virginia. This is an accidental case of foreknowledge reported in a letter sent to Stevenson by Mrs. Schlotterbeck of Dallas, Texas, dated February 19, 1969.[20]

> I think it was around 1950 that my husband left on a business trip from Philadelphia to Boston, and then was planning on going from Boston to

Washington by plane. (He went by train to Boston.) After he left, I told a friend of mine, who was at the house when he left, that I had a feeling I would not see him alive again—and that I felt he should not take the plane from Boston to Washington. I could hardly wait until the next day to call him. When I got in touch with him I begged him not to take the plane to Washington. It turned out that he did not have to go to Washington after all, and he returned to Philadelphia a few days later. I thought no more of my intuition until he told me that he had a reservation on a plane but cancelled at the last minute. That is the plane that was flying from Boston to Washington, and crashed into the Potomac, killing all aboard. The exact date of it can be found in *Life* magazine, as there was a big write-up about the crash.

My husband who is a regional manager of a large electric company, has always traveled . . . and very often by plane—so it was not because it would have been unusual for him to go by plane.

At the end of this letter, a signed testimony by her husband was included as follows:

I will corroborate the above statement in that my wife did call me and tell me not to take the plane from Boston to Washington. And I had a reservation on the plane that crashed into the Potomac but cancelled the reservation at the last minute, because of no need to go to Washington.[21]

In response to Stevenson's questions, the couple clarified that the wife had never before asked her husband to not take an airplane, and the husband clarified that he had felt no anxiety at all about taking this flight. Stevenson made an inquiry at the National Transportation Safety Board, and investigated the details of the accident. On November 1, 1949, a pilot in training at Washington disregarded the instruction of the control tower at Washington National Airport and, as a result, the training plane he was flying collided in midair with an Eastern Airlines DC-4 plane that was in position for landing. The Eastern Airlines plane fell into the lagoon area in the vicinity of the Potomac River, and all passengers aboard had died, even though the pilot of the training plane miraculously survived.[22]

After this, Stevenson went to Dallas and met Mrs. Schlotterbeck, and inquired further for details surrounding the circumstance. While Mr. Schlotterbeck spent three days away from his home, the woman felt anxious immediately after he had left. Mrs. Schlotterbeck confided in the visiting friend about her anxiety, but could not reach her husband in Boston even the following day. She was finally able to reach him on the night before the departure of the reserved flight, around 9 P.M. on October 31, 1949. She pleaded to her husband not to get on the airplane. Although he had consented, he was still intent on taking the flight. However, one hour later, he received a telephone call from a colleague in Washington and was given news of the change of plan. For this reason, without any need to go to Washington, he canceled the next morning's flight and immediately rushed to get on the night train to Philadelphia, and returned home the next morning. The accident was happening around that time.

As in the examples of Bergson or Stevenson cited above, there are often cases of paranormal phenomena that occur spontaneously, that is, in a form wherein it is impossible to have the experimental control of science. And there are many cases that concern the death of a person. What we here need to take note of is *the [qualitative] characteristics of time.* As in these examples, what the subject experiences is the "time" of *chairos* as discussed in the last chapter (i.e., subjective psychological time, as the timing of life), and not the homogeneous physical time that can be objectively calculated. While Jung calls this kind of situation a state of archetypal crisis, this is the state in which we might say that the constellation of the energy of "time" had suddenly altered—the energy operating in the field of the collective unconscious. The essence of the problem rather has something to do with the domain of history and ethics (i.e., meaning and value in human life). Herein can be apprehended a purposiveness different in nature from scientific causality, that is, an activity of the "for the sake of. . . ." This is an issue related to the value and meaning of living human life, different in nature from facts that can be scientifically measured. Nonetheless, such a phenomenon is also an event that occurs in a dimension where scientific observation is possible. Accordingly, when viewing paranormal phenomena, it is necessary to think about it not only in light of the issue of whether this is an objective fact or not, but also in light of the meaning and value that is involved in the living of human life. If I may say so, paranormal phenomena, in their essential significance, may be thought of as phenomena that occur on the borderline between the domain of objective fact discernable by science and the historical and ethical domains that have a bearing on the value and meaning of living human life. I think that this is the reason why the *Yijīng* assumed the principle of not divining the same thing twice.

CONCLUSION

The theoretical foundation that forms the principle of synchronicity is the idea of the collective unconscious. In what way are paranormal phenomena related to this? Let us finally consider this point.

According to Jung's own explanation, the collective unconscious designates the unique structure of the psychic preconditions that have been inherited and formed through generations. The structure of the human mind, like
the structure of the body, is formed by following the principle of ontogenetic
development. And within the structure of the individual organism, there must
belong the characteristics of each generation that have led up to this point.
That is, the collective unconscious refers to the deep structure of the unconscious since the beginning of human life, which humankind gradually and
wholly acquired through thousands and hundreds of millions of people. This
is a far-reaching basis for the general psychic condition that has been inherited from generation to generation without being brought to consciousness
itself. And our individual and conscious soul exists on this basis. In this sense,
we may say that the collective unconscious is a gigantic spiritual asset for the
development of humankind, a substance common to humankind, existing
among all cultural differences.[23]

Jung's student, Jolande Jacobi, describes the content of this explanation
with a diagram similar to Figure 5.1.[24] When we look at the fruits of clinical psychotherapy and depth psychology, we may tend to think that we have

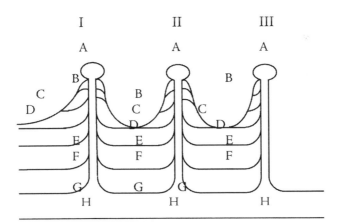

I: Isolated Nation.
II and III: Groups of Nations (e.g., Europe)
A: Individual   E: Ethnic Group
B: Family   F: Primitive Human Ancestors
C: Tribe   G: Animal Ancestors
D: Nation   H: Central Power

Figure 5.1.

gained some degree of understanding about the unconscious. However, if we take into consideration the immensity of its domain, we should recognize that we are merely standing at its entrance gate.

From a theoretical perspective, it will be appropriate to view the standpoint of the collective unconscious from the two aspects of time and space. In light of time, it is an aspect that we might call the form of psychic inheritance that is transmitted from ancestor to descendant through familial genealogy. It may be appropriate to call such a field the *familial unconscious*. In contrast, when seen in light of space, the power of the collective unconscious, for now, may be considered as strongly operative in the field of human relationships (such as family, friends, etc.) where people know one another very well and hold a strong psychological tie. Such a field may perhaps be called the *communal unconscious*. In many cases, paranormal phenomena of spontaneous occurrences are experienced in such a field of the communal unconscious.

If we expand the unconscious as viewed from the aspect of time, from the individual to the group, we may perhaps postulate the field of the collective unconscious that controls the stage of history. In contrast, if we expand the field of the unconscious that transcends the individual body from the viewpoint of space, the characteristic or structure nurtured by a large group, for example, an ethnic group within its climatic environment, comes to be questioned. These two can be respectively called the historical unconscious and climatic unconscious. The phenomenon that we usually call ethnicity, when seen from the viewpoint of the unconscious, takes on the character of the historical-climatic unconscious. Just as time and space are inseparable from each other, history and climate are one, and it weaves the psychological state of each ethnic group.

If the field of the collective unconscious is spread out to the whole of time and space, we would be able to call it the universal (or natural) unconscious. We may summarize the preceding explanation in Figure 5.2. The reason why we call the basis of the collective unconscious, "natural" is because the human being at the basis of the unconscious is a being that resonates with the activity of animals, plants, and physical nature. The East Asian view of life-nature

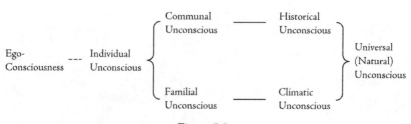

Figure 5.2.

and the cosmology of "interresonating attunement between Heaven and the human being" [*tenjinkannō*, 天人感応] seeks an image of human beings that is connected with such a universal basis of nature.

For the time being, the foregoing explanation merely serves the role of a map for discerning the position in weighing individual issues, and has no further meaning. In response to the question of what the theory of synchronicity teaches us, what we need at present is the attitude that thinks afresh how the external world ought to be, by way of a deep investigation of the internal world into which the idea of the unconscious seems to point as an entry. This is a new path that begins from *knowing one's own self* as an incarnate subject.

PART III

Translator's Note

As there is no explicit transition in the text from Part II to Part III, a few words are in order to establish a connection between them. In Part II, Yuasa has developed Jung's theory of synchronicity far beyond what Jung originally conceived of, by articulating the meaning and the implications of the Yijīng's divination, its view of nature, its idea of space-time inseparability. He has also investigated the theoretical concerns surrounding research on paranormal phenomena, while bringing these topics within the purview of contemporary physics. In so doing, he has proposed how the theory of synchronicity views nature and the human being. As mentioned in the introduction, Yuasa's project in this volume is an attempt to bring science and philosophy together. For this purpose, he sets up in chapter six the project of investigating how science understands time, because, as he states, "science's understanding of time as a theoretical issue" carries a "fundamental importance as it relates to Jung's model," especially in view of the fact that time and space become relativized or zero in synchronistic phenomena. What follows then in Chapter Six is Yuasa's analysis of how science understands time, and he examines the problems it encounters in holding its view of time, when seen from the standpoint developed in Part II. His analysis and examination are directed at establishing the main thesis of this volume: "space-time and mind-body integration."

CHAPTER SIX

Space-Time and Mind-Body Integration

The Resurrection of Teleology

CONTEMPORARY SCIENCE AND EASTERN THOUGHT

In 1984, while I was a faculty member at Tsukuba University, I took charge of organizing an international conference with the theme, "Scientific Technology and the Spiritual World" (the French title: *"Science et Symbole"*) in cooperation with Culture-France, a broadcasting network like the NHK (Japan Broadcasting Company). This conference was attended by scholars of diverse disciplines that ranged from the humanities to the natural sciences. One of the reasons that I was asked to organize it was because people on the French side had a deep interest in C. G. Jung, whom I had been studying for a considerable length of time. Although I was not that familiar with developments in physics, I began to study it out of necessity.

Actually, Culture-France sponsored a conference with the theme "Science and Consciousness" (*"Science et Conscience"*) in Cordoba, Spain, in 1979, in which the figures playing major roles included David Bohm, professor of physics at the University of London, Brian Josephson, professor of physics at Cambridge University and also a Nobel Prize winner, and Fritjof Capra, the author of the best-selling book, *The Tao of Physics*. The issues that were discussed at this Cordoba conference covered the problems of paranormal phenomena (paranormal ability) from the standpoint of parapsychology, along with Jung's theories of the "collective unconscious" and "synchronicity." Moreover, Ms. Isabelle Stengers, a philosopher as well as a collaborator of Ilya Prigogine, was also at the Cordoba conference. At the

Tsukuba conference, we asked a staff member of the Sony branch in London to interview David Bohm.

As I collected information about these Western scholars who gathered at Tsukuba, I found out that there were several among them who were interested in Eastern thought. It appears that Culture-France wanted to hold a conference in Japan, in part, for this reason. I learned that Bohm was interested in Indian mystical thought, and Prigogine was interested in the theory of time as advanced in the Chinese *Yijīng* (the *Book of Changes*) and Daoism. At this conference, I introduced the idea of *ki*-energy (Chin., *qì*: 氣), which Eastern medicine thematizes, and, after the conference was over, many *kikō* (Chin.; *qìgōng*: 気功) masters from China came to visit Japan. This led me to investigate and study *kikō* (i.e., the training of *ki*-energy). I had these masters demonstrate their performing techniques and I also listened to their lectures. Among them were some *kikō* masters who perform healing.

I then went to China in 1987. Since the leaders of *kikō* research there expressed an interest in establishing an exchange program with Japan, we held a symposium in Tokyo in 1988 with the theme "*Ki*-Energy and Human Sciences." The research exploring this area is called "somatic science" (Chin., *réntǐkēxué*: 人体科学) in China, and its members are comprised mainly of scholars of medicine, natural science, and engineering. The central emphasis of this research has three pillars: (1) Eastern medicine, (2) *Ki*-training (Chin., *qìgōng*; Jap., *kikō*: 気功) and (3) extraordinary or special abilities (Chin., *tèyìgōngnéng*: Jap., *tokuikōnō*: 特異効能), which is research on paranormal ability and paranormal phenomena. The Chinese government is funding the Society for Somatic Science, and the executive leader of this association is the well-known scientist Qián Xuésēn, who is the leader in the development of space rocketry in China.

After the Tokyo symposium in 1988, the research exchange with China made progress and we established in 1991 an association called the "Society for Mind-Body Science" (*Jintai kagaku kai*, 人体科学学会), with me as the representative of the founding members. Scholars in various fields such as natural science, engineering, medicine, psychology, and religion are participants of this association.

The conference, held in cooperation with France, arose out of the movement then called New Age Science or the New Age. The New Age Science Movement was triggered by the disputes on American university campuses that occurred in the 1960s at about the time of the Vietnam War. Subsequently, it spread widely. There were many heterogeneous elements included in this movement that had the character of questioning the established values and views of the culture; it was accordingly also called the countercultural movement. For example, Dr. Martin Luther King's movement against the discrimination of Afro-American people, the rise of feminism, and the ecology movement sprouted all at once at this time.

It was about this time when Jung's psychology spread rapidly in the United States of America, and this interest in Eastern thought made Jung famous. Because he had studied Eastern meditation for a long time from the perspective of the unconscious, it evoked an interest among students and youth. What needs to be noted here is that because this movement arose out of the general public or youth, there was no clearly delineated thought or philosophy. It was extremely amorphous. It appears that it also involved the problem of drugs. I have heard that drugs became popular among the students at the time, which enabled them to experience hallucinations. This in turn raised their interest in the unconscious, and consequently the movement spread rapidly. These complex movements came to pass and the issues became scattered in due time. It seems that the movement itself ended in the 1970s.

However, interest in the East has continued, and Americans who are engaged in Eastern meditation methods such as Yoga, Zen, and Southeast Asian Buddhism, have increased to a few million. Study and research by psychologists have also been carried out. Moreover, interest in Eastern medicine has rapidly grown, and the National Institute of Health (NIH), an organization of the [U.S.] federal government, last year issued a report concerning the validity of acupuncture treatment. At present, there are reportedly twelve million Americans who are undergoing treatment by Eastern medicine, where the term *qi* is retained without being translated into English.

It seems that in the background of the rise of interest in the East exists the anxiety of where to seek the meaning of life, due to the increase of people in American society who feel a kind of spiritual dead-end, which is also a psychological situation common to Japanese society.

EINSTEIN AND BERGSON

I have thought afresh of the issues with which I have been concerned in my scholarship. I originally started studying philosophy with an interest in self-cultivation methods, such as Yoga and Zen, which then led me to do research on the psychology of the unconscious, psychosomatic medicine, and Eastern medicine. I came to the realization that these fields have been dealt with in the East collectively as the problem of *ki*-energy.

Furthermore, in the course of interacting with the Japan-China exchange program and through the contact I made with New Age Science, I learned that the theme of *ki*-energy is even connected to the "hard" sciences, such as physics and engineering. Although it is belated, I am now investigating these fields as well.

[In this last chapter,] I will compare and contrast the idea of space-time conceived in physics and the idea of the same seen from the points of view of psychology and philosophy. For therein is a crossing point, I believe, between philosophy and science. Since I am afraid that I may have many misunderstandings in my treatment of them, I would appreciate if the readers can point them out.

Now, the problem of time. The idea concerning the relationship between time and space has considerably changed since Einstein proposed the theory of relativity at the beginning of the twentieth century. According to the special theory of relativity, time and space cannot be separated and they form the four-dimensional space-time continuum. When this theory was proposed, there was a philosopher who criticized Einstein's idea of time. This was the well-known philosopher, Henri Bergson. But after receiving a rebuttal from Einstein, he withdrew the criticism with the admission that he had been mistaken. However, in recent years scientists have reevaluated Bergson's theory of time. For example, a well-known French physicist has made the following remark: "Although this is already noted by Prigogine, there is a similarity between the process of irreversibility ("time's arrow") and Bergson's "pure duration" (durée pure). The dispute between Einstein and Bergson left an impression in the 1920s that physics had won, but it is now regarded that philosophy has been right" (Bernard Despagna).

An argument has been advanced concerning the problem of the possibility of time-travel and time-machines, which is derived from the idea of the four-dimensional space-time continuum, that is, that time and space cannot be separated. If one ejected oneself from the earth into space at an extremely fast speed—for example, ninety percent of the velocity of light—the pace of time becomes slower. Suppose, then, that one travels around space and returns to earth. Such a person will return to the earth as Urashima Tarō did in the Japanese folk tale. After visiting a dragon palace in the deep ocean, he discovered that all of his friends were already dead. Some call this the Urashima-effect. This person returns to a world where the generation of his children or grandchildren is living. This argument suggests that we can go to a future world.

We may entertain this as an argument and it seems plausible. But how about the reverse case? Can we travel back toward the past, or is time-travel toward the past even possible? This seems to be impossible. Suppose that I go back to a past world, meet my ancestor, and kill him. Then, there would be no I presently existing. This is a rather strange argument and it is apparently dismissed, for it destroys the principle of causality that is the foundation of science. In short, these examples show that there has arisen, as one of the fundamental, theoretical problems, the issue of what to think of the distinction

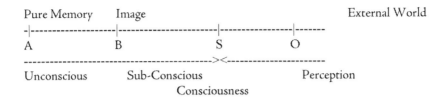

S: Conscious Subject
A|B: Pure Memory's movement toward S.
B|S: Memory-Image's movement toward S.
O S: Perceptual Stimulus from the External World.

Figure 6.1. Perception and Memory

between the past, the present, and the future. This was the very problem that was engaging Bergson when he criticized Einstein's theory of time. It was the problem of what to think of time that is divisible into past, present, and future. Since I am afraid that Bergson's theory of time may be unfamiliar to some readers, I should like to give a brief exposition of it at this point.

Pure memory, represented by A-B, refers to Freud's concept of the unconscious, while the memory-image, represented by B-S, corresponds to his concept of the subconscious. B, which is the demarcating point between the unconscious and the subconscious, is unstable. If we ignore both A-B and B-S, which are to the left of S, then the paradox of pure perception occurs.

To explain it in simple terms, let us suppose that a car is moving. If we look at it, we know that it is moving. Psychologically speaking, we come to know it because there is an after-image of the moving car, that is, because the memory of the after-image is functional. In other words, we come to know that it is moving because a memory regarding the position of a past car is operative. But now suppose a situation in which no memory is operative. Bergson carried out this thought-experiment and called it "pure perception" (*la perception pure*). Pure perception is that activity in which only the present perception occurs and no memory (i.e., the activity of retention) is activated at all in the present perception. Accordingly, the moving car is seen as being always at rest. This creates a situation similar to seeing, one by one, each frame of a reel of film. Bergson's theory states that the moving car must be seen as being always at rest if there is only a present perception, that is, unless memory, the function of the unconscious, or the activity of recollection, is operative. Memory belongs to the unconscious, while perception belongs to consciousness. The relationship between consciousness and the unconscious (memory) cannot in reality be separated. We can have an ordinary perception of motion because the activity of recollecting memory in the unconscious is functional in conjunction with perception. This is Bergson's theory.

Figure 6.1 is a diagram Bergson used to explain the relationship between memory and perception, though I have made a slight modification of it. Memories in the unconscious are of two types; one is a memory-image (*souvenir-image*), which is represented by S-B, that can be recollected in response to the stimulus of perception and the other is the pure memory that cannot be recollected under normal circumstances, which is represented by B-A in the above figure. S-B corresponds to Freud's "subconscious," while B-A corresponds to his "unconscious." Our cognition is established as a meaningful cognition (judgment) when a memory-image (B|S) gives meaning to the perceptual stimulus that comes from the external world (O|S). In connection with Bergson's theory of time, we may recall Zeno's paradox that appeared in ancient Greek philosophy, that is, the argument that a flying arrow is at rest, or that Achilles cannot overtake the tortoise. [See chapter one] This paradox shows that when we try to explain time in light of space, a contradiction arises in regard to the actual experience: no matter how fast Achilles may run, he cannot overtake the tortoise. This is clear sophistry, but it is possible as an argument, as a convoluted use of reason. Even today, this sophistry is still valid.

Bergson took this argument as a problem that connects human psychology with physiology where at the foundation of this idea is his fundamental contention that time cannot be perceived in itself. Our eye cannot perceive time nor can it be heard through the ear. Our sensory organs are capable only of cognizing the state of a thing-event in space, and therefore they cannot directly perceive time. In order to know time, we must perform a certain operation. This is the time of the straight line that Newton constructed, i.e., by drawing a line on a spatially drawn graph; he declared it to be a representation of time.

Concerning this issue, Newton and Leibniz, a philosopher, engaged in a dispute at the time. They were both inventors of differential calculus, and hence also disputed as to who was the first in inventing it. Leibniz criticized Newton's theory of time with the charge that although we come to know time through an event, Newton's method postulates in advance the form of time *prior to* the experience, and then tries to explain the event. To give a concrete example, a farmer who has been working hard, forgetting himself, comes to know the transpiration of time by looking at the sun setting in the west. This is the same situation when we look at our wristwatch. In other words, we come to know time through the cognition of an event in space, and no matter how precise a measurement we may take, it does not change the situation. By contrast, Newton's theory of time is a formal, contentless measure that is presupposed to be prior to experience. He explains an event by presupposing this idea of time. Leibniz's criticism of Newton's theory of time is that it is a theoretical fiction to explain an event.

It appears that Bergson's argument has inherited Leibniz's idea. Einstein's theory of time was a direct inheritance of Newton's theory. Bergson calls it "spatialized time," in virtue of which he says that time becomes a quantity and a volume that can be expressed on a spatial line. That is, time becomes a pure quantity without content. Bergson wanted to argue the point that our experience of time through events is different in nature from the time that is measured as a quantity. In short, the latter is a time that can be expressed on a line, or rather it is that which is *thought* in order to explain an event, based on a certain set of presuppositions. This is what Bergson called "the spatialization of time."

Bergson also says the following. There is Descartes' methodical doubt, but this is a reasoned device he constructed to contend with the certainty of ego-consciousness. His methodical doubt is such that even if a mischievous spirit may deceive me in such a way as to enable me to perceive the world, I who am in doubt, existing here and now, cannot be doubted. Suppose, says Bergson, that there is an evil genius or mischievous god as Descartes proposed and it increases the flow of time by twofold or by threefold, or, reversing the process, decreases it by three-fold. It does not make any difference how much it may be increased or decreased. Even with this thought-experiment, Bergson says that the laws of contemporary physics do not change at all; even if the speed of time is increased by twofold, the contemporary laws of physics suffer no change.

Why is this the case? This is also a kind of thought-experiment, but if time suddenly starts moving twice as fast as the speed of the present time, we will become disoriented with a strange sense of our time-experience. It must be very different from the time we [ordinarily] experience. When a solar eclipse occurs, for example, animals become alarmed and are thrown into confusion. We would probably experience an abnormality comparable to this experience. However, despite the fact that the experience of time is radically different, the laws of physics themselves are not influenced in any way. To be more specific, everyone knows that there are approximately twenty-four hours in a day, and one doesn't have to be a physicist to know this. All human beings in the world have known it through their experience since ancient times when there was no modern science. Physicists of modern times naturally recognized this fact, but this experiential fact is not incorporated into the function of physics as it is mathematically formulated. What Bergson wanted to contend with was that even though the mathematical function may "explain" the time-experience, isn't there a gap between its explanation and the actual experience of time? This is a philosophical problem concerning the gap between mathematics and physics, or, to be more general, between a priori logic and experiential fact.

It needs to be remembered here that Bergson does not denigrate the way science deals with time. But his contention is that time formulated in the mathematical function of physics is different from the human, subjective experience of time, that is, lived time. If I call the time science deals with "objective time," and the time that the human experiences with his or her mind-body "subjective time," the problem is to examine how they are related.

Bergson says that modern science is the daughter of mathematics. Mathematics is the means of calculating all the events in the external world as quantity, and the success of modern science is achieved by depending on it. He says, however, that this success was made possible by discarding and ignoring experiences that cannot be quantified, including phenomena relating to the domain of the mind.

Then, what kind of time is subjective time? Bergson says that the time we actually experience is the "time in which both past and future are entered in a present." Behind the present is enfolded both past and future. To use the terminology of mathematics, it is convoluted time. A past is forgotten as soon as it is sent from the present into the unconscious. But nevertheless it exists, and because of it we can recollect the past. Behind present consciousness, the past is enfolded. What about the future? As long as human beings are alive, they are made to always act toward the future, wherein the activity of pre-grasping the future is enfolded behind the present consciousness. Regardless of whether we are aware of it or not, we anticipate, unconsciously, the future. For this reason, both future and past are in the present or rather they exist behind the present. Bergson uses the expression that both future and past permeate the present. This means that it is the flow (of the mind) that seamlessly ties past and future together, woven within the present. Prigogine calls Bergson's view of time "existential time."[1] He states that, by contrast, what the scientists call time is only a manifest (spatialized) time that appears when the mind is projected upon physical space. That is, (the mind's) time is primarily something alive, and space separate from time is dead.

At the time when Bergson was writing, Freud was not known widely and for this reason Bergson did not use the term "unconscious." In actuality, however, what Bergson discussed is an issue of the unconscious. For example, he cites the case of the near-death experience, which has recently become an issue. With this example, it is extremely easy for us to understand his contention. There are such phenomena as the flashback and the life-review in the near-death experience. These are experienced [for example,] when one is involved in a traffic accident, falling from a cliff, or facing one's death. These are experiences in which the scenes of one's life appear one after another in a split second—those scenes that have left an indelible impression on the experiencer. These phenomena began to be studied fully, beginning in the 1920s, although prior to that time, symptoms of this kind had been reported by psychiatrists. Bergson was making use of them as a point of reference. He explains that all that one has experienced is stored in the unconscious. Out of the totality of past experiences, we select in our normal circumstances a memory necessary for the present action for "the utility of life."

Both Figure 6.2a and Figure 6.2b are diagrams that Bergson used for the purpose of this explanation. AB in Figure 6.2a represents space and the vertical line CI represents the present time in experience. Point I represents consciousness in contact with space, and designates the present time-experience. The flow indicated by I|C represents the process in which the present experience of the mind is constantly pushed back into the past (i.e., historical memory). By contrast, the reverse flow, represented by C|I, indicates the process in which the present perception in I is joined with a memory, while coming to know its meaning (i.e., practical memory). For example, we have memorized the meaning of a word in the English language. We learned it as a past experience. This situation is the same when reading written language. Since the learned memory is stored in the unconscious, we can recognize the meaning of a spoken or written word as it leaps forth out of the memory upon hearing another person speak or when reading a book. We recollect the meaning. We can understand the meaning because the present perception, that is, a perception of the written words in a book, is joined with memory. In other words, under normal circumstances, perception and memory collaborate with each

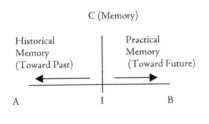

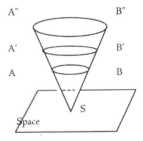

AB: Space (the Present of the Thing-Event)
I: Present Consciousness
C: Memory (the Unconscious Region)

A'–B': Various layers of the unconscious
S: Ego-consciousness based on the body
        (The sensory-motor system in the
        mind-body integration). It is the
        inner experience (i.e., synesthesis)
        that always moves forward

Figures 6.2a and 6.2b.

other, and those that are not necessary for living toward the future are pushed back into the past. However, since the near-death experience is an intuition of one's own death here and now, the concern for the future has been put out of consideration. Concern for the future exists for the sake of action, and for that purpose one selects whatever is necessary from memory. Bergson says that this is the role and function of the brain. But if one intuits that one will die here and now, there is no necessity for a concern for the future. In other words, there is no need for action. At that very instant, those memories that one has experienced in the past gush forth. Even though all the past [experiences] are in actuality stored securely in the unconscious, they do not surface under normal circumstances, nor is there the necessity for them to do so. Should an unnecessary memory surface, it would inconvenience action; but the brain functions in such a way that this does not happen. However, once concern for the future becomes void, past memories flash out in toto. Bergson makes this kind of observation. This flashback experience reveals clearly the structure I mentioned earlier, in which both past and future are enfolded in the present.

In short, in the unconscious region behind consciousness, past and future are entered into in disarray and this is the structure or mechanism of the mind that is connected to the body—which means that both mind and body perceive a surrounding ambience in unison. Why did Bergson think about these things? He advanced this kind of argument as a response to the question of how to think of the integrative relationship between the mind and the body. Figure 6.2b provides an explanation for this. The inverted cone with the apex S indicates the subject's time-experience as CI is depicted in Figure 6.2a. The plane below represents space and S represents present consciousness. This consciousness is joined with the body (i.e., the sensory motor system) and always moves forward in space such that the layers of memory (i.e., the unconscious) are formed behind it. To put it simply, integrated mind-body experience is an experience of time as it relates to space. In this case, while the essence of the mind's activity is the experience of time, the activity of the body expresses the condition of one's existence. The activity of the mind is an experience of time, while the activity of the body is an experience of space. These two orders of experience are joined together as one in the "present" consciousness of the human being who is an integrated mind-body unity. It was along these lines that Bergson was arguing at the time.

IS TIME AN ILLUSION?

Now, I will return to Einstein's theory of time. The theory of relativity, as is known, is divided into the special theory and the general theory. The former is the theory that time and space cannot be separated and it is usually referred to as four-dimensional space-time. Since the general theory of relativity incorporated the idea of gravity within the special theory of relativity, this theory states that mass and space cannot be separated and that space that has mass in it is warped. (To be precise, space-time is warped.) In this case, what needs to be noted is that the special theory of relativity is considered a metaprinciple to which all the laws of physics must conform. Metaprinciple means an a priori form, like a mathematical axiom, that does not require verification by means of experiment or observation. The general theory of relativity was confirmed as to its validity by the observation of an occurrence of a solar eclipse, whereas the special theory of relativity has not been confirmed by experience.

Does the idea of space-time inseparability belong to a metaprinciple? The following episode was reported in regard to this point. When Einstein was thinking about the special theory of relativity, he was hesitant as to whether he should treat time in the same way as space. However, Hermann Minkowski, his math teacher, was impressed by Einstein's paper, and consequently gave a mathematical proof for Einstein's theory, out of which the idea of the four-dimensional space-time continuum was born. Realizing that Minkowski's space was necessary in order to incorporate the problem of gravity, Einstein accepted it. In other words, because a mathematical proof was provided, there was no necessity to obtain any proof based on experience.

When I examined this situation, I learned the following. In the latter half of the nineteenth century, many people questioned Newton's idea of absolute space as electromagnetics developed. Ernst Mach was one of them, and Einstein was greatly influenced by him. Einstein's idea at the time was that space might be closed, unlike Newton's idea of absolute space. However, he didn't pay attention to time and accepted and inherited Newton's idea of absolute time. Suppose that there are observers at each point of cosmic space, then the way space appears to these observers must differ from one another. Despite this, what should we do to guarantee that this space is the one and only space common to everyone? This gave rise to the fundamental principle that the velocity of light is constant. (Light is the fastest means of transmitting information.) Since the concept of velocity includes time in this case, time and space naturally came to be regarded as inseparable.

The issue then returns to the question of whether the idea of four dimensional space-time is a metaprinciple that does not require verification by observation. Prigogine makes the following remark concerning this point:

[t]he biggest concern Einstein had was to guarantee objectivity in the exchange (among the observers). However, for some reason, he didn't follow through on his inferences. For the exchange is an irreversible mechanism;

as soon as an exchange is established, a condition different from the prior condition is generated. That the physical system and the arrow of time common to human beings exist, explains impressively the integration of the cosmos in a way it can not be further conceived.'

According to Prigogine, Einstein initially kept in mind the idea of measurement, but he abandoned it later. This is, as I mentioned earlier, because of Minkowski's proof. In the exposition of the special theory of relativity designed for the general reader, a plurality of observers is often used, but many physicists say that this is not necessary.

Her we run into the question: what meaning does measurement have at all? To omit the details of the issue, the matter of measurement is a problem different in character from the theory of physics itself. The problem of measurement, as is known, is a grave research task in quantum physics, which is the other pillar of contemporary physics, comparable in status to the theory of relativity. I think here is the point where philosophy and the model of physics may be joined.

When we compare the special theory of relativity with the general theory of relativity, in the latter it appears that time does not have any important meaning in the understanding of the structure of the cosmos. When Einstein announced the general theory of relativity to the public, he was thinking of a constant cosmos, that is, the size of the cosmos is definite and it neither contracts nor expands. We learned through Edwin Hubble's discovery, however, that the cosmos expands, through which the time of cosmic history was introduced. Because of this discovery, many solutions to Einstein's equation have been proposed, which is now troubling physicists. Although it is difficult for a neophyte to understand the details, it appears that time was not important in understanding nature according to Einstein's original idea. Rudolf Carnap, who was a philosopher of science, reported the following as Einstein's idea in his later years: Einstein thought that time, being divisible into past, present, and future (the time, should we say, of commonsensical understanding), is a kind of illusion when it is thought through theoretically. However, according to Carnap, Einstein also thought that there is a mystery in the "present," which cannot be solved by science, and this was his biggest concern in his later years.

The fact that this experience cannot be grasped with science was something like a painful resignation difficult for Einstein to avoid.[2] I have pointed out that science is able to account for all that objectively occurs. While physics can describe the temporal ordering of events, psychology (in principle) can account for the uniqueness of human experience regarding time, including the various attitudes toward past-present-future. However Einstein thought that such scientific descriptions will probably fail to satisfy our human demands.

As I think of these remarks, it seems there are two issues. One is that the past and the future cannot theoretically be distinguished at all according to the idea of time postulated by science. This idea is the symmetry of time that was initiated by Newton and inherited without any modification in the contemporary theory of relativity and quantum physics. In the idea of time represented as a line on a graph, both past and future can be dealt with equally. In other words, the characteristics of the mathematical function in physics are such that they do not make any difference at all even if the value of time$_{(t)}$ is changed from positive to negative, for it assumes the symmetrical nature of time.

For this reason, it is not theoretically inconvenient at all to think of a model based on the so-called reverse flow of time. For example, the model of reverse time is used to account for disappearance and generation in the collision between particle and antiparticle (antimatter) in quantum physics (Feynman Diagram). One of the reasons Einstein thought of the commonsensical understanding of time, flowing from the past to the future, as illusory lies in the point that the current scientific worldview is based on the symmetry of time. Einstein thought that, for science, the irreversibility of time was nothing but a seeming phenomenon. He told his friend, Michelle Besso, a scientist, that irreversibility is merely an illusion produced by initial conditions that are "improbable."[3] When Besso died, Einstein wrote in a letter addressed to Besso's younger sister and son as follows: "Michelle has left this strange world (of life) just before me. This is of no importance. For us convinced physicists the distinction between past, present and future is an illusion, although a persistent one."[4]

In recent years, Stephen Hawking has contended that time prior to the Big Bang is an imaginary time that is represented by an imaginary number. Although it is difficult for a person like myself to understand the mathematical explanation, he has proposed this idea in order to dissolve singularities—the critical points that dismantle the current laws of physics—such as black holes and the Big Bang. However, it seems that physicists do not have a clear picture of what imaginary time is. That the essence of time must be represented by an imaginary number sounds as if time is nothing but a form that does not have a reality. At any rate, it seems that this idea points in the same direction as Einstein's question that time flowing from the past to the future via the present, that is, the commonsensical understanding of time, might be an illusion. A physicist who is challenging this question from a new angle is Ilya Prigogine, whom I will deal with later.

Another question Einstein had in his late years was that the "present" cannot be explained by science. Although a mathematical function in physics can explain the process of an event that accompanies a transpiration of time from past to future, or its reverse, from future to past, it does not explain the characteristic of the "present," which is the parameter that marks the distinction between past and future. If there is no clear scientific meaning of "present," it follows that the meanings of past and future cannot be clarified either. He thought that in the present there is something essential that is outside of the domain of science. In the "present," there is something that belongs outside of the realm of science.[5] Needless to say, this is related to the problem of the mind. As stated earlier, as long as one thinks of mind and body as separate, the sensory organs belonging to the body can only perceive the present. For human beings, the past exists only in memory, and the future exists only in the imagination. Pychologically speaking, the past is dormant in the unconscious, and the future emerges out of the fantasy and anticipation that the unconscious pursues. What Bergson calls "pure duration"—living time— is the "time" woven into such past-present-future.

This is the very question that Bergson posed for the understanding of time. He says that the time we actually experience (in our consciousness) is only present and both past and future are enfolded behind them, that is, stored in the unconscious.[6] This means that the "present" is the contact point between objective time in science (in the natural world) and the subjective time the human being experiences. In other words, if we were to theoretically think of the "present," a human element, heterogeneous to physics, enters into the latter. The time that we experience day-to-day ("time" as timing), once gone, does not return. Although the Chinese described "time" with the metaphor "light and shadow fly like an arrow," this means that no one can escape the destiny of aging and dying. In other words, the point is that time is theoretically irreversible.

This may invite criticism, and I may be charged as uttering an meaningless nonsense, but what I want to contend is that it is possible to think of the "present" from the standpoint of science in response to Einstein's question. This is related to Heisenberg's indeterminacy principle, that is, the problem of measurement, for to "measure" an event means to determine the present. Here, the dispute between Newton and Leibniz is revived at the micro level, that is, when the cognition of an event and its explanation are distinguished, what meaning does time have? Bohm, whom I mentioned at the beginning, raises a problem that has a bearing on this point, and I will deal with it later.

RIPENING TIME

Now I will explain Prigogine's idea of time. When he came to visit Japan, a staff member of the Science Division at NHK (Japan Broadcasting Company) contacted me to inquire about the Chinese concept of time, for Professor Prigogine was reportedly very interested in it. What she told me was that Prigogine thinks that the concept of time, as understood by contemporary physics, is missing the mark. What he was referring to was the idea that time is reversible. I wondered about the reversibility of time, and how it is conceived, which led me to many inquiries. The idea of time being reversible is the same as the symmetry of time, which I mentioned earlier. Prigogine's interest in the Chinese concept of time, as I learned through my inquiry, is derived from the philosophy of Lǎozǐ and Zhuāngzǐ, that is, the concept of time that was developed in Daoism. What this means is the following. Physics uses the term "time's arrow," in the sense that time flows unidirectionally, that is, it moves from the past to the future by way of the present. This is a commonsensical (popular) understanding of time, but Prigonine deems that this understanding is commensurate with the idea of time as understood in Daoism. However, I might qualify his understanding by saying that time is not simply a quantity without content, but rather possesses the characteristic of "ripening" (Zeitigen). He says that his idea of time is commensurate with Bergson's idea of time, which the latter calls "existential time."

Contemporary physics' idea that time is reversible indicates the symmetrical nature of time, as I mentioned earlier. However, there is in physics the law of increasing entropy, which maintains that energy phenomena occur following the law of entropy. This law presupposes that time flows only unidirectionally. Although it is a crude example, when I put cream in a coffee cup, the cream and the coffee are separate, but once I stir them, the resultant condition cannot be reversed. In other words, the theory of the increase of entropy states that the cosmos moves toward chaos as time transpires, although there is a definite order (kosmos) in natural phenomena.

The law of the increase of entropy was originally developed in thermodynamics, and it is probably the fundamental law in the theory of energy. The idea of energy was in due time expanded to cover electromagnetics as well as gravity-space (i.e., potential energy), wherein, unlike the case of thermodynamics, the symmetry of time is adopted. However, if this is the case, isn't there a theoretical discrepancy, insofar as it contradicts the idea of "time's arrow"? This is Prigonine's contention. With this in mind, after criticizing Einstein's idea of time, he advances the position that time, as understood in physics, must be reconsidered in light of "time's arrow." Simply put, this idea is analogous to the human being passing away as he or she ages. The physical body that exists in tact is gradually extinguished. This implies that the time of a living organism follows the law of entropy. However, the living organism immanently possesses a process that opposes this law.

Prigogine's position is called the theory of "fluctuation and dissipation." It states that a new order is created out of chaos even under the law of the increase of entropy. According to the hitherto accepted understanding of entropy, the cosmos moves unidirectionally and only to chaos, but his contention is that the reverse process occurs in nature. For example, there occurs a phenomenon with a regulated order, like a cirrocumulus, that is, a cloud formation in the autumn sky. Nature creates order. Prigogine's theory, which is structured in terms of fluctuation and dissipation, expands the system of physics and chemistry to cover the life-system all the way to social systems. His theory has served as a basis for the so-called complex system, a new scientific paradigm that is popular today. His theory is quite understandable when it is applied to the life-system. A living body grows to maturity as a fertilized egg shapes itself into a definite form. This is a process in which cosmos is generated out of chaos, which is the reverse process of the cosmos becoming chaotic. This process is contrary to the usual understanding of the law of entropy, which states that the cosmos ends up in chaos.

Although I use the term "ripening time" (*Zeitigen*), I use it to show Prigogine's understanding of time as being in agreement with that of Daoism. In short, the philosophy of Lǎozǐ and Zhuāngzǐ in regard to the concept of time is that the cosmos is formed out of chaos. To use the terminology of Chinese philosophy, this is due to the activity of *ki*-energy (Chin., *qi*). Behind the order of nature exists an invisible region that is called Dao, out of which issues the activity of *ki*-energy [as I explained it in chapter four]. In other words, the order of myriad things is generated due to the activity of *ki*-energy out of chaos, which exists prior to that which is formed and accordingly the events undergo changes in movement. Prigogine's concept of time endows time with the characteristic of generating order in the natural world. To designate this process, I used the term "ripening of time" (*Zeitigen*).

The term *Zeitigen* has the meaning of suppuration as it is used in medicine, [which I dealt with briefly in chapter four]. It designates a process whereby the content of an event is ripened together with the [temporalization of] time. It was Martin Heidegger, the German philosopher, who introduced this term into philosophy. He is regarded as the founder of Existentialism. He, like Henri Bergson, regarded the question of time as bearing important significance for understanding human experience.

To explain his philosophy of time in simple terms, human existence shoulders the past and the future when living the present. In regard to the past, Heidegger uses such expressions as "being-thrown" into the world. To paraphrase it again in simple terms, it means that we did not come into existence through our own will, but at the foundations of the fact of our living is a fundamental passivity. It is a destiny that cannot be freely altered by us, by our ego-consciousness. In regard to the future, Heidegger uses the term "project" (*Entwerfen*). As long as the human lives in the world, he or she is destined to make a project toward a future, by engaging in work or seeking a meaning for life. In this sense, human existence always shoulders both the past and the future in the midst of the present. Heidegger's understanding of time parallels that of Henri Bergson, who thought that the past and the future are enfolded in the present.

Heidegger calls the understanding of time that accompanies human existence the "ripening of time" (*Zeitigen*). In his later years, he applied this idea to the natural world and stated that "Being" ripens in nature, a difficult thought. The activity of "Being" that exists primordially at the foundations of the myriad things of the world, ripens together with [temporalizing] time, wherein one can discern a similarity with the Dao of Daoism. I think that it is safe to say that his understanding moves in a similar direction as "time's arrow" as conceived by Prigogine and in Daoism. We might say that an invisible power operating behind nature is issued forth and ripens together with time, by virtue of which the myriad of things are generated with a definite form, and are [rendered] alive. Consequently, time comes to be conceived not simply as a quantity, but is endowed with the characteristic of "ripening."

SYNCHRONICITY AND THE COLLECTIVE UNCONSCIOUS

What, then, does it mean to view the world from the perspective of the Chinese understanding of time and space? The issue boils down to this question. It takes us to the *Yijing* (the *Book of Changes*), the book that was the source for the development of Daoism. The idea of change contained in the *Yijing* is the original source of Chinese philosophy. To quickly recapitulate [what I explained in chapter four], it is a view that regards time not as something objective, but as being endowed with definite characteristics such as "chance" and "timely" opportunity (*opportunitum* in Latin or *chairos* in Greek). Temporalizing time is endowed with definite characteristics, and is not simply of quantity.

Although the example may be a bit far-fetched, it is the way of the tea ceremony, as expressed in the phrase, "one encounter for one period" [*ichigoichie*, 一期一会]. This means that a time in which you and I encounter each other is a singular and unique "one encounter" in the history of the cosmos. The essence of time that the human experiences is a situation in life. Time is always experienced for the human being as that which is originally endowed with the characteristic of chance (*opportunitum*) that arises in a situation. However, there are not many encounters in real life where time carries such a high degree of significance. It is for this reason that the *Yijing* teaches the importance of knowing "time." In short, time and space are always inseparable, and due to the activity of ripening time, the event-character is qualitatively in constant change.

It was C. G. Jung who took note of this idea of space-time in the *Yijing*, as I mentioned at the beginning. The *Yijing* is a book of divination. [To recapitulate what I stated in chapters three and four,] divination is a way of knowing the situation a human being is placed in by intuiting the future. In this case, the characteristic of space-time is not known by relying on the cognition of past data based on causality, as is done in science. The process is rather reversed, namely, that by intuiting the future one comes to know the present space-time. Jung explained this way of grasping time by using the difficult expression "synchronicity."

This is based on his idea of the collective unconscious, [as I explained in chapters three and four]. Freud's unconscious is restricted to the interior of the individual, but Jung thought that a transpersonal unconscious level that is shared by the group exists at the base of this kind of personal unconscious. To use an example easy to understand, it refers to a phenomenon such as of group psychology in a given period. For example, when compared to those proposed by modern rationalism, ideas about the human being and nature have changed considerably in the contemporary world at the end of the twentieth century. Everyone senses unconsciously a change in the *Zeitgeist*. In other words, the activity of the collective unconscious moves in a direction with definite characteristics. In a period like this, there tends to occur the phenomenon in which people who are not related to each other think of the same idea. Among people who share a time (or, to be more specific, a time-zone), an event occurs wherein there is a coincidence of meaning. In this manner, a phenomenon occurs to people who are unrelated to each other in which the same idea is thought. The movement of the period controls the group, transcending individuals. In fact, we are moved by the unconscious of the group. Even though we do not consciously become aware of it, everyone will start saying similar things from within this psychological milieu. A genius is a person who can catch the direction in which the period is tending. To take an example from the history of science, both Isaac Newton and Gottfried Leibniz discovered the differential calculus almost contemporaneously, though they had no contact. Both Charles Darwin and Alfred Wallace discovered, at about the same time, how to formulate the theory of evolution.

Jung referred to these instances as synchronicity. When there is a definite movement in the unconscious layer of a group an event simultaneously occurs that is characterized by coincidence in meaning, even though there may be no apparent surface relationship among the persons concerned. Science will regard this kind of case as a meaningless coincidence, but Jung says that a grave meaning is, in fact, concealed in the event that appears to be an accidental coincidence. For this reason, he explained the principle that controls this kind of space-time, by using the term "synchronicity," while contrasting it to causality.

Jung's "collective unconscious" is, as it were, an invisible network of minds that spreads in the "betweenness" (*aidagara*) of each individual.[7] Each of us has a connection in the unconscious dimension in virtue of this network. The "encounter" is that event in which this network is brought to self-awareness.

This is an issue that has bearing on historical study, and I believe that there are people who would agree with this idea of synchronicity. In addition, Jung states that a synchronistic phenomenon is experiencible, close at hand, between the individual and the environment and between one individual and another who are in a special relationship of betweenness.

In thinking through this problem, he had in mind paranormal phenomena such as telepathy and clairvoyance. Paranormal phenomena cannot be explained in terms of the scientific cause-effect relationship. A rationalist would regard it simply as a meaningless coincidence. Note, however, that today's natural science constructs a theory by disregarding the problem of mind. Jung's hypothesis is that if science incorporates within its theory the activity of the mind, a theoretical foundation can be given for these phenomena.

As I mentioned at the beginning [and in the postscript attached at the end of chapter three], the Chinese Society for Somatic Science attempts to elucidate paranormal ability (i.e., extraordinary ability) through the study of *ki*-energy, and the foundation for its thought is the view of nature espoused in the *Yijing*. Jung already grasped this problem about fifty years ago.

In constructing the model of synchronicity, he consulted Wolfgang Pauli, a physicist who received the Nobel Prize. The problem Jung consulted Pauli about was the surprising suggestion of "docking" Einstein's "four-dimensional space-time" with his idea of the collective unconscious. That is, behind space-time that can be physically measured exists the unconscious network that spreads out in one inseparable region, connecting the minds of each individual. Therefore, it is a model in which the qualitative time that constantly ripens can control space. Here, nature is not simply a material substance, but comes to be grasped as "living nature" that immanently houses the unconscious (the mind) and life activity. Paranormal phenomena such as telepathy are generated, based on the network of the collective unconscious that exists latently behind the activity of physical space-time. Pauli told Jung that the latter's idea did not contradict the view upheld by contemporary quantum physics, and he assessed it as one formulation. Because, at that time, the intellectual milieu was such that research in parapsychology was deemed suspect, Pauli thought that Jung's idea was an expression of his "decision." In short, paranormal phenomena can be viewed as instances of synchronicity.

To insert a comment here to facilitate understanding, the reader may recall that there is a compound of the Chinese characters "*u-chū*" (Chin., *yǔ-zhòu*: 宇宙), [as I indicated in chapter four]. The etymological origin of "*u*" (宇) refers to the timber that protrudes from a house, that is, the eaves of a house. It designates that which envelops the place where the human beings dwell. Consequently, it means cosmos. On the other hand, "*chū*" (宙) carries the image wherein a boat, loaded with cargo, moves constantly on a flowing river. It means the flow of time. In other words, Chinese people did not originally separate time from space, but instead grasped them as an integrated space-time continuum. The *Yijing* teaches us to know, through intuition, the characteristic of "time" that reveals a sign in the movement of heaven and earth. Jung's model of synchronicity is derived from this way of thinking.

This chapter has the subtitle, "The Resurrection of Teleology," which represents the current status of my thinking, and that is guided by Jung's model of synchronicity. I am of the opinion that this issue has a bearing on the cognition of value, different in character, for example, from the cognition of fact as is done by science, and is the ethical theme of how to live one's life. Because this issue involves a difficult philosophical discussion, I would like to refrain from it now. Just to elaborate it from the point of view of the theory of time, however, it is related to the *Yijing*'s understanding of time in that the present is seen in this book from the perspective of the future, [as I explained it in chapter four]. Time postulated by science attempts to see the present from the perspective of the past, which is the foundation for the cognition of time based on causality. Contrary to this view, we look at the present from the vantage point of the future. This is the understanding of time, foundational to ethics, in dealing with the question of "how to live one's life."

WHAT IS PRESENT: THE PROBLEM OF MEASUREMENT

Next, I would like to touch on the issues connected to Bohm's ideas, which have attracted attention with the rise of the New Age Science Movement. [As I explained in chapter three,] Bohm has proposed in his later years a model in which he called the natural condition known by the measurements performed in physics the "explicate order," whereas behind the explicate order, there exists an "implicate order" that goes beyond the limitation of observation. His model is commensurate with Jung's model that postulates the dimension of the collective unconscious behind the physicist's space-time controlled by causality. We might say that both Jung and Bohm have provided a new approach to viewing nature: Jung from the side of psychology and Bohm from the side of physics.

Bohm is known in the world of physics for having had a dispute in his youth with Heisenberg concerning the so-called problem of measurement. Indeterminacy in Heisenberg's "indeterminacy principle" means the determination of particle movements by observing the overlapping condition between particles and waves (i.e., the indeterminacy), wherein we obtain through measurement the contraction of the beam of waves in the wave function. What was disputed between them was whether or not it is necessary to take into account the condition prior to measurement. [To elaborate on what I stated in chapter three,] Bohm adopted a position close to the classical viewpoint and attempted to explain the contraction of the beam of waves by postulating a "hidden parameter," whereas Heisenberg rebutted that such a postulation cannot be experimentally verifiable. A majority of people supported Heisenberg's contention at the time, which was settled as the interpretive stance of the Copenhagen school. The stance of the Copenhagen school is a phenomenalism of sorts. More precisely, this school holds that it is meaningless to postulate anything that cannot be measured. At the time, Erwin Schrödinger and Einstein questioned this view. Einstein's analogy is easier to understand for non-experts such as myself. He remarked: "Doesn't the moon exist even though we may not observe it?" The analogy of "Schrödinger's cat" is well known as well, which calls for a rather involved explanation. But to quickly recapitulate it, there is a cat in a basket, although we don't know whether she is alive or dead. When the lid is opened, the cat is dead due to an emission of poisonous gas. In this analogy, the indeterminacy of whether the cat is alive or dead represents the content of mathematical function, that is, the overlapping of particles and waves, while the opening of the lid indicates the act of measurement. In this case, the act of measurement has nothing to do with the theoretical meaning of the mathematical function. Despite this, Heisenberg insisted that the mathematical function is valid as a consequence of the measurement. But Schrödinger questioned its theoretical validity. In the terminology of physics, what he contended was that the quantum jump that occurs due to the measurement cannot be explained by means of the mathematical function. In short, Schrödinger maintained that there is a gap between the description of the mathematical function and the fact that is measured.

At the time, the problem of measurement influenced many scientists to the point of accepting the interpretation that human consciousness has a bearing on material processes and it also exercised great influence even on philosophers. This is the view that nature is not a pure object existing independently of the human being, but rather that there is a mutual connection in cognition between the subject and the object, that is, between nature and the human being. The idea of "field" or the activity of "*basho*" (a place) that supports this mutual connection became a popular, hot topic. However, this problem seemed to have been much more complex and it was in due time forgotten. I think we need to revisit this problem from the viewpoint of the theory of time.

As mentioned in the foregoing, [the act of] "measurement" means the determination of a content that an event signifies, which is the space-time condition of the "present." The meaning of the past and the future is determined by it. Therein lies, I think, the question Einstein posed regarding time, namely, that there is something in the concept of the "present" that science cannot clarify. The previously accepted science follows a procedure in which the theoretician constructs a model by postulating a hypothesis whereby an experiment determines its truth or falsity. In other words, according to this procedure, theory takes precedence over practice. If this is not the case, a theoretical model may prove to be true even without the act of measurement. This I judge to be strange and unreasonable. To put it differently, there is a subtle gap between experiment and theory. Theory is described by mathematical function. However, the experiment inserts the event of "measurement," which is different in character from mathematical logic.

Heisenberg's phenomenalistic view is a standpoint that takes note only of the fact that can be theoretically recognized by means of mathematical description. What Bohm questioned was that there might be a reality behind the mathematical description that cannot appear in the mathematical function. This is commensurate with Bergson's idea, which I mentioned in the beginning, that there is a gap between the experiential fact and the law of physics that is mathematically described.

Einstein, who could not discard his question concerning the fundamental idea of quantum physics, later presented another problem. This is the issue that is called the "EPR paradox," an acronym taken from his collaborators, Boris Podolsky and Nathan Rosen, [which Einstein brought up in order to discount the fundamental ideas of quantum physics]. It refers to a phenomenon in which after a pair of electrons are separated (i.e., the simplex condition) from each other, once the spin of one electron is determined, the spin of the other is also determined, regardless of the distance. No matter how far they are separated from each other, whether the distance may be between Osaka and Tokyo or between Paris and Tokyo, they are simultaneously determined. Einstein contended that it is contrary to reason to assume that there is a kind of communication method like telepathy (i.e., to be precise, a Spuk).

However, the majority of physicists have not shown concern for this issue. Notwithstanding, J. S. Bell clearly proved this theoretical paradox in the 1960s. Was Einstein correct or wrong? It entailed the rather strange result in that he was correct, but was also mistaken, though the issue was extremely complicated. Insofar as the EPR paradox was proven to be true, [which Einstein proposed in order to discount quantum physics], Einstein was correct despite of his intention [insofar as he noted that such a phenomenon exits].

The EPR paradox is an instance of what is called the "nonlocalization function." It means an instantaneous "repercussion" effect on a whole system beyond the activity in the domain of a definitely delineated "field." It is not that a whole is comprehended by adding parts, but that the activity latently existing originally in a whole becomes manifest. It is observation, that is, a human act that determines the "present." The activity that latently exists in the whole is the gigantic field of energy that spreads out in the cosmos (i.e., holism).

The nonlocalization function "moves" at superluminal velocity. Einstein's theory of relativity presupposes the constancy of the speed of light, [and therefore, the nonlocalization function questions Einstein's theory of relativity]. The superluminal velocity is confirmed by the experiments involving the tunnel effect and phase velocity. Since the phase velocity of light is a speed that takes into account angular momentum and is not the speed of photons as a substance, it does not mean that the theory of relativity is destroyed. In Alain Aspect's experiment, it is reported that this effect exceeding 1.7 times the speed of light has been confirmed. [Because of Aspect's experimental verification, the EPR paradox is now known as EPR principle.]

As the problem of measurement has been reconsidered as seen above, the question Bohm raised has surfaced again. The central issue is whether or not a space-time model of holism can be established. This problem has not yet been solved.

METHODOLOGICAL REFLECTIONS ON SCIENCE

As I have given thoughts to the methodology of science, I would like to deal with this issue here. First, the issue of theory ladenness. This means that the methodology for conducting research imposes a definite limitation on the consequences of research. Since scientists are usually interested only in the result of their research, they do not think of what kind of a research method they are using, what problems the method contains, or what limitations it may have. By contrast, philosophers think that science presupposes a certain methodology and that it is a task of epistemology to examine presuppositions. It was Kant who established the epistemology of modern philosophy, and he thought of it when reflecting on Newtonian physics. Consequently, his epistemology has the meaning of methodological reflections on modern science.

Kant mentions two (a priori) conditions that natural science presupposes *prior to* its research. One is concerned with the forms of time and space. This corresponds to Newton's "absolute time" and "absolute space." Another pre-supposition is that science employs logic and mathematics. I will start with the issue of time and space. "Absolute space" refers to empty space without anything in it. This is easy to understand for everyone. However, it is a little difficult to understand "absolute time." What kind of time is a time that is empty of content? This refers to the symmetry of time. To be concrete, it is the time in which there is no distinction between the past, the present, and the future. Just as there is no difference of characteristics in spatial designa-tions such as above and below, and right and left, "absolute time" states that the past and the future cannot be distinguished in terms of their character-istics. This does not refer to time that we actually experience, but it means that no characteristic difference between the past, the present, and the future is given to the measure of time that we employ (i.e., time that is expressed in terms of numerical volumes such as one hour and one minute).

Now, I would like to think through the issue of employing logic and mathematics, which Kant mentions as the other presupposition in epistemol-ogy. Since the situation in contemporary logic differs from what Kant was familiar with, it would be sufficient, for now, to understand that the funda-mental presupposition in scientific research is to think based on the principle of causality, that is, the relationship between cause and effect. In the begin-ning of the twentieth century, Whitehead and Russell collaborated to join logic and mathematics, but it ended in failure. Since Wittgenstein, who was Russell's disciple, the mainstream of logic that is studied in the contemporary period has been symbolic logic. First of all, we need to take note of the fact that there is no involvement of time in logic. Consequently, the idea of causal relationship has nothing to do with logic. This is because to think that there is a causal relationship between thing-events presupposes time. This means that intellectual logic is a priori, that is, prior to experience. When we pro-ceed to think based on intellectual logic, time will be ignored. That is, human life that is inseparable from time fundamentally loses its meaning. Intellec-tual logic refers to the form of thinking that is decided in advance prior to experience. That is, it is a rule stipulated for thinking, and it has no relation with experience in reality. It is probably necessary to reflect on this issue if we are to think of the meaning of life.

Next is the issue concerning mathematics. Because I am completely igno-rant of mathematics—and so I need help from an expert—I will state here a neophyte's dogmatic and prejudiced opinion. There is Gödel's idea of consis-tency. To put this in terms that are easily understandable, this is the conten-tion, as I understand it, that the correctness of a mathematical axiom cannot be proven by mathematics. If this is the case, it means that mathematics is not a discipline that is self-contained, or that the mathematical method in itself contains an essential theory laddenness or contradiction. That is, the use of mathematics itself results in imposing a definite limitation on the result of its research. We can find a problem similar to this in logic. Although I do not know the details of Gödel's contention, according to an introductory book, his mathematical theory is called mathematical logic. And it seems that it is based on ideas derived from logic. To be specific, his idea of consistency is based on the investigation of the law of the excluded middle. I find this to be an extremely important point, but commentaries by math experts just touch lightly on this point, and their expositions continue on to mathematical formula, which is incomprehensible to the uninitiated.

The law of the excluded middle is a principle that states that no sentence (proposition) can be both true and false, and it cannot be in the middle. For this reason, it is also called the principle of bivalence. The philosopher who first thought out this difficult principle was Aristotle, and his logic postulates three principles: the principle of identity, the principle of contradiction, and the principle of the excluded middle. The principle of identity states that "A is A." The principle of contradiction says that "A cannot be both A and not A [at the same time]." The principle of the excluded middle states that "A is either B or not B." [For example], "A is A" means that "I am I." "A is not A" means that "I cannot be anything other than I." The principle of the excluded middle says that "I am either a professor or not" such that there is no middle. These principles apply not only to humans but to things around them.

Although I am afraid that this involves a complicated argument, it has been pointed out that an issue similar to the paradox conceived by Gödel, that is, the issue of theory ladenness, is contained in these principles. An example is often cited that "A Cretan said that the Cretan is a liar." This sentence has the structure of an embedded sentence. It turns out that it is impossible to determine whether this proposition is true or not. We might say that it contains a paradox of two terms that are mutually opposed to each other. To generalize, it means that the validity of logic cannot be proven by logic, just as the validity of a mathematical formula cannot be proven by mathematics. Logic is the rules for thinking, and mathematics is a tool to explain events scientifically. Both of them contain a fundamental contradiction in their foundations. I think that this is the issue foundational to the theory laddenness. The important point in this case is the issue of time. I remarked that there is no time in logic. "A is A" is a principle that is established without any relation to time. Moreover, mathematical formula too has nothing to do with time. Geometry exemplifies well the characteristic of timelessness. Even though the Pythagorean formula was discovered three thousand years ago, it is still valid now. When we ask who knows time, there is no one else but humans. Even though there may be people who say that a dog knows it too, it means that the dog may feel it but it does not know it intellectually. This is because in order to know it intellectually, one needs to understand numbers. It is only humans who understand numbers. However, it does not mean that simply because one understands numbers, one knows time. What knows time is the mind and the body. When we think "the sun has risen" upon seeing it, the body (e.g. eyes) and the mind know that "today is not yesterday." The measures such as of one day and one year become conceived as our experience is repeated. We can in turn know time however short it may be, by using an intricately accurate measuring device. However, time cannot be known without the body and the mind. As I mentioned earlier, the issue with which Bergson and Heidegger concerned themselves is this kind of problem. I think that philosophy and science in the contemporary period or in the near future can come to communicate with each other through such issues involved in the mind-body theory.

PHYSICS AND METAPHYSICS

In order to tackle this problem, I think that cooperation might be needed not only within physics but also with philosophy and psychology, although this may appear to be a wild suggestion. Strange similarities have often been pointed out since the New Age Science Movement arose between the mystical worldview of the East and the worldview proposed by contemporary physics. The issue is whether physics can incorporate in its foundations a holistic understanding of nature, as is represented by the nonlocalization function.

The point where Bohm's idea differs from the majority of physicists is that he adopts the wave-model, rather than the particle-model, as a foundation of his theory in viewing nature. Although it is usually considered that the relationship between the particle model and the wave model has been synthesized in the indeterminacy principle, the actual situation betrays incompleteness. As the quark model demonstrates, many physicists adopt, even now, an explanation of the waves based on the particle model. By contrast, Bohm thinks that we must view nature based on the wave model as its foundation.

The West has constructed a total image of the cosmos based on the particle model since the atomic theory in ancient Greece [see chapter one], and the view of nature proposed by modern science is an extension of this way of thinking. Bohm questioned this way of thinking. The image of nature he saw is a world of total energy that is in constant flow in a vortex. How, then, is it possible to grasp it?

In his later years, he befriended Krishnamurti, the Indian philosopher, and was inclined toward Indian mysticism. He took note of the importance of the concept of *māyā* (illusion) that appears in Indian philosophy. [As I pointed out in chapter three,] the theory of *māyā* states that this world is in reality nothing but an illusion. The term *māyā* is derived from the meaning of "to measure" and "to observe." Accordingly, to observe is to chase after illusion. We might characterize the thinking based on observation as an activity of theoretical thinking, relying on sensory cognition. However, we must recognize the limitation of thinking based on sensory cognition. Bohm thought in this way, similar to Plato's analogy of the cave wherein we only see the shadow of true reality.

His theory is heretical in the world of physics. It has been commented that if one were to adopt his idea totally, the whole theoretical edifice of contemporary physics would be jeopardized. However, I don't think this is his point. What he thought was that the scholarly discipline of physics cannot construct a self-contained and self-sufficient view of nature from within itself. In other words, physics can find a path that enables us to see the true profile of nature when and only when it is connected with metaphysics. I think this was his idea. Might we say that he has moved onto the path of the philosopher, transcending the standpoint of the physicist?

SUMMARY

At the beginning of this chapter [as well as at the end of chapter three], I touched on the movement of *ki*-research, wherein is posed the issue of paranormal phenomena as an extension of *ki*-research. The theme of paranormal phenomena is what triggered Jung to propose the hypothesis of synchronicity and that led Bergson to mysticism in his later years. Jung's space-time model is derived from the *Yijing* and Daoism, [as noted in chapters three and four] and in order to think it through from the contemporary scientific standpoint, he attempted to reinterpret Einstein's four-dimensional space-time model from the standpoint of the collective unconscious. I have felt it necessary to think of science's understanding of time as a theoretical issue of fundamental importance as it relates to Jung's model.

When Bergson criticized Einstein's understanding of time, he had in mind the problem of integrating the mind and the body, for which he took note of the unconscious, while also taking into his purview paranormal phenomena. The new view of time, which both Jung and Bergson problematized, and which concerned Einstein's view of the four-dimensional space-time continuum, is concerned with how to understand space-time integration and mind-body integration. Furthermore, the idea of "ripening time," shared by Heidegger and Prigogine, is compatible with the views of nature and the human being based on *ki*-energy as advocated in the *Yijing*, wherein is found the point of the issue that joins mind-body integration and space-time integration.

The concept of *ki*-energy is originally derived from the ancient philosophy of the *Yìjīng* and Daoism [as I showed, for example, in chapters three and four]. Why has contemporary science come to question anew the meaning of this kind of dated idea? It is because *ki*-energy is not something that is thought (i.e., not a theoretical construct), but is developed inseparably from the practical experience of the concrete bodily technique (or performing technique). *Kikō* (Chin., *qìgōng*: 気功) refers to *ki*-energy training, and is divided broadly into three domains: (1) mind training (e.g. meditation methods such as Zen); (2) bodily training such as *tàijíquán* [Jap., *taikyokuken*, 太極拳]; and (3) the relationship between the human body and the environment, i.e. the understanding of physical nature. Researchers in natural science and engineering are engaged mainly in the domain of (3), research into measuring *ki*-energy that is emitted from *kikō* masters and psychics. It is concerned with the so-called external emission of *ki*-energy. To put it simply, this is a new view that has arisen in China to understand integratively the experience of the three dimensions of the mind, the body, and matter by means of the fundamental concept of *ki*-energy.

In this volume, I could not cover the issues [of *ki*-energy] pertaining to psychology, medicine (Eastern medicine), together with the current situation regarding the experimental measurement of the external emission of *ki*-energy.[8] But I may mention one thing. The psychological function that becomes an issue in meditation is the complex in the unconscious (i.e., the emotions). Moreover, the *ki*-energy that Eastern medicine thematizes is mainly related to emotion. The routes through which *ki*-energy flows are meridians, and the places that are used for the measurement of the external emission correspond to acupoints (curative points) that are plotted along the meridians. In other words, external *ki*-energy connects the human body with the environment by means of the *ki*-energy flowing in the meridians. The psychological function at the unconscious level is connected to matter in a form charged by these characteristics. *Ki*-energy, as of now, is reported in terms of various properties, such as far-infrared rays, magnetic fields, and photons. But since they are carriers of information, when seen from the standpoint of psychology, the issue becomes an inquiry of what characteristics of psychological function are emitted, as they are, I think, charged by affective characteristics. The collective unconscious has this characteristic. It will be a research project, from now on, to connect an experimental approach like this and the model of holism.

At the bottom of the mind's experience of time exists latently the dimension of the unconscious. It transcends the sensory distance between individuals, but connects one person's mind with another person's mind in an invisible dimension. This is Jung's collective unconscious. This is what we may call the system of a network of minds that spreads behind, in the background of the four-dimensional space-time the sensory perception grasps.

This unconscious region constantly changes its quality. It is always being transformed and moves toward a ripening, while issuing a potential energy from within its interior. This energy is great and is the power of [temporalizing] time. That the human being lives means that he or she always exists "here and now." At the base of human existence is concealed the activity connected to the eternal cosmos that synthesizes the past and the future.

Notes

TRANSLATOR'S INTRODUCTION

1. The surname Yuasa here appears first, followed by his personal name, Yasuo, in accordance with Japanese custom.

2. Onuki Yoshihisa, "Yuasa Yasuo's seiyōseishinshi ni furete (II)" [On Reading Yuasa Yasuo's Western Intellectual History (II)], in *Yuasa Yasuo's Complete Works* (Tokyo: Hakua shobō, 2004), Vol. 4, p. 560.

3. Yuasa Yasuo, *Yuasa Yasuo's Collected Works*, Vol. 4, pp. 231–269.

4. This phrase is quoted in Yuasa Yasuo's "*Kindai yōropa no hikari to kage: shinsō shinrigaku ha rekishi to sakai wo domiruka*" [Light and Shadows of Modern Europe: How Depth-Psychology Sees the History and Society], in *Yuasa Yasuo's Collected Works*, Vol. 4, p. 206. [See also C. G. Jung, *Psychology and Religion*, Collected Works, Vol. 11, par. 82ff.]

5. Yuasa Yasuo, ibid., in *Yuasa Yasuo's Collected Works*, Vol. 4, p. 207.

6. An advocate of rationalism may mount the argument that to the contrary, from rationalism comes the very opposite of these evils and that these evils result from the opposite of rationalism. While this is a counterfactual argument, I would like to note one of the problems with rationalism. As Nietzsche points out, the rationalist must *deceive* him or herself, when explaining the motivation for action, for such motivation arises from desire, which is irrational. The person must rationalize the irrational in order to defend his or her rationalism. Behind the façade of the *transparency* of the rational mind lurks an uncultivated, "savage" desire and instinct.

7. Yuasa notes that the phenomenon of death is not included in the definition of the human being proposed in modern rationalism. However, insofar as human beings do die regardless of how one defines human beings, death needs to be addressed squarely. The only exception to this was Martin Heidegger in his *Being and Time*. Yuasa also notes that there is in the contemporary period a will to the nothingness of one's own death. Needless to say, even with the will to the nothingness of

one's own death, this phenomenon of death does not disappear. It simply increases the anxiety and propels people to do all kinds of things that run counter to the realization of authentic human existence.

8. This idea of the "five goings" is sometimes erroneously translated as "five elements." This is clearly misleading because it suggests that the Chinese tradition held a substantialistic ontology, when in fact it held a *fluid* understanding of nature. Recently it has been rendered as the "five phases." Although this rendition seems to be better than the "five elements," it still lacks the sense of *dynamic* movement as found in nature. For these reasons, the new translation "five goings" is used here.

9. When rationalistic thinkers of the Enlightenment period deal with the body, it is thematized either as an idea, that is, as bodyness or as the sensory organs without taking into the purview of their inquiry the lived and living dimension of the body.

10. To fully understand this point, see Yuasa Yasuo, *The Body: Toward an Eastern Mind-Body Theory* (SUNY, 1987) and *The Body, Self-Cultivation and Ki-Energy* (SUNY, 1993).

11. Admittedly there were "nature mystics" like St. Francis in the Christian tradition, who would not take this position, but they are not considered "orthodox."

PREFACE

1. Mier ed., tr. Yuasa et al., *Butsurigaku to shinrigaku no taiwa: pauli and yungu ōfukushokan* [Dialogue Between Psychology and Physics: Correspondences Between Pauli and Jung] (Tokyo: BNP, 2005).

2. Jung and Pauli, tr. Kawai and Murakami, *Shizengenshō to kokoro no kōzō* [Natural Phenomena and the Structure of the *Psyche*] (Tokyo: Narutosha, 1976).

3. As there is a slight difference in translation between what Yuasa quotes here and the English version that appears in Richard Wilhelm, *The Secret of the Golden Flower* (New York: Harvest, 1962), p. 143, we have translated the Yuasa version that is translated from German. The English rendition of this passage reads: "At our point of time the I Ching responds to the need of further development in us. Occultism enjoyed a renaissance in our times which is virtually without a parallel. The light of the Western mind is nearly darkened by it. I am not thinking now of our seats of learning and their representatives. I am a physician and deal with ordinary people, and therefore I know that the universities have ceased to act as disseminators of light. People have become weary of scientific specialization and rationalistic intellectualism." See Richard Wilhelm, *The Secret of the Golden Flower* (New York: Harvest, 1962), p. 143. The passage translated above is from *Ōgon no hana no himitsu* [The Secret of the Golden Flower], tr. Yuasa Yasuo and Sadakata Akio (Tokyo: Jinmon shoin, 1980). —Trans.

4. Richard Wilhelm, *The Secret of the Golden Flower* (New York: Harvest, 1962), p. 141.

5. See the translator's commentary at the end of *Ōgon no hana no himitsu* [The Secret of the Golden Flower], tr. Yuasa Yasuo and Sadakata Akio (Tokyo: Jinmon shoin, 1980).

6. Pauli, tr. Okano Keisuke, *Butsurigaku to tetsugakuni kansuru zuihitsushū* [*Essays on Physics and Philosophy*] (Tokyo: Shupuringā faradei, 1998), particularly chapter 17.

7. K. Wilber, tr. Inoue Tadashi et al., *Kūzō toshiteno sekai* [The World as the Empty Image] (Tokyo: Seidosha, 1983) and Yuasa Yasuo and Takemoto Tadao, ed. *Nyūsaiensu to ki no kagaku* [*New Science and the Science of* Ki-Energy] (Tokyo: Seidosha, 1993).

8. David Bohm, "Beyond Relativity and Quantum Theory" in *Psychological Perspective 2* (Spring-Summer), pp. 25–35, 1988.

9. See Yuasa Yasuo et al., *Kagaku to supirituaritī no jidai* [*Age of Science and Spirituality*] (Tokyo: BNB, 2005)

CHAPTER ONE

1. For basic texts on natural philosophy, see Uchiyama Katsutoshi et al. *Sokuratesu izentetsugakusha danpenshū* [*Collection of the Fragments of Presocratic Philosophers*], 4 vols. with an additional vol., Tokyo: Iwanami shoten, 1995–1998 (a collection of fragments edited by Diels and Kranz). Thanks to this translation, the natural philosophy of Greece has become accessible to beginners. Let me mention in addition to this work other introductory books easily available and recently published.

Yamamoto Mitsuo (ed.), *Shoki girisha tetsugakusha danpenshū* [*Fragments of Greek Philosophers from the Early Period*] (Tokyo: Iwanami shoten, 1958). The first edition came out in 1958, but many editions have since appeared.

Hirokawa Yōichi, *Sokuratesu izen no tetsugakusha* [*Philosophers Before Socrates*] (Tokyo: Kodansha Gakujutsu Bunko, 1997). This one is quite useful because the first part is devoted to the author's commentary and the second part contains the translation of the fragments of major philosophers.

Sekine Seizō, *Rinrishisō no genryū: girisha to heburai no baai* [*The Origin of Ethical Thought: The Case of Greece and the Hebrews*] (Kyoto: Hōsōdaigaku Kyoikushinkōkai, 2001). The first part deals with Greek thought, the latter half deals with Hebrew thought focusing on the Old Testament, and the conclusion deals with a comparative study of both.

Iwata Yasuo, *Seiyōshisō no genryū: jiyū no shishō to ryoinmin no shisō* [*The Origin of Western Thought: The Thought of Free People and the Thought of Captives*] (Tokyo: Hōsōdaigaku Kyoikushinkōkai, 1997).

Katō Nobuo, *Girisha tetsugakushi* [*History of Greek Philosophy*] (Tokyo: Tokyodaigaku shupankai, 1996).

2. Richard McKeon (ed.), *The Basic Works of Aristotle* (New York: Random House, 1941), p. 553 —Trans.

3. Hirokawa, p. 92ff.

4. McKeon, p. 657. —Trans.

5. This appears to be a neologism Yuasa created, and we can trace it to one of the commentaries on the *Yijīng*. In the second chapter of the "Commentary on the

Appended Judgments," 繫辞伝 (*Xìcízhuàn*), we find that "Change *is* a sign [象]. A sign is an image [像]." Here change is understood to be a sign on the part of a cognitive subject who experiences change, where a sign appears in the form of an image. See the section on the divination of the *Yìjīng* chapter four. —Trans.

6. In Buddhist literature, emptiness (*śūnyatā*) is often thematized in analogy with the sky (*ākāśa*) because the latter term can easily conjure up an image of the sky enveloping everything without discrimination since this is one of the salient characteristics of emptiness. Particularly in East Asian Buddhism, the analogical association is easily facilitated in the mind of the language user, because the same character 空 is used to designate both sky and emptiness. —Trans.

7. That is, phenomenal thing-events, by virtue of being dependent on others for their origination and existence, are without substance or essence (*svabhāva*) and thus are empty. —Trans.

8. Dasgupta (trs. Miyasaka and Kuwamura), *Tantora bukkyō nyūmon [Introduction to Tantric Buddhism]* (Kyoto: Jinmonshoin, 1981), chap. 4.

9. Yuasa Yasuo, *Yungu to yōroppa seishin [Jung and the European Spirit]* (Kyoto: Jinmoshoin, 1979), chap. 1. Berthelot, *Renkinjutsu no kigen [Origin of Alchemy]*, tr. Uchida Sōkaku (Tokyo: Uchidarōkakuho shinsha, 1973.), p. 11ff.

10. John Cooper (ed.), *Plato, Complete Works* (Indianapolis: Hackett, 1997), p. 1253. —Trans.

11. McKeon, p. 463. —Trans.

12. McKeon, p. 401. —Trans.

13. I discussed the process by which Jung came across the meditation methods of Daoism and opened his eyes to the psychological significance of alchemy, in chapter three of Yuasa Yasuo, *Yungu to Tōyō [Jung and the East]*, vol. 1 (Kyoto: Jinmon shoin, 1989). This is contained in vol. 6 of *Yuasa Yasuo Zenshū [Yuasa Yasuo Collected Works]*, History of the Eastern Spirit II, (Tokyo: Hakua shobō, 2001).

14. Some scholars have translated them as "elements." This translation does not seem to do justice to this theory because it ignores the ancient Chinese view of nature. To reflect it, we have rendered them as "goings" for the reason Yuasa states in the immediately following sentence. —Trans.

15. On the situation of the thought and science of ancient China, see chapter one of Yuasa Yasuo, *Shintai no uchūsei [Cosmic Nature of the Body]* (Tokyo: Iwanamishoten, 1994).

16. The reference here is to Heisenberg's "indeterminacy principle." —Trans.

17. On the historical situation lying in the background of the origin of the Great Ultimate, see the translators' commentary in Jung and Wilhelm (trs. Yuasa and Sadakata), *Ōgon no hana no himitsu [The Secret of the Golden Flower]* (Kyoto: Jinmon shoin, 1980).

18. Fukunaga Mitsuji, *Rōshi [Lǎozǐ]* (Tokyo: Asahishibunsha, 1968), p. 145. [This footnote is missing from the original text but the translators took the liberty of placing it here. —Trans.]

19. See the Richard Wilhelm Translation of *The I Ching* [*Yìjīng*] rendered into English by Cary Baynes (Princeton: Princeton University Press, 1950), p. 323. —Trans.

20. See Suzuki Yūjirō, *Ekikyō* [*Yìjīng*], 2 volumes, Complete Translations of the Great System of Chinese Literature 10, 1979. Now the *Keijiden* [*xìcízhuàn*] [*Commentary on the Appended Judgments*] is contained in the second volume. The English translation is based on Wing-tsit Chan (trs. and ed.), *A Sourcebook in Chinese Philosophy* (Princeton: Princeton University Press, 1963), p. 152; Philip J. Ivanhoe and Bryan W. Van Norden, *Readings in Classical Chinese Philosophy* (New York: Seven Bridges Press, 2001), p. 171; and D. C. Lau (trs.), *Tao te Ching* (Hong Kong: Chinese University of Hong Kong, 2001, 1982), pp. 37–39. —Trans.

21. Suzuki Yūjirō, ibid.

22. The terms that are rendered here as "original body" and "real body" are usually translated respectively as "essence" and "substance," particularly when they appear in the context of Western philosophy. However, since the ideas of "essence" and "substance" are not part of the Chinese understanding of reality, the translators opted for the present renditions. —Trans.

23. Suzuki Teruo, *Parumenidesu testugakukenkyū* [*Study of Parmenides' Philosophy*] (Kanagawa: Tōkaidaigaku shuppankai, 1999).

24. Yuasa provides a detailed explanation of how this term "*sonzai*" [being: 存在] is used in the context of Chinese and Japanese language in chapter two, "Image-Thinking: Understanding of Being." —Trans.

25. The English translation here has been based on the following: David Gallop, *Parmenides of Elea, Fragments* (Toronto: University of Toronto, 1991, 1984), p. 55; and G. S. Kirk, J. E. Raven, and M. Schofield, *The Presocratic Philosophers* (London: Cambridge University Press, 1983, 1957), p. 245. —Trans.

26. See Friedrich Nietzsche (trs. Greg Whitlock), *The Pre-Platonic Philosophers* (Chicago: University of Illinois Press, 2001), p. 36. —Trans.

27. The English translation here is modified from Heidegger (trs. Joan Stambaugh), *Being and Time* (Albany: State University of New York Press, 1996), p. xix; Seth Bernardete (trs.), *Plato's Sophist* (Chicago: University of Chicago, 1986), p. 36; and Cooper, p. 264. —Trans.

28. For example, Fujisawa Norio's commentary on *The Sophist* contained in Saito, Vol. 3 of *Puraton zenshū* [*The Complete Works of Plato*] (Tokyo: Iwanami shinsho, 1980). Also see, Saito, *Puraton* [*Plato*] (Tokyo, Iwanamishinsho, 1980), p. 195ff.

29. Gallop, p. 57. The translators used "knowing" instead of "thinking" in this passage to reflect Suzuki's interpretation. See also Kirk, Raven, and Shofield, p. 246, fn 1, where the same passage is rendered as: "For the same thing is there both to be thought of and to be." —Trans.

30. Aristotle, *Metaphysics*, Book I, chapter 1, 980a21, in McKeon (ed.), p. 689. —Trans.

31. Heidegger (trs. Joan Stambaugh), *Being and Time* (Albany: State University of New York Press, 1996), p. 160 (p. 171 in original German ed.). —Trans.

32. Heidegger (Stambaugh), p. 196 (p. 212 in the German). The sentence following was included as part of the quotation in the original Japanese edition, but in fact is not part of the original text by Heidegger. —Trans.

33. Heidegger (trs. Kuwaki Tsutomu), *Sonzai to jikan* [*Being and Time*], three volumes (Tokyo: Iwanamibunko, 1961).

34. That is, being in the predicative sense stating *what* something is. —Trans.

35. That is, being in the "existential" sense stating *that* something is. —Trans.

36. Translation based on Gallop, p. 65; and Kirk, Raven, and Schofield, p. 248–249. —Trans.

37. Translation based on Gallop, p. 71; and Kirk, Raven, and Schofield, p. 252. —Trans.

38. Translation based on Gallop, p. 73; and Kirk, Raven, and Schofield, p. 252–253. —Trans.

39. Kirk, Raven, and Schofield, p. 273. —Trans.

40. The actual quotation from Aristotle's *Physics*, Z9, 239b14, is that "the quickest runner can never overtake the slowest." By "quickest runner" is meant Achilles, and by "slowest" is meant the tortoise in Aristotle's discussion of Zeno. See Kirk, Raven, and Schofield, p. 272. —Trans.

41. Ogino Hiroyuki, *Testugaku no genfukei: kodaigirisha no chie to kotoba* [*The Original Scene of Philosophy: The Wisdom and Language of Ancient Greece*] (Tokyo: NHK Raiburarī, Nihonhōsōshuppankai, 1999), chapter five.

CHAPTER TWO

1. Japanese is a multisyllabic language that has three different writing systems. Generally, Chinese characters were imported to stand for meanings while the two phonetic scripts were used for inflectional endings and grammatical particles. Most Japanese characters have two readings, one that is native in origin, and, one adapted from the character's Chinese pronunciation. Thus, "compound" refers to the putting together of two or more Chinese characters (two meaning units), and not to the uniting of two words, as in English or German. It is like putting together multiple morphemes. —Trans.

2. Yuasa thematizes in this chapter the Western concept of "being" in light of two Japanese words "*aru*" and "*sonzai*": the former is an indigenous Japanese word, while the latter is a neologism that consists of two Chinese characters, and it was created for the purpose of translating such Western words as the Greek word "*on*," the English word "being," the French word "*être*," and the German word "*sein*." However, his thematic focus here is on the Japanese word "*aru*," which can be used in both essential and existential predication. His discussion centers on showing how this word "*aru*" behaves differently from those Western counterparts. —Trans.

3. Nishida Kitarō (1870–1945) is considered the "founder of modern Japanese philosophy." Out of his complete works consisting of nineteen volumes, several have appeared in English translation: *Kitarō Nishida: Intelligibility and the Philosophy of Nothingness*, tr. Robert Schinzinger (Honolulu, Hawaii: East-West Center, 1958); *The Fundamental Problems of Philosophy*, tr. David Dilworth (Tokyo: Sophia University, 1970); *Art and Morality*, tr. David A. Dilworth and Valdo H. Viglielmo (Honolulu, Hawaii: East-West Center, 1973); *Last Writings: Nothingness and the Religious Worldview*, tr. David Dilworth (Honolulu: University of Hawaii Press, 1987); *Intuition and Reflection in Self-Consciousness*, tr. Valdo H. Viglielmo (Albany: State University of New York Press, 1987); *Inquiry into the Good*, tr. Abe Masao and Christopher Ives (New Haven.: Yale University Press, 1990). For a good introduction to Nishida's thought, see Nishitani Keiji, *Nishida Kitarō*, tr. Yamamoto Seisaku and James W. Heisig (Los Angeles: University of California Press, 1991). —Trans.

4. Yuasa may have in mind here Zhūzǐ's Neo-Confucian *Li-Qi* philosophy that was developed during the Sōng dynasty. —Trans.

5. See the entry for *"sonzai"* in Yanagiya Akira's *Honyakugo seiritsu jijō* [*Situations Surrounding the Establishment of Translated Words*] (Tokyo: Iwanami shoten, n.a.). As far as I know, there is a sentence in Shinran's *Kōsō wasan* that reads: "when Genkū existed (*sonzai seshitokini*)."

6. The verb *"suru"* is attached to a noun in Japanese to convert a noun into a verb as is in the case of *"sonzai-suru"* mentioned here. —Trans.

7. When one raises a question of being, it may be formulated as "what is it?" Depending on the interest of the questioner, one can place emphasis on any of the words that constitute this question. Hence, the emphasis of the question may fall on the "what," in which case the "whatness" of being is thematized, as in *"what* is it?" This is a question demanding an essence to be disclosed, that is, the being of "what." Or, an emphasis may fall on the "isness" of being, as in what *is* it?" In this case, the "isness" is called into question, that is, the *existence* of what is demanded for a response. Or, an emphasis may fall on the "thatness" of being, as in "what is *it?*" This is a question that demands a being to be disclosed as a particular thing or event. As Yuasa paraphrases *"aru"* with *"that* which is" (*arukoto*), both "it is . . ." and "there is . . ." are framed within *"that* it is." In other words, "it is . . ." is concerned with the *essence* of a being insofar as this statement can fall within the call of "thatness," whereas "there is . . ." is concerned with the *existence* of a being that is thematized within the call of "thatness" of a thing or an event. This analysis shows that the Japanese language demands that the essence shows itself in the concrete thing/event. —Trans.

8. Watsuji Tetsurō (1889–1960) was another major figure in modern Japanese philosophy as well as the teacher of Yuasa Yasuo. His studies ranged from such topics as existential philosophy, early Buddhist philosophy, and Japanese culture and ethics. Out of the twenty-one volumes of his complete works, only two translations have so far appeared in English: *Climate and Culture: Philosophical Study* (New York: Greenwood Publishing Group, 1988), *Watsuji Tetsurō's Rinrigaku: Ethics in Japan*, tr. Yama-

moto Seisaku and Robert E. Carter (Albany: State University of New York Press, 1966). For Watsuji's critique of Heidegger's *Dasein*-Analysis, see Yuasa Yasuo, "The Encounter of Modern Japanese Philosophy with Heidegger" in *Heidegger and Asian Thought*, Graham Parkes, ed. (Honolulu: University of Hawaii Press, 1987). Yuasa is also an author of a definitive version of Watsuji's philosophy. See his *Watsuji Tetsurō: Kindai Nihon no unnmei* [Watsuji Tetsurō: The Destiny of Modern Japan] (Tokyo: Chikuma shobō, 1995). —Trans.

9. An objection that Yuasa is raising here concerning the translation of "*Sein*" as "*yū*" [有] is that this character is a pictograph that depicts someone carrying a concrete thing on the shoulder. As such, it lacks the abstract sense of the term "being," let alone its universalization as Being. —Trans.

10. These are all examples of the character compounds that were mentioned in note 4. —Trans.

11. In addition to the sense of "it is," "*ya*" adds to a statement a speaker's subjective response since it carries a "tone of affirmation and/or exclamation." —Trans.

12. In modern Japanese sentences, final particles written in the phonetic kana syllabary are used instead of Chinese characters. While it is very difficult to translate these particles into English, and though they do not serve any logical grammatical function, they are extremely common, and can change the entire meaning of a sentence or expression. An example of a "negative rhetorical question" in English would be: "You wouldn't be going there, would you?" In Japanese and Chinese, this sense can be captured in one letter or character. —Trans.

13. The Sapir–Whorf hypothesis states that the structure and the grammar of a language condition a speaker of that language to see the world in a way delimited by them. Since there are structural and grammatical differences among languages, speakers of different languages see the world in fundamentally different ways. In this respect, language shapes the worldview of a given linguistic community. This hypothesis was originally proposed by the German scholars Johann Gottfried von Herder and Wilhelm von Humbolt. —Trans.

14. Nakamura Hajime, *Tōyōjin no shii hohō: Chugokujin no shii hohō* [*The Ways of Thinking of the Eastern People: The Chinese Way of Thinking*] (Tokyo: Shinjū sha, 1988), vol. 2.

15. Nishi Junzō, "Shugo nonai kotoba: chūgokugo ni tsuite no shiron" ["*Language without the Subject: An Attempt at the Chinese Language*"] in *Chūgokushisō ronshū* [*Essays on Chinese Philosophy*] (Tokyo: Chikuma shobō, 1969). (There are also subjectless constructions in Japanese, as Yuasa also mentions immediately following Nishi's observation. —Trans.)

16. To use the phenomenologist's category, the embodied subject designates the "subject-body" that is contrasted with "object-body." —Trans.

17. Yuasa seems to be saying here that primacy falls on the presence of an embodied subject when uttering a sentence rather than in the presence of the sentence not accompanied by the speaker. —Trans.

18. "In the back of" is the translation of the character 奥 (*oku*). This character refers to something that is deep inside, and does not mean behind. Thus, here Yuasa is not suggesting a division of being such as in Kant's distinction between phenomena and noumena. —Trans.

19. Note that this "*yama*" is a one word (character) sentence. —Trans.

20. Nishi Junzō, "*Shugo nonai kotoba: chūgokugo ni tsuite no shiron*" ["*Language without the Subject: An Attempt at the Chinese Language*"] in *Chugokushisō ronshè* [*Essays on Chinese Thought*] (Tokyo: Chikuma shobō, 1969).

21. Nishida's basic contention in his "logic of *basho*" is that any being occurs in a place, and without this place nothing can occur, whether it is of the physical, of self-consciousness, or of the absolutely nothing. He distinguished, according to Kōsaka Masaaki, three *basho*s. Nishida calls the first place "*basho* vis-à-vis being," which designates the place where physical thing-events occur, that is, the natural world. He called the second place "*basho* vis-à-vis relative nothing," and it refers to the place where the activity of self-consciousness occurs. He called the third place "*basho* vis-à-vis absolutely nothing." The first is called "*basho* vis-à-vis being" because this is where humans encounter various beings. The second *basho* is called "relative nothing," because self-consciousness does not have its raision d'être apart from the first *basho*, and as such it is relative to the first *basho*. He called the third place as "absolutely nothing" because self-consciousness cannot stand on its own, and therefore he reasoned it is supported from below by "absolutely nothing." He alternatively called "absolute nothing" the "transcendental predicate." He saw the single function of "*basho* vis-à-vis absolutely nothing," to be the self-determintion of itself via its own negation. From this point of view, the activity of self-consciousness, which is linguistically expressed as a predicate, is considered an instance of this negation. According to Nishida's scheme, although there appears to be three kinds of *basho*, the three *basho*s arise as a difference in perspective. Among the three *basho*s so distinguished, however, "*basho* vis-à-vis absolutely nothing" was considered foundational in the sense that apart from it, there is no meaning and significance for the other two *basho*s. —Trans.

22. See Abe Masao's introduction to Nishida Kitarō's *An Inquiry into the Good*, trans. Abe Masao and Christopher Ives (New Haven and London: Yale University Press), pp. vii-xxvi. However, it may be noted that Nishida was adamant that he was developing a philosophy and not presenting Zen in Western guise. His insistence is partly a reflection of the time in which he worked. —Trans.

23. *Genjitsu* [現実], which is translated here as "reality," is a difficult term to render into English. It carries the sense of "what is presenced in fullness." —Trans.

24. See, for example, Martin Heidegger, *The Question of Being*, tr. William Kluback and Jean T. Wilde (Albany: NCUP Inc., 1958), pp. 83–80. —Trans.

25. Here, take the character that means "tree" [木] as an example. Originally, this was a pictograph that depicts a tree standing with its branches and trunk. When this character is written twice, thus indicating many trees, it produces the character that looks like 林. It means "woods." If the same character is written three times, as

in 森, it results in creating a character that means numerous trees, and hence a "forest." —Trans.

26. Here onomatopoetica is excluded from Yuasa's explication. —Trans.

27. F. Saussure, *Ippangengogaku kōgi* [*The Course in General Linguistics*] (Tokyo: Chūkōshinsho, 1986). An English translation is taken from *Critical Theory Since Plato*, ed. Hazard Adams, rev. ed. (Orlando, FL: Harcout Brace Jovanovich, 1992, p. 725.

28. The universality Yuasa is claiming here regarding the "deeper region of the mind" seems to go, at first glance, counter to the "heterogeneity" he mentions in comparing the Chinese language and the Western languages. The universality he has in mind in this connection is probably related to Jung's archetypal images, and the "heterogeneity" he mentions is related to his observation that the Chinese language is a visual language. In order for an image to appear, an image must be connected, by way of "memory," to the unconscious, which is a reservoir of images and at the same time this image is directly a reflection of how the world appears to the speaker. His observation is that this does not occur in the case of the Western languages because they are, as he characterizes them, auditory languages. In the auditory languages, meaning is arbitrarily assigned to a string of sounds for the purpose of interpersonal communication. By contrast, the mode of engagement with the world or nature in the case of the Chinese language is carried out directly without the intervention of an arbitrarily constructed system of meanings. —Trans.

29. See Noam Chomsky, *Syntactic Structures* (1957) and *Aspects of the Theory of Syntax* (1965). —Trans.

30. Gōngsūnlóng was a naïve realist and maintained that form should be strictly distinguished from attribute, wherein he prioritizes the form of a particular over its attributes. This prioritization meant for him that the attribute cannot be substantialized. The gist of his argument is that a "horse" is a form, while "being white" is an attribute, and since the former should be strictly distinguished from the latter, he is led therefore to conclude that "a white horse is not a horse." —Trans.

31. See, for example, Kaji Nobuyuki, *Chūgokujin no ronrigaku* [*Chinese People's Logic*] (Tokyo: Chūōshinsho, 1977).

32. For an explanation and selection from these schools see Wing-Tsit Chan, *A Sourcebook in Chinese Philosophy* (Princeton: Princeton University Press, 1963), chapters 9 and 12. —Trans.

33. For a collection of essays dealing with Zhūzǐ, see *Chu Hsi and Neo-Confucianism*, ed., Wing-tsit Chan (Honolulu: University of Hawaii Press, 1986). —Trans.

34. For an exposition of Wáng Yáng-míng's philosophy, see *Instructions for Practical Living and Other New-Confunfician Writings*, tr. Wing-tsit Chan (New York: Columbia University Press, 1963.). —Trans.

35. Zhūzǐ (朱子, Jap., Shushi,) took "to investigate" to mean "to reach" and so the character 格 comes to mean "one must reach the nature of things," while Wáng

Yáng-míng (王陽明, Jap., Oyōmei) understood it to mean "to correct and to rectify." What needs to be "corrected" and "rectified," according to Wáng Yáng-míng, was the psychological attitude one brings toward "the investigation of things." What needs to be noted in this connection is that the "things" they had in mind were not confined to the physical, but also included the "invisible." —Trans.

36. See F. Th. Stcherbatsky, *Buddhist Logic* (New York: Dover, 1962). —Trans.

37. Xuánzhuàng (602–664) was accorded the title of "dharma-master of *tripiṭaka*" (*sānzàng*), the three baskets of Buddhist learning. He is known for his translation project, sponsored by a Tang emperor. His commentary on Yogācāra Buddhism, *Chéngwéishílún*, is a valuable Chinese contribution to the development of this school of Buddhism. —Trans.

38. Nagasawa Kazutoshi, tr. *Genzōsanzō: Daitōdaijionji sannzōhōshiden* [Xuáng-zhuàngsānzàng: A Biography of the Darma-Master, Xuángzhuàngsānzàng, of the Great Compassion Temple of the Great Tang Dynasty] (Tokyo: Kōfūsha, n.a.), vols. 8 and 9.

39. Nāgārjuna, founder of Mahayana Buddhism, established the emptiness school (*śūnyavādin*). His main philosophical contention was that nothing has a self-nature that can generate itself, that is, everything is dependent on everything else for it to *be*, and therefore everything is empty of substantial or essential nature. —Trans.

40. The Japanese word *kokoro* is the reading of the character 心. It is a picture of a heart, and the pronunciation of this character as *kokoro* is said to be the ono-matopoetica of the beating of a heart. It is variously used to mean "mind," "spirit," or "heart." Needless to say, here there is not a sharp distinction between "mind" and "body." —Trans.

41. Chigi, *Makashikan* [*Móhēzhiguān*], vol. 6 [*Kokuyaku Daizokyō* (Tokyo: Tōhō shoin, n.a.), p. 325.]

42. Here it may call for a further qualification, for in Nāgārjuna's *Karika* we find the statement to the effect that "*saṃsāra is nirvāṇa*" or "*nirvāṇa is saṃsāra.*" This identity statement is made in the case of Nāgārjuna by canceling out the substantial-istic understanding of these terms by relying on "logic." This is the point Yuasa wants to make in this paragraph. —Trans.

43. See, for example, Carl G. Jung, *Two Essays on Analytical Psychology* (Princeton: Princeton University Press, 1966). Yuasa is the author of five books on Carl G. Jung: *Yunngu to kirisutokyō* [*Jung and Christianity*] (Kyoto: Jinmonn shoin, 1978); *Yunngu to Yōroppa seishin* [*Jung and the European Spirituality*] (Kyoto: Jinmonn shoin, 1979); *Yunngu to tōyō* [*Jung and the East*] (Kyoto: Jinmonn shoin, 1989), vol. 1 and 2; *Yunngu chōshinrigaku shokan* [*Jung's Letters on Parapsychology*] (Tokyo: Hakua shobō, 1999). —Trans.

44. The word "*shukan*" (主観) is a compound consisting of two characters, 主 and 観, while the word "*shutai*" [主体] consists of the characters 主 and 体 as are indicated in brackets in the text. Both share the character 主, which means a "host" or a "master." A host is contrasted with a guest, while a master is contrasted with

a disciple. As can be seen, the difference between these two words is in the occurrence of 観 and 体. 観 is derived from a meditation method in which a meditator observes (観) what appears in the field of meditative awareness, and this sense is transferred to the "host" of observation that is the subject. On the other hand, since the character 体 designates the body, it is the body that the host lives, that is, a lived body. This is the "subject-body" that phenomenologists thematize in contrast to the "object-body," that is, the body we live from without. It is the body, for example, that can be measured and quantified. —Trans.

45. For Yuasa's explication of this stance, see Yuasa Yasuo, *The Body: Toward an Eastern Mind-Body Theory* (Albany: State University of New York, 1987). —Trans.

46. The phase "humans cohabiting with nature" appearing in this sentence is "this realm of thought" in the original text, but the translators changed it to read "humans cohabiting with nature" because "this realm of thought" refers to it. — Trans.

47. This passage originally appears in the *Nirvāṇasutra*, and it is a difficult passage to understand if we read it from the homocentric perspective that is based on ego-consciousness. Zen's enlightenment is an experience (satori) in which the distinction between the subject as seer and the object as seen is collapsed. As such it is an opening of a horizon in *samādhic* awareness in which occurs an exchange between the seer and the seen: they become interchangeable. This horizon is nondualistic in nature, and since it is nondualistic, the meditator who achieves a *satori* experience realizes that his *satori* experience is mutually illuminated by the "mountains, rivers, blades of grass, trees, and lands." —Trans.

48. Transcendentalism here refers to the tendency to look for emancipation and meaning outside and apart from the natural world (inner and outer) that we ordinarily experience in our everyday existence. —Trans.

49. This observation echoes a contemporary attitude of seeing the environmental worlds as a biosphere. An increasing number of biologists has begun to notice this in recent years, although a majority of biologists will probably not go so far as to assert that there is spirituality dwelling in nature. —Trans.

50. The reference here is to chapter two of 共時性の宇宙観 [The Synchronistic View of the Cosmos] (Kyoto: Jinmon shoin, 1995), where he speaks of the Daoist idea of "returning to the Void" and Dōgen's characterization of his meditation state. In the case of Daoism, Yuasa quotes a poem that runs as follows: "Without a beginning and without an end. /Without going into the past, and without coming into the future,/A halo of light engulfs the spiritual world. /People forget each other,/ in stillness and purity; /They are powerful and yet empty./ The sky above is illuminated by the mind in heaven. /The ocean water is going smooth./ Whereupon the moon is reflected. /Clouds disappear in blue sky./ And mountains are shining clear./ The mind is dissolved away in *samādhi*,/While the moon-disk rests peacefully alone." For an alternative translation of this poem, see *The Secret of the Golden Flower*, tr. Richard Wilhelm (New York: Harcourt Brace Jovanovich, 1962), pp. 77–78. —Trans.

51. See, for example, Dōgen's "The Sounds of the Valley Streams, the Forms of the Mountains" in Francis Dojun Cook, *How to Raise an Ox* (Los Angeles: Center Publications, 1978), pp. 101–114. —Trans.

52. See *Timaeus* in *The Collected Diaglogues of Plato*, ed., Edith Hamilton and Huntington Cairns (Princeton: Princeton University Press, 1973), 30b, p. 1162. —Trans.

53. See Aristotle, Book I and II of *Physics* and chapters 1–4 in Book XII of *Metaphysics*. —Trans.

54. The form of judgment that Aristotle used is subsumptive judgment in which the predicate is subsumed under the grammatical subject. Taking note of this, Nishida, for example, proposed the predicate-logic that led him to develop his theory of the "logic of *basho*." —Trans.

55. Fukunaga Mitsuji, *Sōshi: Naihen* [Zhuāngzǐ: Inner Chapters] (Tokyo: Asahi shinbunsha, 1978), p. 337. See for an English translation, *Chuang Tzu: Basic Writings* (New York: Columbia University, 1964), p. 95.

56. This use of the phrase "Great Mother" suggests, psychologically speaking, that the feminine principle, as opposed to the masculine principle represented by *logos*, is placed at the foundation of this thought. —Trans.

57. Fukunaga Mitsuji, *Rōshi* [Lǎozǐ] (Tokyo: Asahi shinbunsha, 1968), p. 145. An English translation is taken, with some modifcaitons, from "The Lao Tzu (Tao Tê Ching)," trans. Wing-Tsit Chan in *A Sourcebook in Chinese Philosophy* (Princeton: Princeton University Press, 1963), p. 152.

58. *Meta* means "after" as well as "beyond." —Trans.

59. For the explanations that follow, see Suzuki Yūjirō, *Ekikyō* [Yìjīng] (Tokyo: Shūeisha, 1974), vol. 2, p. 8 and p. 368.

60. We find, for example in chapter forty-two of *Dàodéjīng* a passage that reads: "One gives rise to two, two gives rise to three, and three gives rise to myriad things. Myriad things carry *yīn* and embraces *yáng*." For a comprehensive treatment of this concept from a point of view of Chinese intellectual history, see *Ki no shisō* [Ki Thought], Onozawa Seiichi, ed. et al. (Tokyo: Tokyo University Press, 1980). Also, for a theoretical interpretation of the function of *ki*-energy in its relation to Eastern methods of self-cultivation and theories of the body, see Yuasa Yasuo, *The Body, Self-Cultivation and Ki-Energy* (Albany: State University of New York Press, 1993). —Trans.

CHAPTER THREE

1. Yuasa Yasuo, *Yungu to Tōyō* [Jung and the East] (Kyoto: Jinmon shoin: 1989–1990), 2 vols.

2. C. G. Jung, Foreword to Abegg, "*Osten denkt anders,*" in Collected Works, Vol. 18, par. 1485. English version: *Psychology and the East* (Princeton: Princeton University Press, 1978), p. 188. —Trans.

3. Carl G. Jung, *"Eki to gendai"* [*The* Yìjīng *and the Contemporary Period*], trs. Yuasa Yasuo and Kuroki Mikio in *Tōyōteki meisō no shinrigaku* [*The Psychology of Eastern Meditation*] (Osaka: Sōgensha, 1983).

4. Carl G. Jung and Wolfgang Pauli, *Shizen genshō to kokoro no kaimei* [Clarification of Natural Phenomena and the Mind], tr. Kawai Hayao and Murakami Yūichi (Tokyo: Kaimeisha, 1976); German, *Naturerklärung und Psyche*; English: *The interpretation of Nature and the Psyché*], and *"Hiingateki Renkan no Genri toshite no Kyōjisei"* ["Synchronicity: An Acausal Connecting Principle"] (Princeton: Princeton University Press, 1976). The essay Pauli contributed to this volume was "The Influence of Archetypal Ideas on the Scientific Theories of Kepler."

5. Wolfgang Pauli (1900–1958) was a theoretical physicist of Switzerland, and contributed to the development of the theory of relativity; he worked on the systematization of quantum mechanics together with Heisenberg, and introduced the innovation of the spin for the first time. He predicted Pauli's so-called exclusion principle. He also predicted the existence of the neutrino, and made a huge contribution to the development of field theory and the principle of mediation. He was a recipient of the 1945 Nobel Prize in physics.

6. Carl G. Jung, *Yobu e no Kotae* [*An Answer to Job*], tr. Nomura Mikiko (Kyoto: Yorudansha, 1981).

7. Carl G. Jung, *Ketsugō no Shinpi* [*Mysterium Conjunctionis*], 1955 (not translated into Japanese yet).

8. M. L. von Franz, *Zahl und Zeit: Psychologische Überlegungen zu einer Annahrung von Tiefen-psychologie und Physik* (Stuttgart: Ernst Klett Verlag, 1970). English translation: *Number and Time* (Chicago: Northwestern University Press, 1974).

9. Jean Shinoda Bolen, M.D., *The Tao of Psychology: Synchronicity and the Self* (San Francisco: Harper and Row, 1979), p. 16.

10. Tenge Shirō, *Kōfukuna jinsei no himitsu* [*The Secret of a Happy Life*] (Tokyo: PHP Kenkyūjo, 2000), pp. 63–64.

11. Tenge Shirō, *Kōfukuna jinsei no himitsu* [The Secrete of a Happy Life] (Tokyo: PHP Kenkyūjo, 2000), pp. 63–64.

12. Carl G. Jung, *Synchronicity* (Princeton: Princeton University Press, 1973), p. 22 (par. 843) and p. 109 (par. 982). This incident also appears in Jung's letter to A. D. Cornell, dated February 9, 1960.

13. Carl G. Jung, *Jiden* [*Memories, Dreams, Reflections*] I, tr. Kawai Hayao (Tokyo: Misuzu Shobō, 1972), p. 200ff.

14. Carl G. Jung, *Memories, Dreams, Reflections* (New York: Vintage Books, 1965), p. 138. —Trans.

15. Carl G. Jung, *Tōyōteki meisō no shinrigaku* [*Psychology of Eastern Meditation*], tr. Yuasa Yasuo and Kuroki Mikio (Osaka: Sōgen sha, 1983), p. 273. Because this passage differs in content between the English version and the original German version, what does not show in the English version was translated from the German version.

16. Yuasa (note 1), p. 272ff.

17. Carl G. Jung, *Synchronicity* (Princeton: Princeton University Press, 1973), p. 3. —Trans.

18. Carl G. Jung, Foreword to Abegg, *"Osten denkt anders," Collected Works,* Vol. 18, par. 1485.

19. Austin in his *Zen and the Brain* characterizes this feeling as "unconscious circumspatial awareness," although it is not clear whether he will be willing to include "destiny" in the scope of the meaning of this phrase. See James H. Austin, *Zen and the Brain* (Cambridge: MIT Press, 1998), p. 488. —Trans.

20. The succeeding line refers to a second reading that follows a first reading that is a divination in response to an inquiry. This reading then is an instruction about the succeeding situation that follows the first situation.

21. Xenophon, *Sokuratesu no omoide* [*The Recollection of Socrates*] (Tokyo: Iwanami shoten, N.D.), p. 232.

22. Sigmund Freud, *Yumehandan* [*Interpretation of Dreams*], tr. Takahashi Yoshitaka (Kyoto: Jinmon shoin, 1968).

23. This connotes a pulsating , invigorating life-activity. —Trans.

24. The translation mentioned here refers to: J.B. Rhine & Pratt, *Parapsychology: Frontier Science of the Mind—A Survery of the Field, the Methods, and the Facts of ESP and PK Research* (Springfield, IL: Charles C. Thomas, 1957). The Japanese version of this translation appeared as J. B.Rhine, *Chōshinrigaku gaisetsu,* trs. Yuasa Yasuo and Motoyama Hiroshi (Tokyo: Shūkyōshinri shupan, 1964).

25. Carl G. Jung, "Synchronicity: An Acausal Connecting Principle," in C. G. Jung and W. Pauli, *The Interpretation of Nature and the Psychē* (NY: Bollingen Foundation and Pantheon Books, 1955), p. 22; and also in C. G. Jung, *The Structure and Dynamics of the Psychē* (Princeton: Princeton University Press, 1969; New York: Bollingen Foundation, 1960), p. 432.

26. The "power of thinking" includes not only an image but also a special mode of de-tensionalized intentionality that is different from the intentionality that is operative when taking the everyday standpoint. It operates when one enters the experiential dimension of the "one world." —Trans.

27. In addition, we can also mention retrocognition, clairaudience, and reading other people's minds, as instances of paranormal phenomena. —Trans.

28. Carl G. Jung, *Modern Man in Search of a Soul* (San Diego: Harcourt Brace, 1933).

29. J. B. Rhine, *Extra Sensory Perception*, 1934 (Boston: Bruce Humphries, 1964).

30. Carl G. Jung, *Shinrei Genshō no Shinri to Byōri* ["On the Psychology and Pathology of So-called Occult Phenomena" in Jung, *Psychiatric Studies*; and also in *Psychology and the Occult*], trs. Uno Masato et al. (Tokyo: Hōsei Daigaku Shupan, 1982).

31. Carl G. Jung, *Jiden* [*Memories, Dreams, Reflections*] (note 9), p. 157ff.

32. The reference is to Carl G. Jung's letter to J. B. Rhine, dated November 27, 1934. This letter is contained in *C .G. Jung Letters*, tr. R. F. C. Hull (Princeton: Princeton University Press, 1973), p. 180. —Trans.

33. The following correspondence between Jung and Rhine are based on letters included in C.G. Jung, *Letters* 1,2 (Princeton: Princeton, 1973). Their content was introduced with detail in my *Yungu to Tōyō* [*Jung and the East*] (Kyoto: Jinmon shoin, 1989), p. 203ff.

34. R. F. C. Hull, tr. *C. G. Jung Letters* (Princeton: Princeton University Press, 1973), p. 495.

35. C. G. Jung, foreword to *The I Ching* (Princeton: Princeton University Press, 1950), p. xxii.

36. See, for example, Whilhem/Baynes trs., *The I Ching* (Princeton: Princeton University Press, 1950), p. 318. —Trans.

37. Wolfang Pauli, "*Shizenkagakuteki tachibakara mita muishiki toiu gainen*" ["*Idea of the Unconscious from the Standpoint of Natural Science and Epistemology*"] in *Butsurigaku to tetsugaku ni kannsuru zuihitsushū* [*Essays on Physics and Epistemology* (*Aufsätze und Verträge über Physik und Erkenntnistheorie*, Frieder Verlag & Sohn, Verlag Braunschweig, 1961)], ed., Namiki Mikio, tr. Okano Keisuke (Tokyo: Springnet Verlag Tokyo, 1998), chapter 17. [Originally in *Dialectica* 8, no. 4 (15 Dec, 1954), pp. 283–303; English version: Pauli, *Writings in Physics and Philosophy* (Berlin: Springer-Verlag, 1994)].

38. Pauli, tr. Okano Keisuke, *Butsurigaku to tetsugaku ni kansuru zuihitsushū* [*Essays on Physics and Philosophy*] (Tokyo: Shupuringā faradei, 1998), particularly Chapter 17.

39. Fritjof Capra, *Tāningu Pointo* [*Turning Point*], trs. Yoshifuku et al. (Tokyo: Kōsakusha, 1984), p. 606ff.

40. Ryle Watson, *Seimei Chōryū* [*Lifetide: A Biology of the Unconscious*], trs. Mikihata et al. (Tokyo: Kōsakusha, 1981). This work is divided into four sections; at the beginning of each section, there is a quotation from Jung's *Memories, Dreams, Reflections*.

41. David Bohm, *Danpen to Zentai* [*Fragmentation and Wholeness* (Jerusalem: The Van Leer Jerusalem Foundation)], tr. Sano Masahiro (Tokyo: Kōsakusha, 1985). David Bohm, "*Uchū no anzaikei to meizaike*" ["The Implicate Order and the Explicate Order of the Cosmos"], tr. Takemoto Tadao, "*Ryōshi Rikigaku to ishiki no yakuwari*" ["Quantum Mechanics and the Role of Consciousness"], Kagaku to Ishiki Shirīzu [Science and Consciousness Series] Part II (Tokyo: Tama shupan, 1984).

42. This term "implicate order" has been translated in various ways in Japanese. Here the translators omit the following passage: "Although this has been translated as 'built-in order' or 'woven order,' since Professor Takemoto Tadao of Tsukuba University has provided an easy-to-understand translation, I will follow his translation." —Trans.

43. The translators took the liberty of omitting the following sentence: "Mr. Takemoto translates this as '明在系.'" See previous note. —Trans.

44. This is not an exact quotation. See David Bohm, *Wholeness and the Implicate Order* (London: Routledge & Kegan Paul, 1980), pp. 150–157, where Bohm discusses the "holomovement." For example, on p. 151,Bohm states, " . . . what 'carries' an implicate order is *the holomovement*, which is an unbroken and undivided totality." —Trans.

45. David Bohm, "Anzaikei to Tōyōteki Meisō" ["The Implicate Order and the Eastern Meditation"], trs. Yuasa Yasuo and Takemoto Tadao, *Nyèsaiensu to ki no kagaku* [*New Age Science and the Science of Ki*] (Tokyo: Seidosha, 1987).

46. David Bohm, "Anzaikei to Tōyōteki Meisō" ["The Implicate Order and the Eastern Meditation"], trs. Yuasa Yasuo and Takemoto Tadao, in *Nyūsaiensu to Ki no Kagaku* [*New Age Science and the Science of Ki*] (Tokyo: Seidosha, 1987).

47. To express this idea, Kegon Buddhism (Chin.; *Huáyán*) uses the metaphor of Indra's net. Indra's net is a cosmic net wherein a diamond hangs in every intersection of the net. In this net, every diamond reflects every other diamond in the mesh. Therefore, there is non-obstruction and interpenetration between the diamonds; what occurs in one diamond, be it a movement of mind or body, gets reflected in every other diamond. The diamond is used to designate "pure mind" (*amalacitta*) that is achieved through religious self-cultivation. —Trans.

48. For Yuasa's view on *ki*-energy, see Yuasa Yasuo, *The Body, Self-Cultivation and Ki-Energy* (Albany: State University of New York Press, 1993). —Trans.

49. Yuasa Yasuo, ed., *Ki to ningen kagaku: Nichū shinpōjiam kōenshū* [*Ki and Human Science: Proceedings of the Japan-China Symposium*] (Tokyo: Hirakawa shuppan, 1990).

CHAPTER FOUR

There was a section at the end of this chapter with the title "Living Time and Dead Time," which occupies three and a half pages in typescript. The translators took the liberty of deleting this section, for the content overlaps with some of the content contained in chapter six. The overlapping content deals with Yuasa's comparison of the theories of time advanced by Bergson, Einstein, and Prigogine. However, because there are paragraphs that are not contained in chapter six, the translators inserted them in appropriate places in chapter six with permission from Professor Yuasa. —Trans.

1. In the original text, the word "*eki*" appears as in *Ekikyō*, that is, the *Yìjīng* (the Book of Changes) but the translators took the liberty of changing it to read the *Yìjīng* instead of "changes" which the word "*eki*" suggests.–Trans.

2. Yuasa Yasuo, *Shintai no uchūsei: Tōyō to Seiyō* [The Cosmic Order of the Body: East and West] (Tokyo: Iwanami shoten, 1994).

3. Henri Bergson, *Bushitsu to kioku* [*Matter and Memory*] (Tokyo: Hakusuisha, 1965). Yuasa Yasuo, *Shintairon: Tōyōteki shinshinron to gendai* [*The Theory of the*

Body: An Eastern Theory of Mind and Body, and the Contemporary World] (Tokyo: Kōdansha gakujutsu bunko, 1990), p. 211ff.

4. Miura Kunio, *Ekikyō* [*Yìjīng*] (Tokyo: Kadokawa Shoten, 1988), p. 31.

5. Ibid., p. 57.

6. Richard Wilhelm (German trs.) *The I Ching or Book of Changes* (rendered into English by Cary F. Baynes) (Princeton: Princeton University Press), 1950, p. 48. In this quote, the phase "*Yang-chi*" is spelled as "*yáng-qi*" and *Yin-chi* as "*yīn-qì*." All quoted passages of the *Yìjīng* will refer to this English version of Wilhelm's German translation. —Trans.

7. Wilhelm, pp. 441–442, translation slightly modified.–Trans.

8. The hexagram presented here in the original essay seems to contain a typographical error; since the correct hexagram is number twenty-seven instead of forty-one, the translator took the liberty of changing it to hexagram number twenty-seven.–Trans.

9. C. G. Jung, trs. Yuasa Yasuo and Kuroki Mikio, *Tōyōteki meisō no shinrigaku* [*The Psychology of Eastern Meditation*] (Osaka: Sōgensha, 1983).

10. Here "civilizing" is a translation of the compound "*wén*" and "*míng*" [Jap., "*bunmei*": 文明], which means illumination by means of letters, to become literate in the Chinese written system.–Trans.

11. Yuasa Yasuo, *Shintairon* [*The Theory of the Body*]. See note 2, p. 211.

12. "Life-time" is a translation of *seimeiteki jikan* [*seimeiteki jikan*, 生命的時間], and one literal rendition of this phrase would be "time filled with life activity."–Trans.

13. See Richard Wilhelm's translation of *The I Ching* [*Yìjīng*] rendered into English by Cary Baynes (Princeton: Princeton University Press, 1950), p. 323.–Trans.

14. In the English version of Richard Wilhelm's translation this is rendered as "That which lets now the dark, now the light appear is *tao*." See ibid., p. 297.–Trans.

15. See note 12 on "life-time."–Trans.

16. On Tillich's opinion, see his essay dealing with the beginnings of political romanticism (Tokyo: Hakusuisha, n.a.), contained in Pual Tillich *Zenshū* [*Collected Works*], vol. 11.

17. Nishi Junzō, "*Chūgokutetsugaku no jikanron no dōki*" ["The Motive of the Theory of Time in Chinese Philosophy"] in *Chūgokushisōshū* [*Anthology of Chinese Thought*] (Tokyo: Chikuma shobō, 1969).

18. On the following, see Ryu Bunei, *Chūgoku no jikuron* [*The Chinese Theory of Time and Space*] (Tokyo: Tōhō shoten, 1992).

19. Prigogine and Stengers, *Konton kara no chitsujo* [*Order Out of Chaos*] (Tokyo: Misuzu Shobō, n.a.). See Toffler's foreword to the edition. English edition: *Order Out of Chaos*, p. xviii.–Trans.

20. The phrase that is translated here as "succeed or not" is "*ataruka dōka*" in the original, which, when translated literally, may be rendered "whether it will hit

(the mark) or not." "Hitting (the mark)" suggests an actor initiating an action onto an object outside of him or her; in the present case, a diviner is giving a reading on a certain concern. Here is involved a theory of truth that emphasizes an action, the fulfillment of which determines the truth, that is, "hitting" the targeted object, rather than, for example, a correspondence between a proposition and the state of affairs. This theory is closer to the pragmatic theory of truth, where the workability of things becomes a defining feature. The difference comes down to which aspect, theory or practice, one emphasizes more in envisioning what truth is.–Trans.

CHAPTER FIVE

1. See note 21 in chaper four.–Trans.

2. William McDougal (1871–1938), a British-American pioneer in psychical and parapsychological research, was born in Lancashire, England, and educated in Germany. Since Yuasa seems to be under the mistaken impression that McDougall originally was from the United States, the translator took the liberty of changing the present sentence to reflect this fact. —Trans.

3. The Duke University Parapsychology Laboratory was established by Rhine in 1935. In 1962, Rhine took his research away from Duke to establish a privately funded nonprofit organization, Foundation for Research on the Nature of Man (FRNM) next door to Duke University in Durham, North Carolina. In 1995, the FRNM was renamed as the Rhine Research Center Institute for Parapsychology. — Trans.

4. Yuasa Yasuo, *Ki towa nanika* [*What Is Ki?*] (Tokyo: NHK Books, 1992); see pp. 169ff.

5. Jung's letters to Rhine have been translated in *AZ* no. 29, "*Yungu kokoro no shinpi* [*Jung, Mystery of the Mind*]" (1999, Fall, Shinjinbutsu Ōraisha). On the relationship between the two, see Yuasa Yasuo, *Jungu to tōyō* [*Jung and the East*], vol. 2 (Kyoto: Jinmon shoin, 1989–1990), pp. 190ff.

6. Ibid., *AZ*, pp. 51ff. [This note (#3 in Jap ed.) is missing from the original text but the translators took the liberty of placing it here. —Trans.]

7. See "*Kyōjisei: hiingatekirenkan no genri*" in Jung and Pauli, *Shizengenshō to kokoro no kōzō* (Tokyo: Kaimeisha, 1976) [English ed.: "Synchronicity: An Acausal Connecting Principle" in *Interpretation of Nature and the Psyche*. —Trans.]

8. F. D. Peat, *Sinkuronishitī* [*Synchronicity*] (Tokyo: Asahishuppansha, 1989), pp. 31ff. [This is another missing footnote (#5 in Jap ed.) from the original text; the translators took the liberty of placing it here. —Trans.] [English ed.: F. David Peat, *Synchronicity: The Bridge Between Mind and Matter* (New York: Random House, 1988)].

9. Pauli, "*Muishiki no gainen no shizenkagakuteki ninshikironteki sokumen*" ["*Ideas of the Unconscious from the Standpoint of Natural Science and Epistemology*"], in *Butsuri to ninshiki* [*Matter and Cognition*] (Tokyo: Kōdansha, 1984), pp. 32ff.

[Originally in *Dialectica* 8, no. 4 (15 December, 1954), pp. 283–303; English version now in Pauli, *Writings in Physics and Philosophy* (Berlin: Springer-Verlag, 1994), p. 155.] Yuasa, pp. 251ff.

10. English: Pauli, "Ideas of the Unconscious from the Standpoint of Natural Science and Epistemology" in *Writings in Physics and Philosophy*, p. 153. —Trans.

11. This passage is taken from the Preface Jung wrote to Richard Wilhelm's translation of *The I Ching* that Mrs. C. F. Baynes translated into English in 1950, but the corresponding passage is not translated into the English version. The translated passage is from C. G. Jung, *Tōyōteki meishō no shinrigaku* [*The Psychology of Eastern Meditation*] that Yuasa Yasuo and Kuroki Mikio translated, which is based on the German original. (Osaka: Sōgensha, 1983, p. 274). This volume is a compilation of various essays that Jung wrote on Eastern philosophies and religions. —Trans.

12. C.G. Jung, *Tōyōteki meishō no shinrigaku* [*The Psychology of Eastern Meditation*] tr. Yuasa Yasuo and Kuroki Mikio (Osaka: Sōgensha, 1983), p. 273. [Again, there is no corresponding passage in Baynes' translation of this text, and the present passage is translated from *Tōyōteki meishō no shinrigaku* [*The Psychology of Eastern Meditation*], translated by Yuasa Yasuo and Kuroki Mikio. —Trans.]

13. Jung and Wilhelm, *Ōgon no hana no himitsu* [*The Secret of the Golden Flower*] (Kyoto: Jinmonshoin, 1980), p. 18. Yuasa, *Yungu to Tōyō* [*Jung and the East*] (Kyoto: Jinmon shoin, 1989–1990) volume II, pp. 118ff. [English ed.: C. G. Jung and Richard Wilehlm, *The Secret of the Golden Flower, A Chinese Book of Life*, trs. Cary F. Baynes (New York: Harvest, 1962, 1931), p. 141.]

14. Tachibana Takashi, *Rinshi taiken* [*Near Death Experience*], Vol. II (Tokyo: Bungeishunjūsha, 1994), p. 190.

15. Bergson, *"Ikiteiruhito no maboroshi to shinreikenkyū"* ["'Phantasma of the Living' and 'Psychical Research'" in *Beruguson Zenshū* [*Collected Works of Bergson*] Vol. V, *Seishin no Enerugī* [*The Energy of the Spirit*] (Tokyo: Hakusuisha, 1965). [English ed.: Henri Bergson, "'Phantasms of the Living' and 'Psychical Research'" in *Mind-Energy; Lectures & Essays*, trs. H. Wildon Carr (London: Macmillan, 1921). See chapter III. —Trans.]

16. Bergson, *Mind-Energy*, pp. 66–67. —Trans.

17. Bergson, *Mind Energy*, p. 67. —Trans.

18. Bergson, *Mind-Energy*, p. 69. —Trans.

19. Bergson, *Mind-Energy*, p. 66. —Trans.

20. Kasahara Toshio, *Chōshinrigaku handobukku* [*Parapsychology Handbook*] (n.a.: Purën shuppan, 1989), pp. 90ff. [The reference is to Ian Stevenson, who began a Division of Parapsychology within the Department of Psychiatry at the University of Virginia Medical School. For an account of this incident in English see Ian Stevenson, *Telepathic Impressions, A Review and Report of Thirty-five Cases* (Charlottesville: University Press of Virginia, 1970), pp. 105–108. —Trans.]

21. Stevenson, pp. 105–106. —Trans.

22. See Stevenson, p. 107. —Trans.

23. Jung, *Two Essays on Analytical Psychology, Collected Works*, vol. 7 (Princeton: Princeton University Press, 1966), pp. 64ff.

24. Jacobi, *Yungu shinrigaku* (Tokyo: Nippon kyōbunsha, 1973), p. 65. [English ed.: Jolande Jacobi, *Psychology of C.G. Jung* (New Haven: Yale University Press, 1973). —Trans.]

CHAPTER SIX

1. This sentence and two sentences following it are taken from the last section of chapter four, "Living Time and Dead Time." The quotation is from Prigogine and Stengers, *Konton kara no chitsujo* [*Order Out of Chaos*] (Tokyo: Misuzu Shobō, n.a.). English edition: *Order Out of Chaos*, see, for example, p. 214 and p. 294.

2. This paragraph is inserted here from the section "Living Time and Dead Time" that originally appeared at the end of chapter four.–Trans.

3. Prigogine and Stengers. English edition: *Order Out of Chaos*, p. 294. —Trans.

4. Prigogine and Stengers, p. 294 [Eng. ed.]–Trans.

5. The translators took the liberty of inserting the sentence that starts here to the end of this paragraph, and they are taken from the last section of chapter four, "Living Time and Dead Time."–Trans.

6. Again, the translators took the liberty of inserting the sentence that starts here to the end of this paragraph, and they are taken from the last section of chapter four, "Living Time and Dead Time."–Trans.

7. For the development of this idea, "*aidagara*," see *Watsuji Tetsurō's Rinrigaku: Ethics in Japan*. Tr. Yamamoto Seisaku and Robert E. Carter (Albany: State University of New York Press, 1996). —Trans.

8. For this topic, see Yuasa Yasuo, *The Body, Self-Cultivation and Ki-Energy* (Albany: State University of New York Press, 1993). —Trans.

Selected Bibliography

Aristotle. *Metaphysics* in *Basic Works of Aristotle*, ed. Richard McKeon. New York: Random House, 1941.

———. *Physics* in *Basic Works of Aristotle*, ed. Richard McKeon. New York: Random House, 1941.

Austin, James H. *Zen and the Brain*. Cambridge: MIT Press, 1998.

Bergson, Henri. *Busshitsu to kioku* [*Matter and Memory*]. Tokyo: Hakusuisha, 1965.

———. *Busshitsu to kioku* [*Matter and Memory*]. Tokyo: Hakusuisha, 2001.

———. *Dureé et Simultaneité: A Propos de la Theorie D'Einstein*. Paris: n.a., 1951.

———. "*Ikiteiruhito no maboroshi to shinreikenkyū*" ["'Phantasma of the Living' and 'Psychical Research'"] in *Beruguson Zenshū* [*Collected Works of Bergson*]. Vol. V. Tokyo: Hakusuisha, 1965.

———. *Jikan to jiyū* [*Time and Free Will: An Essay on the Immediate Date of Consciousness*]. Tokyo: Iwanami shoten, 2001.

———. *L'Énergie Spirituelle*. Paris: F. Alcan, 1920.

———. *Matter and Memory*. London: G. Allen & Urwin, 1913.

———. "'Phantasms of the Living' and 'Psychical Research'" in *Mind-Energy; Lectures & Essays*, tr. H. Wildon Carr. London: Macmillan, 1921.

———. *Seishin no Enerugī* [*The Energy of the Spirit*]. Tokyo: Hakusuisha, 1965.

———. *Time and Free Will: An Essay on the Immediate Data of Consciousness*. New York: Dover, 2001.

Bernardete, Seth (trs.). *Plato's Sophist*. Chicago: University of Chicago, 1986.

Berthelot. *Renkinjutsu no kigen* [*Origin of Alchemy*], tr. Uchida Sōkaku. Tokyo: Uchidarōkakuho shinsha, 1973.

———. *Wholeness and the Implicate Order*. London: Routledge & Kegan Paul, 1980.

Bohm, David. *"Anzaikei to tōyōteki meisō"* ["The Implicate Order and the Eastern Meditation"], trs. Yuasa Yasuo and Takemoto Tadao in *Nyūsaiensu to ki no kagaku* [*New Age Science and the Science of Ki*]. Tokyo: Seidosha, 1987.

———. *Danpen to zentai* [*The Fragments and the Whole*], tr. Sano Masahiro. Tokyo: Kōsakusha, 1985.

———. *Fragmentation and Wholeness.* Jerusalem: Van Leer Jerusalem Foundation, 1976.

———. *Kagaku to ishiki shirīzu* [*Science and Consciousness Series*], Part II. Tokyo: Tama shupan, 1984.

———. *Ryōshi rikigaku to ishiki no yakuwari* [*Quantum Mechanics and the Role of Consciousness*]. Tokyo: Tama shupan, 1984.

———. *Uchū no anzaikei to meizaike* [*The Implicate Order and the Explicate Order of the Cosmos*], tr. Takemoto Tadao. Tokyo: Tama shupan, 1984.

———. *Wholeness and the Implicate Order.* London: Routledge & Kegan Paul, 1980.

Bolen, Jean Shinoda. *The Tao of Psychology: Synchronicity and the Self.* San Francisco: Harper and Row, 1979.

Born, Max. *Physics in My Generation.* New York: Pergamon, 1956.

Boss, Medard. *Yume* [*The Analysis of Dream*], tr. Miyoshi Ikuo. Tokyo: Misuzu shobō, 1970.

Capra, Fritjof. *Tāningu pointo* [*Turning Point*], trs. Yoshifuku et al. Tokyo: Kōsakusha, 1984.

———. *Turning Point.* New York: Simon & Schuster, 1982.

Cassidy, David. *Uncertainty: The Life and Science of Werner Heisenberg.* New York: Freeman, 1992.

Chan, Wing-Tsit, ed. *Chu Hsi and Neo-Confucianism.* Honolulu: University of Hawaii Press, 1986.

———, tr. *Instructions for Practical Living and Other New-Confucian Writings.* New York: Columbia University Press, 1963.

———. *A Sourcebook in Chinese Philosophy.* Princeton: Princeton University Press, 1963.

Chigi, *Makashikan* [*Móhēzhǐguān*] [*Kokuyaku daizokyō*], vol. 6. Tokyo: Tōhō shoin, n.a.

Chomsky, Noam. *Aspects of the Theory of Syntax.* Cambridge: MIT Press, 1965.

———. *Syntactic Structures.* The Hague: Mouton, 1957.

Cooper, John (ed.). *Plato, Complete Works.* Indianapolis: Hackett, 1997.

D. Albert. *Ryōshirikigaku no kihongenri* [*The Fundamental Principles of Quantum Physics*]. Tokyo: Nippon hyōronsha, 1997.

Dasgupta. *Tantora bukkyō nyūmon* [*Introduction to Tantric Buddhism*], tr. Miyasaka and Kuwamura. Kyoto: Jinmon shoin, 1981.

Dōgen. "The Sounds of the Valley Streams, the Forms of the Mountains" in Francis

Dojun Cook, *How to Raise an Ox*. Los Angeles: Center Publications, 1978.

Freud, Sigmund. *Yumehandan [Interpretation of Dreams]*, tr. Takahashi Yoshitaka. Kyoto: Jinmon shoin, 1968.

Fukunaga Mitsuji. *Rōshi [Lǎozǐ]*. Tokyo: Asashi shinbunsha, 1968.

———. *Sōshi: Naihen [Chuāngzǐ: Inner Chapters]*. Tokyo: Asahi shinbunsha, 1978.

Gallop, David. *Parmenides of Elea, Fragments*. Toronto: University of Toronto, 1991, 1984.

Hawking, S.W. *Hōkingu: Uchū o kataru—biggu ban kara burakku hōru made [The Cosmos: From Big Bang to Black Hole]*. Tokyo: Hayakawa shobō, 1997.

Heidegger, Martin. *The Question of Being*, tr. William Kluback and Jean T. Wilde. Albany: NCUP, 1959.

———. *Being and Time*, tr. John Macquarrie and Edward Robinson. New York: Haper, 1962.

———. *Being and Time*, tr. Joan Stambaugh. Albany: State University of New York Press, 1996.

———. *Sonzai to jikan [Being and Time]*. Tokyo: Iwanami shoten, 1963.

———. *Sonzai to jikan [Being and Time]*, tr. Kuwaki Tsutomu. Tokyo: Iwanami-bunko, 1961. Three volumes.

———. *Martin Heidegger and National Socialism*. New York: Paragon, 1990.

Hirokawa Yōichi. *Sokuratesu izen no tetsugakusha [Philosophers Before Socrates]*. Tokyo: Kodansha Gakujutsu Bunko, 1997.

Ivanhoe, Philip J., and Van Norden, Bryan W. *Readings in Classical Chinese Philosophy*. New York: Seven Bridges, 2001.

Iwata Tetsuo. *Seiyōshisō no genyrū: jiyū no shishō to ryoinmin no shisō [The Origin of Western Thought: The Thought of Free People and the Thought of Captives]*. Tokyo: Hōsōdaigaku Kyoikushinkōkai, 1997.

Jacobi, Jolande. *Psychology of C. G. Jung*. Tr. K. W. Bash. New York: Routledge, 1973.

———. *Yungu shinrigaku*. Tokyo: Nippon kyōbunsha, 1973.

Jung, C. G., and Pauli, W. *An Answer to Job*. Tr. R. F. C. Hull. London: Routledge & Kegan Paul, 1954.

———. *C. G. Jung Letters*, ed. G. Adeler. New York: Vintage, 1972.

———. *C. G. Jung Letters*, tr. R. F. C. Hull. Princeton: Princeton University Press, 1973.

———. Foreword to Abegg, "Osten denkt anders" in *Collected Works*, Vol. 18.

———. Foreword to *The I Ching*. Princeton: Princeton University Press, 1950.

———. *Jiden [Memories, Dreams, Reflections]* I, tr. Kawai Hayao. Tokyo: Misuzu Shobō, 1972.

———. *Ketsugō no shinpi [Mysterium Conjunctionis]*. Kyoto: Jinmon shoin, 1995.

———. "Kyōjisei: hi-ingatekirenkan no genri" in *Shizengenshō to kokoro no kōzō.* Tokyo: Kaimeisha, 1976.

———. *Memories, Dreams, Reflections.* New York: Vintage, 1965.

———. *Modern Man in Search of a Soul.* San Diego,: Harcourt Brace, 1933.

———. *Mysterium Conjunctionis.* Zürich: Rascher, 1955.

———. *Psychology and the East.* Princeton: Princeton University Press, 1978.

———. *Psychology and the Occult,* trs. Uno Masato et al. Tokyo: Hōsei daigaku shuppan, 1982.

———. "Richard Wilhelm: In Memoriam," in *The Spirit in Man, Art, and Literature* tr. R. F. C. Hull. New York: Bollingen Foundation, 1966.

———, and Richard Wilhelm. *The Secret of the Golden Flower, A Chinese Book of Life,* trs. Cary F. Baynes. New York: Harvest, 1962, 1931.

———. *Shinrei Gensō no Shinri to Byōri* ["On the Psychology and Pathology of So-called Occult Phenomena"] in Jung, *Psychiatric Studies.* Tokyo: Hōsei daigaku shuppan, 1982.

———. *Shizen genshō to kokoro no kaimei* [*Clarification of Natural Phenomena and the Mind*], tr. Kawai Hayao and Murakami Yūichi. Tokyo: Kaimeisha, 1976.

———. *The Structure and Dynamics of the Psyche.* Princeton: Princeton University Press, 1969. NY: Bollingen Foundation, 1960.

———. "Synchronicity: An Acausal Connecting Principle" in *Interpretation of Nature and the Psyche.* Princeton: Princeton University Press, 1973.

———. *Tōyōteki meishō no shinrigaku* [*The Psychology of Eastern Meditation*], tr. Yuasa Yasuo and Kuroki Mikio. Osaka: Sōgensha, 1983.

———. *Two Essays on Analytical Psychology.* Princeton: Princeton University Press, 1972.

———. *Yobu e no Kotae* [*An Answer to Job*], tr. Nomura Mikiko. Kyoto: Yorudan-sha, 1981.

———. *Yungu no chōshinri shokan* [*Jung's Letters on Parapsychology*], ed. and tr. Yuasa Yasuo. Tokyo: Hakua shobō, 1999.

Kaji Nobuyuki, *Chūgokujin no ronrigaku* [The Logic of the Chinese People]. Tokyo: Chūōshinsho, 1977.

Kasahara Toshio, *Chōshinrigaku handobukku* [*Parapsychology Handbook*]. Tokyo: Burën shuppan, 1989.

Katō Nobuo. *Girisha tetsugakushi* [*History of Greek Philosophy*]. Tokyo: Tokyodaigaku shupankai, 1996.

Kirk, G. S., Raven, J. E., and Schofield, M. *The Presocratic Philosophers.* London: Cambridge University Press, 1983, 1957.

Kyasshidi, D. *Fukakuteisei: Haizenberugu no kagaku to shōgai* [David Cassidy, *Uncertainty: The Life and Science of Werner Heisenberg*] Tokyo: Hakuyōsha, 1998.

Lau, D. C. (trs.). *Tao Tê Ching*. Hong Kong: Chinese University of Hong Kong, 2001, 1982.

Matsuda and Nimase. *Jikan no gyakurūsuru sekai [The World Where Time Is Reversed]*. Tokyo: Maruzen, 1990.

McKeon, Richard (ed.). *The Basic Works of Aristotle*. New York: Random House, 1941.

Miura Kunio, *Ekikyō [Yìjīng]*. Tokyo: Kadokawa Shoten, 1988.

Nagasawa Kazutoshi, tr. *Genzōsanzō: daitōdaijionji sanzōhōshiden [Xuángzhuàng-sānzàng: A Biography of the Darma-Master, Xuángzhuàngsānzàng, of the Great Compassion Temple of the Great Tang Dynasty]*. Tokyo: Kōfūsha, n.a., vols. 8 and 9.

Nagatomo, Shigenori. "The Logic of the *Diamond Sutra*: A is not A, Therefore A," *Journal of Asian Philosophy*, vol. 10. no. 3, 2000, pp. 213–244.

Nakamura Hajime, *Tōyōjin no shii hohō: chugokujin no shii hohō [The Ways of Thinking of the Eastern People: The Chinese Way of Thinking]*. Tokyo: Shinjū sha, 1988.

Nietzsche, Friedrich. *The Pre-Platonic Philosophers*, tr. Greg Whitlock. Chicago: University of Illinois Press, 2001.

Nikkei saiensu, ed. *Ryōshirikigaku no paradokkusu* [The Paradox in Quantum Physics]. Tokyo: Nippon Keizai shinbunn, 1995.

Nishi Junzō. "*Chūgokutetsugaku no jikanron no dōki*" ["The Motive of the Theory of Time in Chinese Philosophy"] in *Chūgokushisōshè [Anthology of Chinese Thought]*. Tokyo: Chikuma shobō, 1969.

———. "*Shugo nonai kotoba: chūgokugo ni tsuite no shiron*" ["*Language without the Subject: An Attempt at the Chinese Language*"] in *Chūgokushisō ronshū [Essays on Chinese Philosophy]*. Tokyo: Chikuma shobō, 1969.

Nishida, Kitarō. *Art and Morality*, tr. David A. Dilworth and Valdo H. Viglielmo. Honolulu, Hawaii: East-West Center, 1973.

———. *The Fundamental Problems of Philosophy*, tr. David Dilworth. Tokyo: Sophia University, 1970.

———. *Inquiry into the Good*, tr. Abe Masao and Christopher Ives. New Haven: Yale University Press, 1990.

———. *Intelligibility and the Philosophy of Nothingness*, tr. Robert Schinzinger. Honolulu, Hawaii: East-West Center, 1958.

———. *Intuition and Reflection in Self-Consciousness*, tr. Valdo H. Viglielmo. Albany: State University of New York Press, 1987.

———. *Last Writings: Nothingness and the Religious Worldview*, tr. David Dilworth. Honolulu: University of Hawaii Press, 1987.

Nishitani Keiji. *Nishida Kitarō*, tr. Yamamoto Seisaku and James W. Heisig. Los Angeles: University of California Press, 1991.

Ogino Hiroyuki. *Testugaku no genfukei: kodaigirisha no chie to kotoba* [*The Original Scene of Philosophy: The Wisdom and Language of Ancient Greece*]. Tokyo: NHK Raiburarī, Nihonhōsōshupankai, 1999.

Pauli, W. *Butsuri to ninshiki* [*Physics and Cognition*]. Tokyo: Kōdansha, 1984.

———. "Muishiki no gainen no shizenkagakuteki ninshikironteki sokumen" ["Ideas of the Unconscious from the Standpoint of Natural Science and Epistemology"] in *Butsuri to ninshiki* [*Matter and Cognition*]. Tokyo: Kōdansha, 1975.

———. *Writings in Physics and Philosophy*, Berlin: Springer-Verlag, 1994.

Peat, F. D. *Sinkuronishitī* [*Synchronicity*]. Tokyo: Asahishuppansha, 1989.

———. *Synchronicity: The Bridge Between Mind and Matter*. New York: Random House, 1988.

Pessis-Pasternak, Guitta. *Dekaruto nakka iranai?* Tokyo: Sangyōtosho, 1993.

———. *Faui-il Brûler Descartes?* Paris: Éditions La Découverte, 1991.

Plato. *Timaeus* in *The Collected Diaglogues of Plato*, ed., Edith Hamilton and Huntington Cairns. Princeton: Princeton University Press, 1973.

Prigogine, Ilya, and Stengers, Isabelle. *Konton kara no chitsujo* [*Order Out of Chaos*]. Tokyo: Misuzu shobō, 1992.

———. *Order Out of Chaos*. New York: Bantam Books, 1984.

Puraton Zenshū [*The Complete Works of Plato*], vol. 3 (Tokyo: Iwanamishoten, 1980), containing a commentary of the *Sophist*, Fujisawa Yoshio and Mizuno Arinobu, *Puraton* [*Plato*].

Rhine, J. B. and J. G. Pratt. *Chōshinrigaku gaisetsu*, trs. Yuasa Yasuo and Motoyama Hiroshi, Tokyo: Shèkyōshinri shupan, 1964.

———. *Extra Sensory Perception*, 1934. Boston: Bruce Humphries, 1964.

———. *Parapsychology: Frontier Science of the Mind—A Survey of the Field, the Methods, and the Facts of ESP and PK Research*. Springfield, Charles C. Thomas, 1957.

Ryū Bunei. *Chūgoku no jikūron* [*The Chinese Theory of Time and Space*]. Tokyo: Tōhō shoten, 1992.

Saussure, F. *The Course in General Linguistics*. New York: Philosophical Library, 1959.

———. *Ippangengogaku kōgi* [*Lectures on General Linguistics*]. Tokyo: Iwanami shoten, 1986.

Sekine Kiyomitsu. *Rinrishisō no genryu: girisha to heburai no baai* [*The Origin of Ethical Thought: The Cases of Greece and the Hebrews*]. Kyoto: Hōsōdaigaku Kyoikushinkōkai, 2001.

Stcherbatsky, F. Th. *Buddhist Logic*. New York: Dover, 1962.

Stevenson, Ian. *Telepathic Impressions, A Review and Report of Thirty-five Cases*. Charlottesville: University Press of Virginia, 1970.

Suzuki Teruo. *Parumenidesu tetsugakukenkyū* [*Study of Parmenides' Philosophy*]. Kanagawa: Tōkaidaigaku shupankai, 1999.

Suzuki Yūjirō. *Ekikyō* [*Yijing*]. Tokyo: Shūeisha, 1974.

Tachibana Takashi. *Rinshi taiken* [*Near Death Experience*], Vol. II. Tokyo: Bungeishunjūsha, 1994.

Takemoto Tadao and Yuasa Yauso, ed. *Kagaku gijutsu to seishin sekai* [*The Scientific Technology and the Spiritual World*]. Five volumes. Tokyo: Seidosha, 1987.

———, ed. *Ryōshirikigaku to ishiki no yakuwari* [*Quantum Physics and the Role of Consciousness*]. Tokyo: Tama shuppan, 1984.

Tenge Shirō. *Kōfukuna jinsei no himitsu* [*The Secret of a Happy Life*] Tokyo: PHP Kenkyèjo, 2000.

Thorn, K. S. *Burakku hōru to jikūnohizumi* [*Black Hole and Space-Time Warps: Einstein's Outrageous Legacy*]. Tokyo: Hakuyōsha, 1998.

Tillich, Paul. *Zenshū* [*Collected Works*], vol. 11. Tokyo: Hakusuisha, n.d.

Tsuzuki Takuji. *Jiikan no fushigi: taimu mashinn kara Hōkingu made* [*The Mystery of Time: From the Time-Machine to Hawking*]. Tokyo: Kōdansha, 1996.

Uchiyama Katsutoshi, et al. *Sokuratesu izentetsugakusha danpenshū* [*Collection of the Fragments of Presocratic Philosophers*]. Tokyo: Iwanami shoten, 1995–1998 (a collection of fragments edited by Diels and Kranz). 4 vols., with a supplementary volume.

von Franz, M. L. *Number and Time*. Chicago: Northwestern University Press, 1974.

———. *Zahl und Zeit: Psychologische gberlegungen zu einer Annahrung von Tiefen-psychologie und Physik*. Stuttgart: Ernst Klett Verlag, 1970.

Wada Sumio. *Nijūseiki no shizen kakumei* [*The Revolution of Nature in the Twentieth Century*]. Tokyo: Asahi shinbunsha, 1997.

Watanabe, Satoshi. "Sōtaiseiriron to Beruguson" in *Toki* ["The Theory of Relativity and Bergson," in *Time*]. Tokyo: Kawaide shobōshinsha, 1976.

Watson, Ryle. *Seimei Chōryū* [*Lifetide: A Biology of the Unconscious*], trs. Mikihata et al. Tokyo: Kōsakusha, 1981.

Watsuji, Tetsurō. *Watsuji Tetsurō's Rinrigaku: Ethics in Japan*. tr. Yamamoto Seisaku and Robert E. Carter. Albany: State University of New York Press, 1996.

Wilhelm, Richard. *The I Ching or Book of Changes*, tr. Cary F. Baynes. Princeton: Princeton University Press, 1950.

Xenophon. *Sokuratesu no omoide* [*The Recollection of Socrates*]. Tokyo: Iwanami shoten, n.a.

Yamamoto Mitsuo, ed. *Shoki girisha tetsugakusha danpenshū* [*Fragments of Philosophers from the Early Period of Greece*]. Tokyo: Iwanami shoten, 1958.

Yanagiya Akira. *Honyakugo seiritsu jijō* [*Situations Surrounding the Establishment of Translated Words*]. Tokyo: Iwanami shoten, 1982.

Yuasa Yasuo. *The Body, Self-Cultivation and Ki-Energy*. Albany: State University of New York Press, 1993.

———. *The Body: Toward an Eastern Mind-Body Theory*. Albany: State University of New York Press, 1987.

———. "The Encounter of Modern Japanese Philosophy with Heidegger" in *Heidegger and Asian Thought*, Graham Parkes, ed. Honolulu, Hawaii: University of Hawaii Press, 1987.

———. *Ki towa nanika [What Is Ki?]*. Tokyo: NHK Books, 1992.

———. *Kyōjisei no uchūkan [The Synchonistic View of the Cosmos]*. Kyoto: Jinmonn shoin, 1995.

———, and Sadakata Akio, trs. *Ōgon no hana no himitsu [The Secret of the Golden Flower]*. Kyoto: Jinmonn shoin, 1980.

———. *Shintai no uchūsei: Toyō to seiyō [The Cosmic Nature of the Body: East and West]*. Tokyo: Iwanami shoten, 1994.

———. *Shintairon: Toyōteki shinshinron to gendai [The Theory of the Body: An Eastern Theory of Mind and Body, and the Contemporary World]*. Tokyo: Kōdansha gakujutsu bunko, 1990.

———. *Shūkyō to kagaku no aida [Between Religion and Science]*. Tokyo: Meicho kankōkai, 1994.

———. *Tetsugaku no tanjō: danseisei to joseisei no shinrigaku [The Birth of Philosophy: The Psychology of Masculinity and Femininity]*. Kyoto: Jinmonn shoin, 2004.

——— and Kuroki Mikio. *Toyōteki meisō no shinrigaku [The Psychology of Eastern Meditation]* Osaka: Sōgensha, 1983.

———. *Yungu chōshinrigaku shokan [Jung's Letters on Parapsychology]*. Tokyo: Hakua shobō, 1999.

———. "Yungu kokoro no shinpi" ["Mystery of the Mind in Jung"] in *AZ*, no. 29, fall, 1999, Shinjinbutsu Ōraisha.

———. *Yungu to kirisutokyō [Jung and Christianity]*. Kyoto: Jinmonn shoin, 1978.

———. *Yungu to tōyō [Jung and the East]*. Kyoto: Jinmonn shoin, 1989–1990. vol. 1 and 2.

———. *Yungu to yōroppa seishin [Jung and the European Spirituality]*. Kyoto: Jinmonn shoin, 1979.

———. *Watsuji Tetsurō: Kindai nihon no unmei [Watsuji Tetsurō: The Destiny of Modern Japan]*. Tokyo: Chikuma shobō, 1995.

———. *Yuasa Yasuo's Complete Work*. Vol. 4. Tokyo: Hakua shobō, 2004.

Watsuji Tetsurō. A *Climate*, tr. G. Bownas. Tokyo: Ministry of Education, 1961.

———. *Rinrigaku: Ethics in Japan*, tr. Yamamoto Seisaku and Robert E. Carter. Albany: State University of New York Press, 1966.

Index